Hard Disk Power
with
The Jamsa Disk Utilities™

Walter Lawrence

Hard Disk Power

with
The Jamsa Disk Utilities™

Kris Jamsa

SAMS

A Division of Macmillan Computer Publishing

11711 North College, Carmel, Indiana 46032 USA

International Standard Book Number: 0-672-22761-4
Library of Congress Catalog Card Number: 90-61031

Development Editor: *Allen Wyatt*
Technical Editor: *Greg Guntle*
Manuscript Editors: *Sara Black and Kathy Grider-Carlyle*
Production Editor: *Kathy Grider-Carlyle*
Illustrators: *Don Clemons and Tom Emrick*
Cover Art Director: *Glenn Santner*
Cover Photo: *Dick Spahr Photography, Inc.*
Indexers: *Hilary Adams and Joelynn Gifford*
Compositor: *Cromer Graphics*
Production: *Sally Copenhaver, Tami Hughes, Bill Hurley, Jodi Jensen,
Lori Lyons, Jennifer Matthews, Diana Moore, Dennis Sheehan,
Bruce Steed, Mary Beth Wakefield, Nora Westlake*

Printed in the United States of America

Trademarks

For information about our audio products, write us at:
Newbridge Book Clubs, 3000 Cindel Drive, Delran, NJ 08370

Overview

Contents

Part 2
Installing and Using the Jamsa Disk Utilities

Introduction

► About the Book

► About the Jamsa Disk Utilities

Introduction

Hard disks are wonderful tools. They let us store and access millions of pieces of information quickly. Almost every personal computer in use today has a hard disk installed.

Hard disk management is the process of organizing the files on your disk to achieve the best performance. Hard disk management is not difficult, nor is it time consuming. In fact, once you apply a few of the key concepts presented in this book, your system will be faster, which will make you more productive. Best of all, you can work with total control of your files, rather than with fear of making a drastic error. Almost every user working with a hard disk has encountered one or more of the following error messages:

```
File not found

Non-System disk or disk error

Invalid drive specification

Abort, Retry, Ignore, Fail?

General Failure error
```

This book will help you fully understand the causes of these errors, as well as the solutions. Although they must work with hard disks everyday, most users are never taught the techniques they need. This book was written to make hard disks easy for everyone to use.

This book and disk combination is unique because it not only provides you with the information you need to maximize your disk's capabilities, it provides you with a collection of essential software programs that normally cost between $150 and $200. If you are working with a hard disk, you can't afford to be without these utilities.

About the Book

If you aren't familiar with DOS, subdirectories, or other file manipulation concepts, don't worry. This book begins with the basics. You will begin with the essential DOS commands and concepts needed on a daily basis. When you are comfortable with those concepts, you can apply them to boost your disk's performance.

As you advance through the book, you will learn the actions DOS performs behind the scenes when you store files or create subdirectories. You'll fully understand the use of the file allocation table, disk clusters, and the how and why of disk fragmentation. If you are looking for answers to your hard disk questions, you'll find them inside this book.

Successful hard disk management only requires the knowledge of a few key DOS commands. This book contains the secrets for using these commands to maximize your system performance.

About the Jamsa Disk Utilities

Disk utilities provide you with the services DOS forgot, such as recovering deleted files, quickly locating a specific file on your disk, eliminating unused directory entries to maximize your disk performance, and providing the ability to bring your disk back to life after a previously fatal disk format operation. Hard disk users need disk utilities. The obvious question becomes, "Which ones?"

When we talked with users, their primary criticism of existing disk products was that the products were hard to use and hard on the pocketbook.

We took the "everyday user's" input to heart and built a collection of easy-to-use, essential disk utilities. The Jamsa Disk Utilities provide the power you need and the ease of use you want, at a cost you can afford.

The Jamsa Disk Utilities won't scare, confuse, or intimidate you. They'll just help you get the job done.

Instead of just reading about them, put The Jamsa Disk Utilities to work. In minutes you can improve your disk's performance.

Acknowledgments

Thorough, precise, cooperative, dedicated, and a great pleasure to work with; there simply aren't enough words to express my gratitude for the contributions to this book made by the talented and unselfish professionals at SAMS. Although you won't find their names on the book's cover, their hard work appears on every page. From its start, *Hard Disk Power with the Jamsa Disk Utilities* was a very special book. The staff at Sams has combined their talents to produce a book of exceptional quality.

To the editors, artists, word processors, proofreaders, typographers, and manuscript designers, my sincere thanks.

Please join me in introducing *Hard Disk Power with the Jamsa Disk Utilities*.

Part One

HARD DISK POWER

Depending on your level of expertise, the term *Hard Disk Power* can mean many things. To the novice, it may mean understanding DOS file and subdirectory manipulation well enough to increase disk organization and daily productivity. To the expert, Hard Disk Power means maximizing disk performance.

Because every DOS user has a different level of experience, this book begins with disk and file basics. If you are new to DOS or to hard disks, this book's first few chapters build the foundation you will need to control your files and to use your system effectively and confidently. With that foundation in place, you will quickly master the essential DOS commands you will use each day.

If you are already familiar with DOS file and subdirectory manipulation, the chapters in Part One will teach you time-saving shortcuts and optimal settings for maximum system performance, as well as a detailed understanding of DOS file and subdirectory manipulation from behind the scenes. Few DOS users actually understand how DOS stores files on disk. As a result, most users don't perform several simple steps that can protect their data and significantly improve their system performance. All the concepts discussed in Part One relate strictly to DOS.

Computer technology is increasing on a daily basis. It's almost impossible to keep up with the newest and fastest computers and disk drives. As such, users need to maximize the performance of their existing hardware. The easiest and least expensive way to do that is with DOS. Throughout Part One you will learn DOS techniques you can use immediately to maximize your disk, directory, and system performance. Best of all, DOS provides these power techniques free!

If you perform the techniques presented in Part One, your disk will be configured for maximum performance when you begin using the Jamsa Disk Utilities discussed in Part Two.

1

Hard Disk Basics

- ► How Your Computer Stores Information
- ► Looking at Floppy Disks
- ► Microfloppy Disks
- ► Hard Disk Drives
- ► Disk Layout
- ► How Disks Store Information
- ► Understanding Disk Performance
- ► Disk Storage System
- ► Preparing a Disk for Use
- ► Disk Head Parking
- ► More Advanced Concepts
- ► Summary

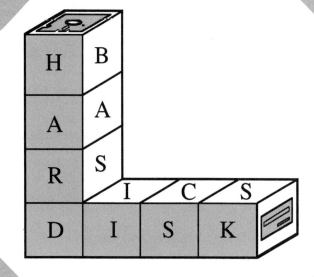

1

Hard Disk Basics

Computers store programs and information, such as letters, reports, and numerical data, on disks. Personal computers use two types of disks: removable floppy disks and hard disks. Both disk types store information. Hard disks, however, are much faster and have much greater storage capacities than floppy disks.

Although hard disks provide more storage space for information, they are as easy to use as floppy disks. In fact, as soon as you understand a few basic DOS concepts, you'll find storing and retrieving information on your hard disk is much easier and faster than continually inserting and removing floppy disks.

If you are using a hard disk, you may have already encountered long lists of file names that scroll past on the screen faster than you can read them. You may have difficulty locating a specific file or command on your disk. An errant DOS command may have overwritten or deleted your files, or worse yet, you may continually work in fear of damaging your disk.

Hard disk management is the art of organizing your disk and files. Good hard disk management makes the best use of your disk's storage space, improves your system performance, and makes your computer easier to use. Best of all, hard disk management doesn't require programming or using difficult commands. You don't need to be a computer scientist to organize your disk. Just follow the steps discussed in the next few chapters and you'll have total control over your hard disk.

How Your Computer Stores Information

As discussed, your computer uses both floppy and hard disks to store programs and information. Information recorded on disk provides your computer's long term storage. If, for example, you store a letter on a disk, you can access the letter a few minutes later, a few days later, or even several years later. Once recorded on disk, the information remains there until you erase it.

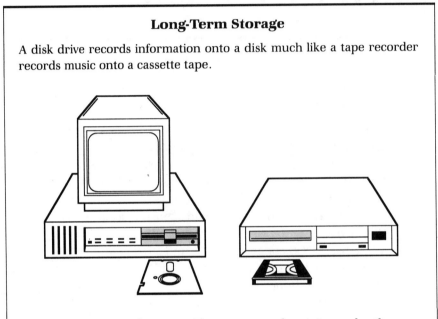

Long-Term Storage

A disk drive records information onto a disk much like a tape recorder records music onto a cassette tape.

Once you record a song with a tape recorder, you can play the song back immediately, a few days later, or even after several years. The song remains on tape until you erase it or tape over it. Just as you can record several songs on the same tape, you can place many pieces of information on a disk. Like a cassette tape, your disk can eventually run out of storage space.

To execute programs, your computer uses a second, short term storage area known as your computer's memory. Unlike items recorded on disk in long term storage, information in your computer's memory is stored temporarily as electronic signals in memory chips called RAM (RAM stands for random-access memory). When you turn off your computer, the information in memory is lost.

Short-Term Storage

Think of your computer's memory as an electronic chalk board. When a program executes, the program temporarily stores information in memory.

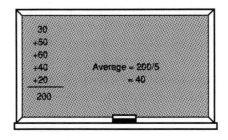

The program can access this information as long as it remains in memory. When the program ends or if the information is erased by another program, the information in memory is no longer available, just as if you had erased the chalk board.

Understanding Memory

Your computer's memory is made up of many memory chips that reside on a hardware board inside your computer, similar to that shown in the following figure.

Because memory chips hold electronic signals, they must have power to store information. When you turn off your computer's power, the memory chips can no longer store information; hence, the term temporary storage.

Before your computer can execute a program, the program must reside in your computer's memory. Most of the programs you execute, such as a word processor, reside on a disk. When you run these programs, DOS locates the program on disk and loads it into memory so it can be used, as illustrated in the following figure.

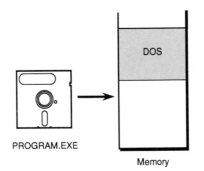

Without memory, your computer could not execute programs.

Bits, Bytes, KBytes, and MegaBytes

Disks store programs and information. Computer memory temporarily stores programs and calculations while the program executes. Because both disks and memory have a fixed size, we must have a way to express the size of their storage capabilities. Computers store information using electronic signals. A signal can be either present (on) or absent (off). To represent a signal's presence, computers use the value 1. The value 0, on the other hand, indicates the signal is absent. Computers use collections of ones and zeros (called *binary digits*) to represent numbers and characters. The word bit is an abbreviation for binary digit (a value that is either 0 or 1).

Because most of us don't think in terms of bits, we often group bits into collections of eight called *bytes*. As you will learn in Chapter 3, DOS always refers to the size of your files in terms of bytes.

Byte

Think of a byte as a character of information. A file containing the word *DISK* has four characters or bytes of information. A single-spaced typed page, for example, requires approximately 4,000 characters or bytes.

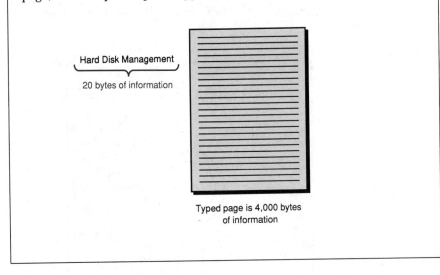

Hard Disk Management

20 bytes of information

Typed page is 4,000 bytes
of information

When referring to the computer's memory or disk storage capabilities, you will often encounter the term *KByte* or the initial *K*. The letter K stands for the value 1,024. The value 64K, for instance, actually becomes 64 * 1,024 or 65,536 bytes.

For most purposes, you can round the value for K to 1,000. If you are told your computer has 640K of memory (RAM), you know your computer can store over 640,000 characters of information.

The terms megabyte, meg, and the initial M refer to one million bytes. A hard disk, for example, may have 20 meg of storage (20,000,000 bytes). Knowing a typed page requires 4,000 bytes, you can estimate that a 20 meg hard disk will store 5,000 typed pages of information.

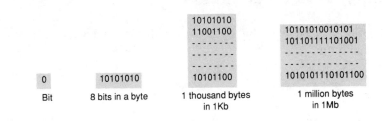

0

Bit

10101010

8 bits in a byte

10101010
11001100

10101100

1 thousand bytes
in 1Kb

10101010010101
101101111101001

1010101110101100

1 million bytes
in 1Mb

Looking at Floppy Disks

When the IBM PC first became available in 1981, it used a small removable disk called a "floppy disk" for long term storage. The floppy disk was so named because it is housed in a flexible cardboard jacket. If you open an unused floppy disk, you will find a circular plastic disk, as shown in the following figure.

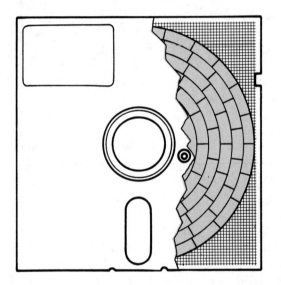

The plastic disk is coated with a magnetic material similar to the tape in a cassette that records information. Never touch the plastic disk when you handle the floppy. If you inadvertently scratch the disk's surface, the disk may not be able to record information in the future, or worse yet, you may damage or lose the information the disk currently contains.

Floppy Disk Components

The floppy disk actually has several distinct parts, as shown in the following figure.

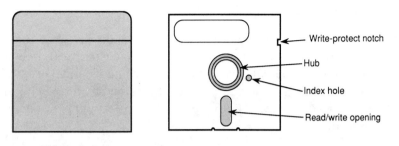

Disk envelope

The Disk Envelope

The disk envelope is a protective paper sleeve that covers the floppy disk's read/write opening. Always place your floppy disk back into the disk envelope when the disk is not in use. The envelope protects the disk from dust, smoke, and accidental spills.

The Disk Jacket

The disk jacket is the cardboard that surrounds the disk. The jacket provides you with a way to pick up the disk and gives the disk the rigidity needed to insert it into the disk drive.

The Disk Hub

Each time you place a floppy disk into a disk drive and close the drive latch, the disk drive spins the disk inside the disk jacket. In some cases, you can hear the disk spinning. Within the disk drive, a spindle grips the disk at the hub and rotates it. A floppy disk spins in the disk drive at approximately 300 RPMs (revolutions per minute). Most floppy disks have a small reinforcement ring at the disk hub.

The Index Hole

The floppy disk index hole assists your computer in formatting a floppy disk drive. If you carefully rotate a floppy disk within the disk jacket by gripping the disk hub, you will eventually see a small hole in the disk. This hole provides an initial starting point for disk formatting.

The Write-Protect Notch

As discussed, once you record information on disk, the information remains on disk until you erase it or overwrite it with new information. To avoid accidentally erasing or overwriting essential programs or information stored on a floppy disk, cover the small opening at the upper right corner of your disk with a write-protect tab provided with a box of new disks.

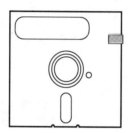

When you cover a floppy disk's write-protect notch, your computer can read the programs and information the disk contains, but the computer cannot change them. You should always ensure that your original software disks have write-protect tabs to protect them.

The Read/Write Opening

To read and record information, the disk drive must access the floppy disk's magnetic surface. The floppy disk's read/write opening provides the disk drive with access to the disk. Because the disk rotates within the disk jacket, the entire disk surface is available to the disk drive.

Different Types of Floppy Disks

Since the release of the IBM PC in 1981, floppy disk storage capabilities have increased. Initially, floppy disks could only store information on one side. These disks, called single-sided disks, were capable of storing only 160,000 bytes. By improving disk drives to use both sides of a disk, disk storage capacity grew to 320K. As disk technology improved, disk manufacturers were able to record more information on disk by packing the information closer together, increasing the density of information stored

Accessing Disk Information

A disk is very much like a record album on a phonograph. When you play the record, the record spins allowing the phonograph's needle to access the entire album.

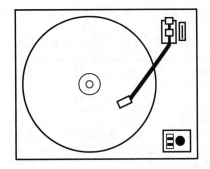

When the disk drive reads or records information, the drive uses a device called the read/write head to manipulate the disk's information in much the same way as the phonograph's needle plays a record album.

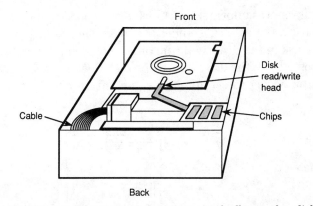

Just as the needle moves across a record album, the disk drive's read/write head moves in and out to access information stored on different parts of the disk.

on disk. These "double-density" disks store up to 360K and are the primary floppy disk type in use today.

With the IBM PC AT came the newest floppy disks capable of storing 1.2 million bytes each. These disks pack four times as much information as the original floppy disks and are thus known as quad-density disks.

Table 1.1 summarizes the evolution of the 5¼-inch floppy disk.

Table 1.1. *Floppy disk storage capabilities.*

Disk Type	Storage	Sides	Density
160K	163,840 bytes	1	Single
180K	184,320 bytes	1	Double
320K	327,680 bytes	2	Single
360K	368,640 bytes	2	Double
1.2M	1,213,952 bytes	2	Quad

Floppy Disk Drives

A disk stores information. A disk drive records information on your disk. To use a floppy disk, remove the disk from the paper envelope and place the disk in the drive with the disk label facing up and the end of the disk inserted into the drive last. If the disk doesn't have a label, insert the disk so the write-protect notch is to the left, inserted last as shown.

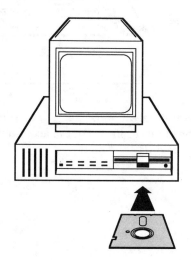

Next, close the disk drive latch. The latch may be one of several types, as shown in the following figure.

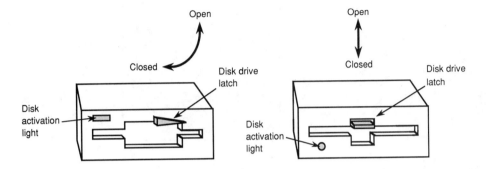

If you attempt to access the disk without having closed the latch, DOS will display the following error message:

```
Not ready reading drive A
Abort, Retry, Fail?
```

Should this error occur, close the disk drive latch and type R to retry the operation.

All disk drives have a disk activation light that illuminates when the disk is in use. Never open the disk drive latch or turn off your computer while the disk activation light is turned on. Doing so may damage the disk, losing the information it contains.

To remove a disk from the disk drive, simply open the drive latch and gently remove the disk. Make sure you place the disk in its protective paper envelope when it is not in use.

Microfloppy Disks

Although 5¼-inch floppy disks have provided the bulk of disk storage for personal computers since 1981, many newer computers and all laptop computers use a smaller, more durable disk called a microfloppy or 3½-inch disk. Although the microfloppy is smaller in size, it has greater storage capabilities than the standard 5¼-inch floppy disk.

Unlike the floppy disk, which uses a flexible cardboard jacket, the microfloppy uses a hard plastic jacket. If you could open a microfloppy disk, you would again find a small magnetically coated disk.

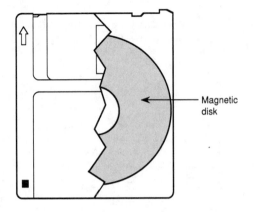

Microfloppy Disk Components

The microfloppy disk stores information in the same manner as the standard floppy disk. The disk drive's read/write head accesses information recorded on the disk's surface.

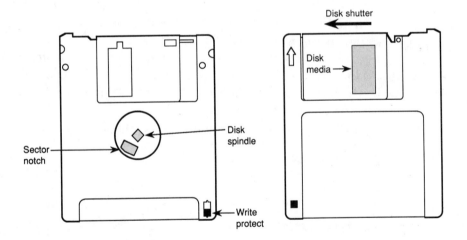

The Read/Write Shutter

The first thing you may notice when you handle a microfloppy disk is that you can't actually see the disk media. The microfloppy disk has a metal shutter at the top that slides to the left to expose the disk's surface. As with all disks, never touch the recording surface.

When you place a microfloppy disk in the disk drive, the disk drive actually slides the shutter open to access the disk.

The Disk Spindle and Sector Notch

If you turn a microfloppy disk over, you will find the disk spindle and sector notch.

The microfloppy disk only fits into the disk drive shutter-first with the disk spindle and sector notch facing down. The disk drive uses the disk spindle to spin the disk.

The sector notch serves as the microfloppy disk's index hole. The disk drive uses the sector notch during disk formatting.

The Write-Protect Hole

Unlike the floppy disk that has a write-protect notch, the microfloppy disk has a write-protect hole.

Once you write-protect a microfloppy by sliding the write-protect cover up and exposing the hole, the computer can read the programs and information recorded on the disk but it cannot change or delete them.

Different Types of Microfloppy Disks

Initially, microfloppy disks held 720K of information. Many laptop computers, as well as the smaller PS/2 computers, use 720K disks. The newer, larger PS/2 systems support 1.44M microfloppy disks. Many disk manufacturers are working on microfloppy disks that hold more than 2 megabytes. Table 1.2 summarizes the microfloppy disk sizes.

Table 1.2. *Microfloppy disk types.*

Disk Type	Storage	Sides	Density
720K	737,280 bytes	1	Double
1.44M	1,457,664 bytes	2	Double

Microfloppy Disk Drives

Depending upon the computer type, the location of the microfloppy disk drives may differ. Most microfloppy drives, however, are similar to the drive shown here.

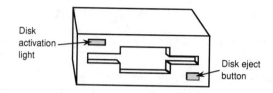

Disk activation light

Disk eject button

To insert a microfloppy disk into the drive, place the disk into the drive shutter end first, with the sector notch and disk spindle facing down, as shown in the following figure.

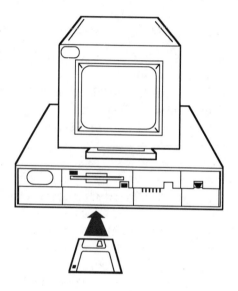

Note that the microfloppy drive also uses a disk activation light to tell you when the drive is in use. To remove the microfloppy disk from the drive, press the eject button. Because the microfloppy disk does not expose the disk's surface, you do not have to insert the microfloppy into a protective envelope. However, you should still place the disk into a storage container to prevent it from getting lost.

Hard Disk Drives

Floppy disks provide several essential functions. First, floppy disks allow users to exchange programs and information. All new software programs are distributed on either floppy or microfloppy disks. Floppy disks also provide a way to start or *boot* your computer when the hard disk fails. They allow users to back up the files from their hard disk to reduce the possibility of data loss and they will remain an essential part of computer usage for a long time. However, because floppy disks are slow (in comparison to the computer's fast electronic components) and have limited storage capabilities, users have become dependent upon hard disks.

A hard disk, like a floppy disk, stores programs and information. However, because of its design, a hard disk can store much more data than a floppy and can access the data much faster. As you have seen, a floppy disk uses a single disk surface. (If you open a floppy disk, you will see only one circular recording media.) In most cases, the disk drive can record data on both sides of this surface. A hard disk, however, may have several stacks of these recording surfaces, known as platters, stacked on top of each other.

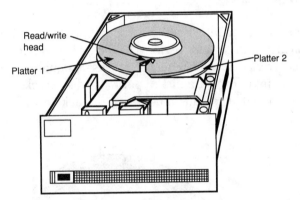

The hard disk drive has read/write heads for both sides of each platter which let the disk drive store data on both sides of the disk surface. Unlike the floppy disk that uses a flexible plastic surface, the hard disk uses an aluminum disk coated with a metal oxide. Because the recording surface is solid, the hard disk can store data more compactly, which increases the disk's storage capabilities. Also, the disk drive can rotate the platters past the read/write heads at a much faster rate. Hard disk platters spin at 3600 RPMs, more than ten times faster than a floppy disk. The faster a disk spins, the less time the drive needs to record or access information. The less time your system spends performing disk operations, the more productive your time at the computer becomes.

Hard disks have tremendous storage capabilities ranging to billions of bytes. Table 1.3 describes several of the more commonly used hard disk sizes.

Table 1.3. *Common hard disk sizes.*

Disk Type	Storage	Equivalence
10M	10,485,760 bytes	2,500 typed pages
30M	31,457,280 bytes	7,500 typed pages
60M	62,914,560 bytes	15,000 typed pages

Note that the front of the hard disk contains a disk activation light. The disk drive illuminates this light when the disk is in use. Do not turn off your computer while the disk activation light is on. Doing so may damage your disk or files.

Disk Layout

To organize the information recorded on disk, each platter of your disk is divided into distinct regions. The disk is divided into circular patterns called *tracks*. The number of tracks assigned to your disk will vary, depending upon your disk type. Each disk track has a unique number assigned to it. The outermost track is track zero.

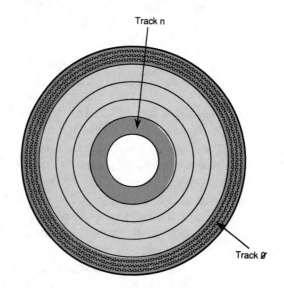

Track n

Track Ø

Table 1.4 lists the number of tracks assigned to commonly used disks.

Table 1.4. *Tracks per side for commonly used disks.*

Disk Type	Number of Tracks
360K	40
720K	80
1.2K	80
1.44M	80
10M	306
20M	615

Disk Tracks

Think of disk tracks as the grooves in a record album. By looking at the grooves in an album, you can move the needle to the correct song.

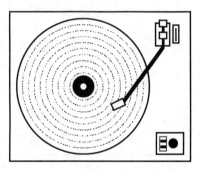

By looking at disk tracks, the disk drive can move the read/write heads to the correct disk location.

Each track is further divided into individual storage locations called *sectors*. For most disks, each sector stores 512 bytes.

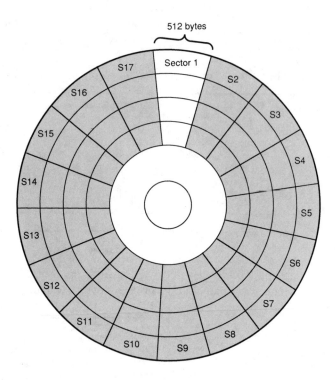

Table 1.5 defines the number of sectors per track for commonly used disk types.

Table 1.5. *Sectors per track for commonly used disks.*

Disk Type	Sectors Per Track
360K	9
720K	9
1.2M	15
1.44M	18
Hard disk	17

If you know a disk's sector size, number of tracks, and tracks per sector, you can determine the disk's storage capability using the following equation.

$$\text{Bytes of Storage} = (\text{sides per disk}) * (\text{tracks per side}) * (\text{sectors per track}) * (\text{sector size})$$

Using a 360K floppy disk, the equation becomes the following:

```
Bytes of Storage = (2) * (40) * (9) * (512)
                 = 368,640 bytes
```

Likewise, the storage capabilities of a 20M hard disk is determined in the following manner:

```
Bytes of Storage = (4) * (605) * (17) * (512)
                 = 21,063,680 bytes
```

As discussed, hard disks contain multiple platters. To improve performance, equivalent track positions on each platter are combined into groups called *cylinders*. In other words, track 1 on each platter is collectively referred to as cylinder 1. Likewise, track 500 on each platter forms cylinder 500. Pictorially, a cylinder can be envisioned as shown in the following figure.

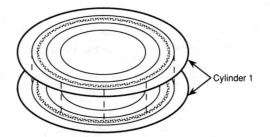

You need to understand the term cylinders because hard disk manuals refer to them. For the discussion throughout this book, think of tracks or cylinders as the circular ring of storage locations on your disk.

How Disks Store Information

The aluminum hard disk is coated with a metal oxide that can store magnetic charges. Each track contains thousands of individual storage units called *domains*. Each domain is capable of representing a zero or a one, which directly corresponds to a bit.

Actually, each domain holds a magnetic charge. For simplicity, assume that domains representing the value 1 hold a magnetic charge that points north, while domains representing the value 0 have magnetic charges that point south.

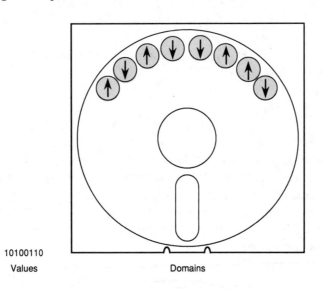

10100110
Values   Domains

To read information, the disk drive's read/write head passes over the disk sensing the individual domain charges.

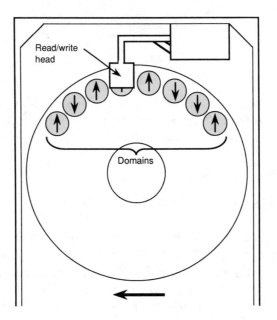

To record information, the read/write head passes over the disk, sensing the individual domain charges. To record information, the read/write head acts like a magnet, assigning the correct charges to specific domains. The read/write head works with tremendous speed and accuracy. One side of a hard disk platter for a 20M disk, for example, contains over 4,000,000 domains. With the disk platter spinning at 3600 RPMs over 522,240 bytes, more than 4 million bits spin past the read/write head every second!

To obtain the accuracy required to access individual domains, the read/write head floats very close to the disk's surface, but does not touch it. The following illustration shows the relationship between the read/write head and the disk platter compared to several other very small objects.

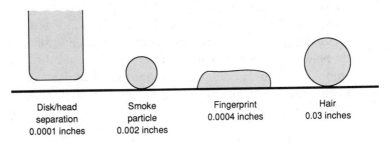

Disk/head	Smoke	Fingerprint	Hair
separation	particle	0.0004 inches	0.03 inches
0.0001 inches	0.002 inches		

With this illustration in mind, you can better understand why hardware repairmen cringe when PCs with hard disks are bumped and moved while turned on. If the disk head comes in contact with the spinning platter, the head essentially scrapes the magnetic surface off the disk, throwing pieces of the disk surface across the remainder of the disk. This event is called a *head crash*. It is normally accompanied by a loud scraping noise, lost information, and an expensive bill for a new disk. A disk head crash is comparable to an airplane landing with its gear up and skidding down the runway. In rare instances, you may be able to recover some information after a head crash, but such cases are the exception.

To reduce the possibility of a head crash, keep your computer area free from smoke and dust. Also, never move your computer while the disk is spinning. If you are moving your computer a substantial distance, park the disk heads as discussed later in this chapter.

The disk drive stores information by magnetizing domains. With this in mind, you must keep your disks, both floppy and hard, away from powerful electronics capable of emitting magnetic pulses that can change the information magnetized on the disk. Such devices include the telephone and pencil sharpener that sit on most desks.

Understanding Disk Performance

As you can guess, the disk drive performs a tremendous number of steps to record and access information. Considering the fact that the read/ write head examines over 4 million bits per second, the disk drive appears to be quite fast. As discussed, however, the disk drive moves the read/write head in and out to access data stored on different parts of the platter. Because a mechanical movement is required, the disk is actually much slower than the computer's very fast electronic counterparts, such as the central processing unit or random-access memory.

Because the disk drive is slow in comparison to your computer, you can improve your system performance by reducing disk operations. A major benefit of hard disk management is reduced disk operations for common tasks. As you improve your disk organization, you will also improve your system performance, which makes your time at the computer more productive.

Disk Storage System

All three of the disk drive types discussed—floppy, microfloppy, and hard disk drives—record or access information on disk. The disk drive places the read/write head at the correct disk location and then begins the read or record operation. Your computer accesses the disk drive through a hardware board called the *disk controller*. The disk controller directs the drive, places the read/write heads at the correct location, and then supervises the disk operation. Your disk drive plugs into the disk controller which in turn plugs into your computer.

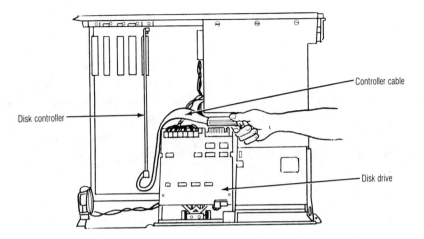

In general, DOS asks the controller for a specific disk sector. The controller initiates the disk read operation and returns the data to DOS. There are three primary disk controller types. Each controller type has advantages and disadvantages.

In the past, the Shugart Technologies (ST) 412 and 506 controllers were the standard hard disk controllers. Presently, Enhanced Small Device Interfaces (ESDI) controllers are providing faster disk access for higher priced machines. Unfortunately, many older disks aren't compatible with ESDI controllers, so you may not be able to boost your performance by installing a new controller. Check with your manufacturer. Many users connect SCSI (pronounced scuzzy) drives to their computers. SCSI drives are external drives with a controller built-in. The drives connect to a serial or parallel port. In fact, many newer computers even offer SCSI adapters. SCSI drives provide hard disk access to computers lacking expansion ports.

Preparing a Disk for Use

Regardless of whether you are using a floppy disk or hard disk, you must perform several steps to prepare the disk for use. The steps you perform will differ, depending upon your disk type.

Floppy and Microfloppy Disk Preparation

Because disk manufacturers have no idea which operating system you will be using with their disks, new disks are not specifically prepared for use with your computer. Before you can use them, you must prepare new disks for use with DOS by using the FORMAT command. Your DOS disk contains a file named FORMAT.COM. You can locate this file on your DOS floppy disk by placing your DOS system disk in drive A and issuing the following command:

```
A> DIR FORMAT.COM

 Volume in drive A is MS330PP01
 Directory of  A:\

FORMAT   COM      11671 07-24-87  12:00a
         1 File(s)        5120 bytes free
```

If your screen displays the message `File not found`, the disk in drive A does not contain the file FORMAT.COM. Insert your original DOS disks in drive A one at a time and use the DIR command just shown to locate FORMAT.COM.

Next, with the DOS disk in drive A, type **FORMAT A:** at the DOS prompt and press Enter. DOS will respond with the following message:

```
Insert new diskette for drive A:
and press ENTER when ready...
```

Remove the DOS disk from drive A. Insert a new, unused disk in drive A, close the drive latch and press Enter. DOS will begin preparing your disk for use.

Earlier in this chapter, we discussed the fact that your disk is divided into circular rings called tracks and that each track was further divided into fixed-size sectors. The DOS FORMAT command performs this disk division.

FORMAT examines your disk, creating and dividing one track of sectors at a time. As FORMAT prepares your disk for use, FORMAT tests each sector to make sure that it can store data. In some cases, the disk surface may be slightly damaged. Rather than letting DOS store information in the damaged sector, FORMAT marks the sector as unusable.

When FORMAT is complete, it displays a summary of the available disk space:

```
Format complete
    362496 bytes total disk space
    362496 bytes available on disk
```

If FORMAT encountered bad sectors, the summary message will include the number of damaged bytes on the disk as shown here:

```
Format complete

    nnnnnn bytes total disk space
      nnnn bytes in bad sectors
    nnnnnn bytes available on disk
```

Next, FORMAT asks if you want to format another disk:

```
Format another (Y/N)?
```

If you do, type **Y**, otherwise, type **N**. After FORMAT completes, your disk is ready for use by DOS.

Understanding Bad Sectors

Your disk has a magnetic coated surface that stores information. In some cases, defects in the disk surface make it impossible for the disk to store information in those areas. When FORMAT examines your disk, it locates these unusable areas and marks the corresponding sectors as unusable. If your floppy disk continually formats with bad sectors, strongly consider purchasing a different brand of disks.

Building a Bootable Disk

The process of turning on your computer and starting DOS is often referred to as *booting* DOS. To *boot* DOS from a floppy disk, the disk in drive A must contain several DOS system files. If the disk does not contain these files, your system will display the following error message when you turn it on:

```
Non-System disk or disk error
Replace and strike any key when ready
```

By default, FORMAT does not place the system information needed to boot DOS on every disk. The information takes up considerable disk space which, in most cases, would simply be wasted.

As you work with DOS, there may be times when you need to create bootable floppy disks for a specific purpose. If so, place the /S switch at the end of your FORMAT command, as shown here:

```
A> FORMAT A: /S
```

The /S switch directs FORMAT to copy the essential files that DOS needs to start. In other words, /S directs FORMAT to create a bootable disk.

The figure below represents how a system disk appears after formatting with the /S switch. The critical DOS files have been copied to the proper locations.

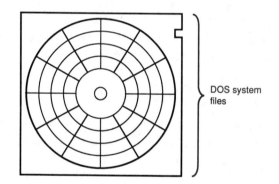

DOS system files

Hard Disk Preparation

A new hard disk requires several preparation steps before it is ready for use. In most cases, your computer manufacturer or retailer performs the first step, low-level formatting.

Because the original manufacturer does not know which controller a system will use, most disks leave the manufacturing plant blank, without track and sector information. After the disk and controller are installed, a low-level format program examines the disk, marking defective regions and recording track and sector information. The low-level format program is not FORMAT.COM. It is controller-specific and is provided by the controller manufacturer.

The low-level format program rigorously tests the disk, writing and reading information to ensure that the disk is recording correctly. A "good" low-level format program may require up to 24 hours to finish formatting. As the low-level format locates damaged locations, it displays the location's address (normally a side and track address) on your screen. Many disks have a certification sticker attached to the outside of the drive that lists the damaged locations.

You may never have to use a low-level format program; most retailers perform it for you. If, however, your disk begins to encounter many errors and reformatting the disk with the DOS FORMAT command does not reduce the number of errors, a low-level format may be your next step after you verify that the disk controller and cable to the controller work correctly.

After low-level formatting completes, your disk is ready for partitioning and formatting, as discussed in Chapter 2.

Disk Head Parking

As discussed, a disk crash occurs when the disk head comes in contact with a spinning disk platter. As such, never move your computer while it is powered on.

To prevent the disk head from contacting the disk platter when you turn off your computer, many disk controllers move the disk heads to an unused cylinder called a *landing zone* and actually set the heads down on the platter. Parking the disk heads in this way prevents the heads from colliding with the platter if the PC is moved. If your disk controller parks the heads automatically, you may actually hear the controller park the disk when you turn off your computer.

If your controller does not automatically park your disk, your manufacturer or retailer can provide you with a program that does so.

Parking your disk heads is a smart protective step. Many users park their disk immediately before turning off their system, every time. Never move your computer without first parking the heads.

More Advanced Concepts

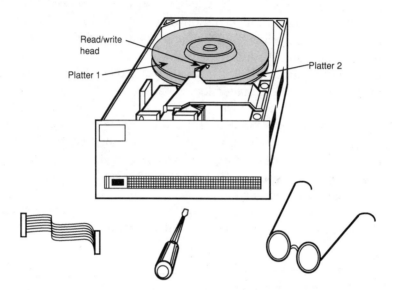

The first part of this chapter provided an overview of the fundamental concepts needed to understand and work with your hard disk. If you are new to DOS, or to using hard disks, continue your hard disk preparation by skipping ahead to Chapter 2. The following section discusses several disk concepts aimed at the more advanced hard disk user.

Understanding the Data Route

Each time you access information stored on disk, the data follows the same route from your disk to your computer's memory. To begin, the disk controller supervises the reading of a sector of bytes from the disk. The controller buffers the sector in its own memory before providing the data to DOS, as shown in the following figure. When the data is available, the disk controller signals the CPU (central processing unit).

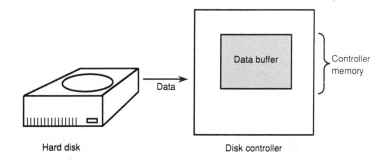

Next, depending upon your PC type, either the CPU or a DMA (direct memory access) chip places the information into an area in memory DOS sets aside for disk transfers called a *disk buffer,* as shown in the following figure. The CONFIG.SYS BUFFERS = entry discussed later in this book specifies the number of available disk buffers. Newer PCs use the CPU to transfer data from the disk controller memory to a DOS buffer. In other words, the CPU must oversee the transfer of every byte moved from the controller memory into the DOS memory buffer. However, the CPUs in older PCs cannot keep up with the disk controller's speed and must rely on the faster DMA chip. The DMA chip is a fast, specialized chip whose function is to move data directly into memory.

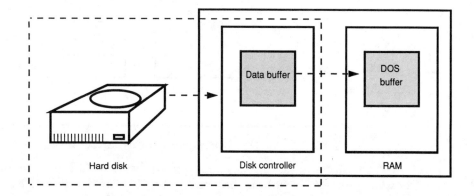

Once the data resides in the DOS buffer, DOS moves the data into the memory buffer set aside by the application, as illustrated in the following figure.

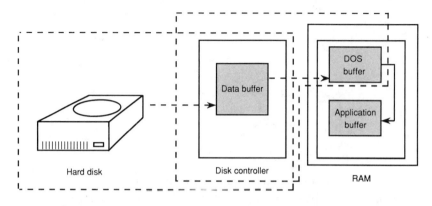

When your application saves information to disk, DOS first moves the data from the application memory buffer into a DOS buffer. Next, the CPU (or DMA chip) transfers the data to the controller memory and signals the controller to begin supervising the disk write operation. This is the reverse process of reading information, as illustrated in the following figure.

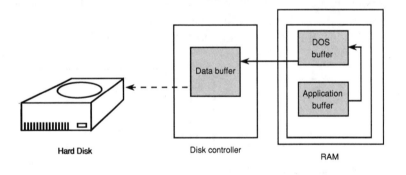

Examining the Data Flow from Your Disk

Assume that you just invoked your word processor. To edit a file, the word processor must bring portions of the file from disk into memory. The word processor first requests DOS to read the file. DOS in turn requests the disk controller to read a specific sector from disk. When the controller finishes reading the sector into its memory, it notifies DOS. Depending upon the computer type, either the CPU or DMA chip transfers the sector into a DOS buffer. DOS then moves the data from the DOS buffer to the application buffer. If the word processor needs additional file data, this process is repeated. When the word processor later saves the file, the data flow is reversed and the file is recorded to disk a sector at a time.

Disk Drive Performance Considerations

Because disk drives are mechanical devices, they are inherently slower than your computer's fast electronic components. The longer it takes your program to access data on disk, the slower your programs appear to run. As a result, most users naturally want to maximize disk drive performance.

Disk Head Movement

All hard disks spin at the same rate of 3600 RPMs. As a result, the only performance gain the disk drive itself can provide is head movement. As the disk spins, the read/write head moves in and out across the disk to locate specific tracks. A device called a *disk head actuator* moves the disk head.

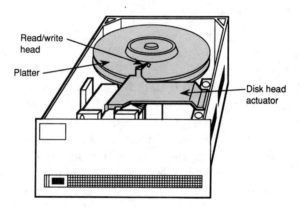

There are two types of disk head actuators in use today: *stepper motor* and *voice coil actuators*. A stepper motor is a small motor that can spin in either direction. Connected to the stepper motor is a band which in turn moves the disk drive head in and out across the disk tracks. The motor is calibrated such that each movement places the disk head over a track.

A voice coil actuator uses a magnet to push or pull a rod connected to the disk heads. Because voice coil actuators don't have mechanical parts, they are much faster than stepper motor actuators. However, in addition to higher performance, the voice coil actuator also has a higher cost. Whereas the mechanical nature of the stepper motor actuator ensures that the heads are always positioned over a track, many voice coil actuators rely upon position information magnetically recorded between tracks. Using this information (called *servo data*), the voice coil actuator can quickly align the disk heads on the correct track.

The amount of time a disk drive takes to move from one track to another is called *seek time*. Manufacturers often advertise an average seek time for their disks. A more important timing consideration, however, is disk *access time*. Access time measures the amount of time required to locate and read a sector of data. Access time considers the seek time and the settling time delays (delays occurring while the head stops vibrating from the move before it begins reading).

The disk controller has a tremendous influence over performance. As discussed, ESDI controllers using run length limited (RLL) encoding techniques provide very good response. Keep in mind that the controller oversees every disk operation. A faster controller will naturally improve performance.

Disk Interleaving

For simplicity, our discussion has assumed that disk sectors reside on disk in order, with sector 2 immediately following sector 1, and so on. If you have a fast 80386 based system, your computer may be fast enough to keep up with data transfers from successive sectors. However, assume you have a slower PC. Also assume that a program needs to read sectors 1 and 2 from a specific track. First, DOS initiates the disk read operation, directing the controller to transfer the data for sector 1 from disk into a DOS buffer as discussed earlier. Unfortunately, by the time the data transfer completes and DOS is ready for the next sector, sector 2 may have already spun past the read/write head and the controller must wait for the disk to complete another revolution before it can read sector 2. Although the disk is spinning at 3600 RPMs and the delay is minimal, the cumulative delay for several such sector misses in a disk-intensive program (such as a database) can become a performance factor. To reduce the possibility of sector misses, many disks physically separate successively numbered sectors. The separation distance lets the computer complete one disk operation in time to access the next sector as it spins past the head. Separating disk sectors in this way is called *disk interleaving*. Disk interleaving improves system performance by better synchronizing the disk to the CPU speed. The following illustration shows a 2:1 and 4:1 disk interleave.

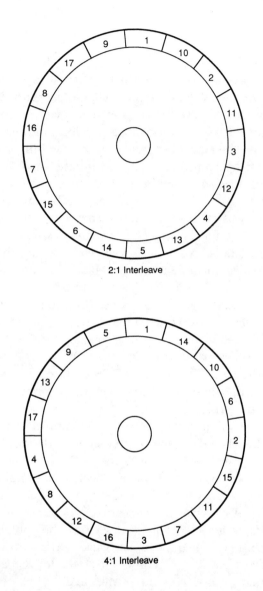

2:1 Interleave

4:1 Interleave

Faster PCs will have a smaller interleave value. The disk interleave is set during the low-level formatting process discussed earlier. Third-party software packages are available that determine and then implement the disk interleave value that provides the best performance for your PC.

Disk Errors

A hard disk crash is the most fatal error that your disk can experience. Floppy disks don't experience head crashes because the floppy drive read/write head is always in actual contact with the disk. In addition to head crashes, a disk can experience several different errors. Keep in mind that disks are mechanical devices and, as such, will eventually wear out. The controller card may lose a chip, or a pin in the wire that connects the controller to the computer may break. Disk errors are categorized as *soft* or *hard errors* depending upon the type of error and its source. Soft errors occur when the hardware is working correctly, but data was read or written incorrectly. Most controllers catch soft errors by performing *cyclic redundancy checks* (CRC) on the data each time the data is accessed. A cyclic redundancy check applies a complex mathematical formula to the data bits. The controller records the result of the formula on the disk immediately following the sector. When the controller reads data, it performs a CRC to ensure the value it calculates matches the value recorded for the sector. If the values differ, the controller reads the data again, repeating the test. If the data is correct, the controller passes the data to DOS. If the CRC check fails several times, the controller notifies DOS of the soft error. DOS will in turn display a disk read error message and prompt you to Abort, Retry, or Ignore the error.

When writing data to disk, the controller calculates and stores a CRC value. The controller then reads the data, calculates a second CRC, and compares it to the first. If the CRCs are equal, the data is correct. If an error occurs, the controller repeats its attempt to record data several times before reporting the soft error to DOS. After a write soft error, DOS displays a write error message.

Finally, a seek error occurs when the controller cannot place the read/write head at the correct track. If the controller cannot correct a seek error, it will return an error status to DOS and DOS will display a seek or sector not found error message.

Although these errors can occur, they are normally very rare. If you perform regular disk backups as discussed later in this book, you will greatly reduce your loss of data, time, and money should a disk error occur.

Understanding Data Encoding

As discussed, your disk contains many tracks which are further divided into sectors. During formatting, the disk records a unique sector address on the disk at the start of each sector. The sector address, like all information on the disk, is a combination of zeros and ones (binary digits). Unfortunately, the same binary digit sequence could inadvertently occur within one of your data files, which could confuse the disk controller. To prevent file data from inadvertently matching sector addresses, the disk controller encodes the information it records on disk. Data encoding also simplifies the controller's task of reading data. The controller doesn't actually read ones and zeros from the disk. Instead, the controller reads changes in magnetic polarity. The data encoding schemes optimize the controller's capabilities. In the past, controllers used a modified frequency modulation encoding scheme (MFM). Today, however, most controllers use Run Length Limited (RLL) encoding. RLL encoding translates the data recorded on a disk to restrict the number of consecutive zeros that can occur in a given space. RLL 2,7 encoding, for example, limits the run length of zeros from 2 to 7. One of the most important benefits that RLL encoding provides is increased disk capacity. In the future, advanced RLL encoding techniques will let drives store even more sectors per track, increasing capacity and performance.

Summary

Computers use disks to store programs and data. Depending upon your application, the data stored on disk may be letters, reports, or other information. Disks are classified by their size and removability. Floppy disks normally store close to one million characters, or bytes, of data. Users insert specific floppy disks into a hard drive when the disks are needed. Users frequently use floppy disks as backups and to exchange information from one computer to another. Hard disks are not removable, but are capable of storing much larger amounts of information than floppy disks. Additionally, hard disks are at least ten times faster than floppy disks. Despite their physical differences, both disk types store information by using the same techniques. As a result, the commands are the same for both hard and floppy disks. Before you can use a disk, you must format it. Formatting defines the disk's storage locations (tracks, sectors). This chapter taught you how to format a floppy disk. Chapter 2 presents hard disk formatting.

2

Preparing Your
Hard Disk for Use

- ► Understanding Hard Disk Partitions
- ► Partitioning Your Hard Disk
- ► Using FDISK
- ► Low-Level Formatting Versus the DOS FORMAT Command
- ► Formatting Your Hard Disk
- ► Placing DOS on Your Disk
- ► Summary

2

Preparing Your Hard Disk for Use

As mentioned in Chapter 1, most computer retailers perform your disk's low-level format for you. After the low-level format successfully completes, you must still perform several steps to prepare the disk for use by DOS. The first step is to partition the disk using the DOS FDISK command. Partitioning defines the regions on your disk that DOS can use to store information. Depending on your disk size, the steps you must perform to partition your disk will differ. After partitioning your disk, you must format it using the DOS FORMAT command.

Some retailers also partition and format your hard disk for you. If your system already boots DOS from your hard disk, you won't need to perform the steps discussed in this chapter. Instead, you may want to read the chapter to gain an understanding of partitioning and formatting.

Understanding Hard Disk Partitions

When the first hard disks were released for the IBM PC and PC compatibles in the early 1980s, affordable disks were only capable of storing up to 10 megabytes of information. To support the 10M disks and prepare for future growth in disk storage capabilities, the programmers who wrote DOS developed a file system based upon a maximum disk size of 32M. However, rapid technological advances in hard disk capabilities soon created disks able to store 40, 60, and even greater than 100M of information.

To use disks larger than 32M, users must divide their disks into multiple *partitions* using FDISK. Using a 60 megabyte hard disk, for example, a user could create two 30M partitions. Each disk partition has its own drive letter. The first partition (or *primary partition*) is assigned the drive letter C. This partition is called the primary partition because it is the partition the computer uses to boot DOS. The second partition, called the *extended partition* is assigned the drive letter D. Although the extended partition can hold DOS files, the system will not use it for booting.

Primary Versus Extended Partitions

If your hard disk is larger than 32 megabytes and you are not using DOS version 4, you need to divide your disk into multiple disk partitions. One of the partitions must be a bootable disk. Each time your computer starts, it will attempt to boot using this primary partition. Additional disk partitions are called extended disk partitions because they extend your disk storage capabilities beyond 32 megabytes.

When divided into partitions, a single hard disk appears to the user, as well as to DOS, as if it were multiple disk drives. Given a disk with partitions for drives C and D, operations performed on one drive, such as formatting, do not effect the other drive.

Partition Boundaries

A partition is a group of consecutive disk cylinders. Each partition has a fixed size. DOS assigns each partition a unique drive letter and treats each partition as a unique drive. Just as formatting a floppy disk in drive A cannot effect a floppy disk in drive B, performing a disk operation on one DOS partition cannot effect another.

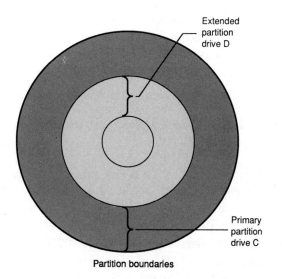

Partition boundaries

When you create partitions, you are not restricted to creating only two partitions of equal size. Again using a 60 megabyte fixed disk, you could create one 30 megabyte partition (drive C) and two 15 megabyte partitions (drives D and E).

One of the major changes to DOS under version 4 is the ability to create partitions larger than 32 megabytes. Under DOS 4, you can create partitions up to 512 megabytes, which temporarily exceeds today's affordable disk drives.

To keep track of partition boundaries, hard disks store the partition information in the first sector of your hard disk (side 0, track 0, sector 1). The partition information is often called the *master boot record.*

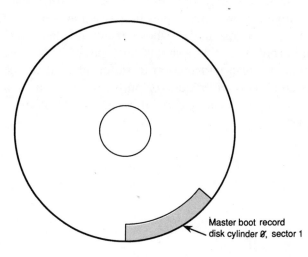

Master boot record
disk cylinder 0, sector 1

Not only does the master boot record contain the cylinder boundaries for each partition, but it also holds information used during booting. This information lets the computer know which partition contains the operating system it is supposed to use when booting.

Partitioning Hard Disks Smaller than 32 Megabytes

If your disk is smaller than 32 megabytes, you may wonder how partitions concern you. Each time a PC boots, the startup procedures built into the PC read the master boot record from your hard disk. If you have not defined the partition information, the PC will not recognize that the hard disk even exists. As a result, the PC will only boot DOS from the floppy disk in drive A. When you later try to access the hard disk, DOS will display the following error message:

```
Invalid drive specification
```

The bottom line is that to use your hard disk, you must create at least one partition using FDISK.

Other Uses for Hard Disk Partitions

DOS is the disk operating system for the IBM PC and PC compatibles. When hard disks first became available for PCs in the early 1980s, DOS was not the only operating system in use. Many users were slowly changing from other operating systems, such as CP/M. The PC developers recognized that those users needed to be able to place two different operating systems on their disk. Because different operating systems store information in different formats, each operating system needed its own unique region on the disk. By creating two disk partitions, a user can place both DOS and CP/M on a disk in separate partitions.

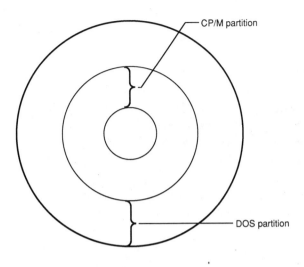

Partitioning Your Hard Disk

To partition a new hard disk, you must start your system by placing a bootable DOS system disk in floppy drive A and turning on your computer. If you are using an IBM PC AT or AT compatible, your system may display the following error message:

```
161 - System Options Not Set-(Run SETUP)
```

The IBM PC AT and AT compatibles use a battery powered chip called a CMOS (Complementary Metal Oxide Silicon) chip that stores the current date and time, as well as system options such as hard disk drive types. The CMOS chip allows the AT to remember the current date and time, as well as the hardware configuration after you turn off your computer's power. Should your computer display such an error when starting, you must boot the system using the SETUP disk provided with your computer's *Guide To Operations* manual. The SETUP program will prompt you to enter the current date and time, as well as fixed and floppy disk information. You must provide SETUP with a value that represents your fixed disk type. Your retailer should note your drive type on your system documentation. In some cases, a small sticker on the outside of the drive specifies the drive type. Record the drive number in a safe location. When the SETUP program completes, your system will restart and you can then begin partitioning your hard disk.

If you are using a system other than an AT or AT compatible, you won't need to worry about running SETUP. Instead, your system should display the familiar DOS DATE and TIME commands followed by version specific copyright information and the DOS prompt.

```
Current date is Sun   9-30-1990
Enter new date (mm-dd-yy):
Current time is 1:26:52.04
Enter new time:

Microsoft(R) MS-DOS(R)     Version 3.30
(C)Copyright Microsoft Corp 1981-1987

A>
```

Using FDISK

The DOS file FDISK.COM contains the FDISK program which lets you partition your disk. Using the DOS DIR command, you can locate the floppy disk containing FDISK.COM.

```
A> DIR FDISK

Volume in drive A is MS330PP01
Directory of  A:\

FDISK    COM    48919   7-24-87  12:00a
     1 File(s)        5120 bytes free
```

When you invoke FDISK under DOS version 4.0, FDISK displays the menu shown in the following figure. Depending upon your version of DOS, the actual screens FDISK displays may differ slightly. However, FDISK's function (letting you create partitions on your disk) remains the same.

```
                    IBM DOS Version 4.00
                    Fixed Disk Setup Program
                 (C)Copyright IBM Corp. 1983, 1988

                        FDISK Options

    Current fixed disk drive: 1

    Choose one of the following:

    1. Create DOS Partition or Logical DOS Drive
    2. Set active partition
    3. Delete DOS Partition or Logical DOS Drive
    4. Display partition information


    Enter choice: [1]




    Press Esc to exit FDISK
```

With the FDISK main menu, you can create DOS primary and extended partitions, select a specific partition as the boot partition, delete the DOS primary or an extended partition, and display the cylinder boundaries that make up each partition. To select an FDISK option, type the number that corresponds to the option and press Enter. To return to DOS without selecting an option, press the Esc key.

To create a DOS partition, select option 1. FDISK will display the following menu.

```
                Create DOS Partition or Logical DOS Drive

        Current fixed disk drive: 1

        Choose one of the following:

        1. Create Primary DOS Partition
        2. Create Extended DOS Partition
        3. Create Logical DOS Drive(s) in the Extended DOS Partition


        Enter choice: [1]




        Press Esc to return to FDISK Options
```

To begin, create a primary DOS partition by selecting option 1. FDISK will display the following.

```
                    Create Primary DOS Partition

Current fixed disk drive: 1

Do you wish to use the maximum available size for a Primary DOS Partition
and make the partition active (Y/N).....................? [Y]




Press Esc to return to FDISK Options
```

If you are using DOS version 4, you can use the entire disk for a single partition. If you are not using DOS 4, you may need to create multiple partitions based upon your disk drive size. As you create your partitions, keep the following guidelines in mind.

If you are using a hard disk that is 30 megabytes or smaller, you will probably only want to create a single partition that uses the entire disk. If you are using a 40 or 60 megabyte disk, consider using two partitions of the same size. As you will learn in later chapters, DOS allocates file space more efficiently for partitions larger than 16 megabytes. By creating partitions larger than 16, you reduce the amount of unused disk space that DOS may waste for each file it creates. For disks larger than 60 megabytes, create your partition sizes with the goal of the keeping the smallest partition larger than 16 megabytes.

The FDISK prompt asks if you want to create the maximum size partition for this disk. (If you create the maximum partition size and it consumes your disk space, it reboots.) In most cases you will, so simply press Enter. When you do so, FDISK will create the partition and display the following screen telling you that your system will now restart.

```
System will now restart

Insert DOS Install diskette in drive A:
Press any key when ready . . .
```

With your DOS system disk in drive A, press any key to restart your system. If your disk is large enough to support extended partitions, invoke FDISK once again. When FDISK displays its main menu, again select option 1 to create a DOS partition. From the Create DOS Partition menu, select option 2 to create an extended partition. FDISK will display the following screen.

```
                        Create Extended DOS Partition

        Current fixed disk drive: 1

        Partition Status    Type    Size in Mbytes   Percentage of Disk Used
           C: 1             PRI DOS       10              49%




        Total disk space is   20 Mbytes (1 Mbyte = 1048576 bytes)
        Maximum space available for partition is   10 Mbytes ( 51%)


        Enter partition size in Mbytes or percent of disk space (%) to
        create an Extended DOS Partition............................: [  10]



        Press Esc to return to FDISK Options
```

In this case, FDISK is prompting you for the number of cylinders that you want to use for the extended partition. In most cases, you will simply use the default. Keep in mind the goal to create partitions greater than 16 megabytes. You can determine the partition storage capabilities using the following equation:

```
PartitionStorage = (Sides)*(Cylinders)*(Sectors Per Cylinder)*(Sector Size)
```

When you press Enter, FDISK will create the extended partition while displaying the following information.

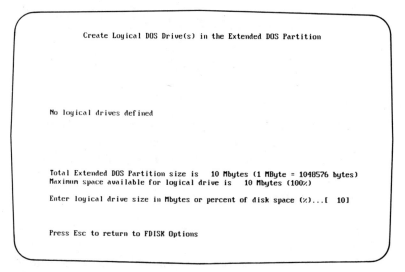

```
                          Create Extended DOS Partition

        Current fixed disk drive: 1

        Partition Status    Type    Size in Mbytes   Percentage of Disk Used
          C: 1              PRI DOS       10             49%
             2              EXT DOS       10             51%






        Extended DOS Partition created


        Press Esc to continue
```

When you press the Esc key to return to the FDISK menu, FDISK will display the following message telling you that you have not defined a logical disk for the extended partition.

```
              Create Logical DOS Drive(s) in the Extended DOS Partition





        No logical drives defined





        Total Extended DOS Partition size is   10 Mbytes (1 MByte = 1048576 bytes)
        Maximum space available for logical drive is   10 Mbytes (100%)

        Enter logical drive size in Mbytes or percent of disk space (%)...[  10]


        Press Esc to return to FDISK Options
```

The logical drive letter in this case is D. Press Enter to create the logical drive, FDISK will display the following screen describing the starting and ending cylinders for the logical drive.

```
               Create Logical DOS Drive(s) in the Extended DOS Partition

Drv Volume Label  Mbytes  System  Usage
D:                    10  UNKNOWN  100%











            All available space in the Extended DOS Partition
            is assigned to logical drives.
            Press Esc to return to FDISK Options
```

When you press Esc, your system will return you to the FDISK main menu. Repeat this process for any additional extended partitions you need to create. If you don't need to create additional extended partitions, press Esc to exit FDISK. Your system will restart, and you can continue with the DOS format command.

Warning! Never change the partition information for a disk containing files that you have not backed up to floppy disk. In fact, once your hard disk is operational, you should consider deleting the file FDISK.COM from your fixed disk to prevent an inadvertent partition modification.

Low-Level Formatting Versus the DOS FORMAT Command

In Chapter 1, you learned that the disk low-level format thoroughly tests each disk storage location and physically records the disk track and sector information onto the disk for use by the disk controller. The low-level format, therefore, is often called a *physical disk format.*

Every operating system stores information on disks differently. DOS is no exception. FORMAT creates and writes to the disk a series of tables DOS needs to manage the disk system. These tables allow DOS to track disk space containing files, disk space available for storing files, and disk space determined to be unusable. In addition, FORMAT places files on your disk that DOS needs in order to boot from the hard disk. Because FORMAT does not actually change your hard disk's physical characteristics, it is often called a *logical format*.

Formatting Your Hard Disk

Formatting a disk prepares it for use by the operating system. DOS stores information on disk in files. To manage the files on your disk, DOS must keep track of where each file's data resides, as well as the locations of the unused disk space. To track disk usage, DOS uses a table called the *file allocation table* or *FAT*. The FAT tracks the disk sectors in use, the available (unused) sectors, as well as damaged sectors marked unusable by the low-level format. The DOS FORMAT command creates the FAT and writes it to disk. Each time you create or delete a file, DOS updates the FAT.

Understanding the FAT

The file allocation table is your disk's road map. The FAT tracks the disk space currently in use, the space available for file allocation, and the space consumed by damaged sectors.

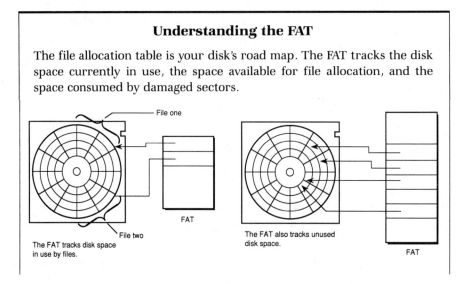

File one

FAT

File two

The FAT tracks disk space in use by files.

The FAT also tracks unused disk space.

FAT

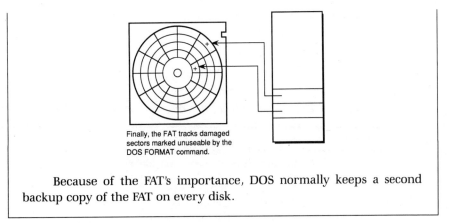

Finally, the FAT tracks damaged
sectors marked unuseable by the
DOS FORMAT command.

Because of the FAT's importance, DOS normally keeps a second backup copy of the FAT on every disk.

The FAT is your disk road map; it tells DOS where each file's information resides. If the section of your disk containing the FAT is damaged, DOS can no longer access your files. To reduce the possibility of such an error, DOS places two copies of the FAT on your disk. Should the first FAT become damaged, DOS uses the second.

A *directory* is a list of file names. To keep track of files on your disk, DOS stores information about each in a directory. When you issue the DOS directory command, DIR, DOS displays information about files in the current directory or the directory specified.

```
A> DIR

Volume in drive A is MS330PP01
Directory of  A:\

4201      CPI      17089    7-24-87   12:00a
5202      CPI        459    7-24-87   12:00a
ANSI      SYS       1647    7-24-87   12:00a
APPEND    EXE       5794    7-24-87   12:00a
ASSIGN    COM       1530    7-24-87   12:00a
ATTRIB    EXE      10656    7-24-87   12:00a
  :        :          :        :         :
RECOVER   COM       4268    7-24-87   12:00a
SELECT    COM       4132    7-24-87   12:00a
SORT      EXE       1946    7-24-87   12:00a
SUBST     EXE      10552    7-24-87   12:00a
SYS       COM       4725    7-24-87   12:00a
        34 File(s)         5120 bytes free
```

DOS keeps track of the name, extension, size, and creation/last modification date and time stamp for each file on your disk. DOS stores this information in a 32-byte entry called a *directory entry*. Table 2.1 describes the directory entry format.

Table 2.1. *Fields in the 32 byte DOS directory entry.*

Bytes	Use
1– 8	Contain the eight character file name
9–11	Contain the three character extension
12	Contains the file attributes
13–22	Reserved for use by DOS
23–24	Contains the file's time stamp
25–26	Contains the file's date stamp
27–28	Contains the file's starting cluster number
29–32	Contains the file's size in bytes

Understanding File Directories

Picture a DOS directory as a filing cabinet for the files on your disk. To find out what files are stored on a disk, you can search the directory, just as you would open a drawer of the filing cabinet and thumb through files. As you will learn in later chapters, DOS lets you add, rename, and delete files from the directory, just as you might in an office.

Every DOS disk begins with only one directory called the *root directory*. The directory is named the root because the subdirectories you later create to organize your disk grow out from it like a tree and its branches grow from the root.

In addition to creating the file allocation table, FORMAT also reserves several disk sectors to store the root directory. The number of files you can create in the root is fixed and is dependent upon the number of sectors set aside for the root directory by the FORMAT command. For example, for most hard disk partitions, FORMAT allocates 32 sectors for the root directory. Knowing each sector contains 512 bytes and each directory entry is 32 bytes, you can determine the maximum number of files DOS can store in the root directory using the following equation:

```
Root files = (reserved sectors) * (sector size) / (directory size)
           = (32) * (512)/(32)
           = 512
```

In this case, the value 512 tells you the number of files and sub-directories you can create in the root directory. Your disk can store many more files than this in other subdirectories. The root directory, however, can store only a fixed number of files because its size is constrained by the number of sectors FORMAT allocates for the root. All subdirectories other than the root can grow as needed to store an essentially unlimited number of files. Chapter 4 discusses DOS subdirectories in detail.

FORMAT's last major function is to make your hard disk bootable. To do so, FORMAT places a boot record at the first sector of the disk partition.

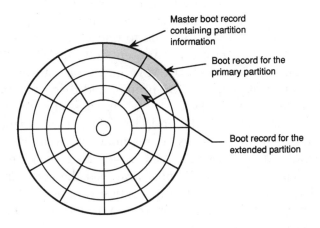

Master boot record containing partition information

Boot record for the primary partition

Boot record for the extended partition

Every disk partition, bootable or not, has a boot record as the first sector. This boot record is specific to the operating system used on the partition. When you turn on your system, the PC startup routine reads the master boot record to locate the partition containing the operating system to boot.

Next, the startup routine locates the partition and reads the operating system's boot record. If the partition is bootable, the boot record contains information the PC uses for booting. If the partition is not bootable, the boot record contains information which in turn displays the following message:

```
Non-System disk or disk error
```

When the PC startup routine finds a bootable partition, it passes control of the PC to software contained in the boot record. The boot record software in turn takes over the responsibility of booting DOS.

For DOS to successfully boot, DOS requires three specific files to reside in the root directory: two DOS hidden files and COMMAND.COM. *Hidden files* are files that reside on your disk but do not appear in the directory listing. DOS hides two key files to prevent you from inadvertently deleting or moving them. If you are using MS DOS, the two hidden files DOS needs to boot are IO.SYS and MSDOS.SYS. If you are using PC DOS, the hidden files are IBMBIO.COM and IBMDOS.COM. Although PC DOS and MS DOS use different names for these files, the file's functions are the same. IO.SYS and IBMBIO.COM contain extensions to the ROM-BIOS basic input and output routines built into your computer. MSDOS.SYS and IBMDOS.COM contain the DOS system services. These services perform DOS file, date and time, and program execution operations. It isn't necessary for you to understand what these files do, just realize that the files must be present on your disk for DOS to start.

The file COMMAND.COM is the DOS command processor responsible for displaying the DOS prompt and then executing commands as you enter them. COMMAND.COM contains all of the DOS *internal commands* such as CLS, DATE, and TIME. Internal commands are commands that DOS always stores in memory. *External commands*, such as FDISK.COM and FORMAT.COM, reside on disk. When you execute an external command, DOS must first load the command from disk into memory. If the DOS startup routine cannot locate COMMAND.COM when DOS is booting, your screen will display the following error message:

```
Bad or missing Command Interpreter
```

To quickly review, FORMAT performs several major steps:

1. FORMAT examines your disk to locate any unusable (damaged) sectors.

2. FORMAT then creates two copies of the file allocation table, placing markers in the FAT for each damaged location which prevent DOS from later trying to use an unusable sector.

3. FORMAT creates and stores a boot record on the partition's first sector.

4. Depending upon the partition size, FORMAT reserves a number of sectors to store the disk's root directory.

5. If FORMAT is creating a bootable system disk, FORMAT copies the DOS hidden system files to the disk.

6. Depending upon your version of DOS, FORMAT will copy the file COMMAND.COM to the root directory.

Be very careful with the DOS FORMAT command. If you format a floppy disk containing files, the information is lost forever. Depending on your version of DOS, you may be able to recover from a hard disk error using the UNFORMAT utility provided with the Jamsa Disk Utilities. You can use UNFORMAT, but don't rely on it! This is on the companion disk that accompanies this book.

Warning! Never rely on third party utility programs to recover your disk after an inadvertent formatting. Instead use FORMAT.COM with care and caution.

With your DOS system disk in drive A, invoke the FORMAT command as follows:

```
A> FORMAT C: /S
```

The command contains two parameters. The first is the disk drive to format, which in this case is drive C. The /S directs FORMAT to create a bootable system disk. For DOS to boot from your hard disk, you must use the /S qualifier. When you press Enter to invoke the command, FORMAT will respond with the following warning message:

```
WARNING, ALL DATA ON NON-REMOVABLE DISK
DRIVE C: WILL BE LOST!
Proceed with Format (Y/N)?
```

FORMAT displays this message to help keep you from formatting a hard disk you are currently using. If you type **N** and press Enter, the command ends and the disk is unchanged. If instead, you type **Y** and press Enter, FORMAT will begin the logical format of your disk and display the side and cylinder number it is currently formatting as follows:

```
Head:  0 Cylinder:   3
```

When FORMAT completes, your screen displays the following:

```
Format complete

System transferred
   nnnnnnnnn bytes total disk space
       nnnnn bytes used by system
   nnnnnnnnn bytes available on the disk
```

The `System transferred` message informs you that FORMAT has created a bootable disk by transferring the hidden system files to the hard disk, as well as creating a boot record. Next, FORMAT displays a summary of the total disk space available, the amount used for operating system files, and the amount of space currently available.

Placing DOS on Your Disk

Select drive C as the current drive and perform a directory listing of the root.

```
A> C: <Enter>
C> DIR
```

If the root contains the file COMMAND.COM, your system is bootable from the hard disk.

```
C> DIR
 Volume in drive C has no label
 Directory of  C:\

COMMAND COM      25276    7-24-87  12:00a
        1 File(s)  28057600 bytes free
```

If the root directory is empty and DOS displays the message `File not found`, you must copy COMMAND.COM from drive A to your fixed disk, as shown here:

```
C> COPY A:COMMAND.COM C:\
```

Chapter 4 discusses the DOS subdirectory commands in detail. For now, however, issue the following commands to place the DOS external commands on your hard disk.

```
C> MKDIR DOS
```

The MKDIR command creates a subdirectory (storage location) for files. In this case, name the subdirectory DOS, since it will store your DOS commands. Next, with your DOS system disk still in drive A, issue the following command:

```
C> COPY A:*.* DOS
```

The command directs DOS to copy all of the files on the floppy disk in drive A to the DOS subdirectory. When the command completes, place the DOS supplemental programs disk in drive A and repeat the COPY command.

```
C> COPY A:*.* DOS
```

In Chapter 6, which discusses the DOS system startup process in detail, you will learn a great deal about the AUTOEXEC.BAT and CONFIG.SYS files.

For now, understand that each time it starts, DOS uses the contents of the file CONFIG.SYS to customize itself for your system. Using the following DOS COPY command, you can create a minimum CONFIG.SYS file.

```
C> COPY CON CONFIG.SYS
```

The command directs DOS to copy the information that you type at the keyboard (the CON device) into the file CONFIG.SYS. When you press Enter to execute the command, DOS advances the cursor to the start of the next line. Type in the following two lines, pressing Enter at the end of each line.

```
BUFFERS=25
FILES=20
```

Your screen should now contain the following:

```
C> COPY CON CONFIG.SYS
BUFFERS=25
FILES=20
```

To end the file copy operation, press the F6 function key followed by Enter. This lets DOS know you are through with the file. You have now created CONFIG.SYS, and your display should appear as follows:

```
C> COPY CON CONFIG.SYS
BUFFERS=25
FILES=20
^Z

    1 File(s) copied
```

The ^Z character (pronounced *control Z*) marks the end of your file. When DOS encounters this character, DOS knows the file is complete.

Understanding CONFIG.SYS

Each time DOS starts, DOS searches the root directory for the file CONFIG.SYS. If DOS locates the file, DOS uses the file's contents to configure itself in memory. If CONFIG.SYS does not exists, DOS uses its own default values to configure itself in memory. At a minimum, the CONFIG.SYS file for a hard disk system should contain the following entries:

```
FILES = 20
BUFFERS = 25
```

Next create the file AUTOEXEC.BAT in the same fashion you created CONFIG.SYS. When you are done, your screen should appear as follows:

```
C>COPY CON AUTOEXEC.BAT
PATH C:\DOS
^Z

    1 File(s) copied
```

Each time DOS starts, it searches the root directory for the file AUTOEXEC.BAT. If the file does not exist, DOS executes the DATE and TIME commands. If DOS locates AUTOEXEC.BAT, it automatically executes (auto exec) each command the file contains. As you will learn in Chapter 5, the PATH command provides DOS with a list of subdirectories that it should search to locate external commands or programs. In this case, the PATH command in your AUTOEXEC.BAT file directs DOS to search the subdirectory DOS on drive C. As you will recall, you just copied all of the external DOS commands to this subdirectory.

Understanding AUTOEXEC.BAT

After DOS processes CONFIG.SYS and configures itself in memory, DOS searches the root directory for a file named AUTOEXEC.BAT. If DOS locates the file, DOS executes each of the commands contained in the file. With AUTOEXEC.BAT, you can specify one or more DOS commands that you want DOS to execute each time it starts. At a minimum, AUTOEXEC.BAT should contain the following PATH command which simplifies the execution of DOS commands:

```
PATH C:\DOS
```

With these files in place, your hard disk is ready to boot DOS. Remove any floppy disks from drive A and use the Ctrl+Alt+Del keyboard combination to restart DOS. When you do so, your screen will clear, the disk activation light for drive A will light momentarily, and your computer will then boot from the hard disk.

It is important that you understand why your computer always attempts to boot from the floppy disk in drive A before using the hard disk. If the PC attempts to boot from your hard disk first and the hard disk becomes damaged, the computer may not be bootable. By letting your computer boot from a floppy disk first, you can boot your system using drive A and then run a third party utility program to recover as much of the damaged hard disk as possible.

Finally, if you have created extended DOS partitions, you must format each partition individually before you can use it to store files. Because you won't use these partitions to start DOS, format them without the /S switch, as shown here:

```
C> FORMAT D:
```

You also do not need the CONFIG.SYS or AUTOEXEC.BAT files for your other drives. Repeat the DOS FORMAT command for each disk partition you have created.

Summary

A disk partition is a collection of consecutive cylinders on your hard disk grouped together to store information. Each partition corresponds to a specific disk drive. If your disk is 30 megabytes or smaller, your entire disk will very likely make up the disk partition for drive C. If you are using a larger hard disk, you can divide it into several partitions, allocating disk space for several logical disk drives on the same physical disk.

DOS versions 3.3 and earlier support hard disk partitions up to 32 megabytes in size. If your disk is bigger than 32 megabytes, you must create multiple partitions for these DOS versions to use your entire disk. The first partition you create is called the primary partition. It is the partition containing the DOS system files used to boot your computer. The remaining partitions are called extended partitions because they let you access your disk beyond 32 megabytes. If you are using DOS version 4, you can create partitions up to 512 megabytes.

Regardless of the size of your hard disk, you must create at least one partition. The DOS FDISK command creates partitions on your disk. Depending upon your computer retailer, your hard disk may arrive partitioned for you. In such cases, you can use FDISK to display the current partition information, and possibly modify it if the partition division is not satisfactory. If your disk is not partitioned, you must use FDISK to do so.

Once FDISK completes, you must format each partition using the DOS FORMAT command. Because the primary partition must be able to boot DOS, format the partition using the /S qualifier. The DOS FORMAT command initializes your disk file allocation tables and the root directory. Once FORMAT completes, your disk is ready for use. Should you inadvertently format a disk in error, the UNFORMAT program provided with the Jamsa Disk Utilities may be able to recover your disk.

Working with DOS Files

► DOS File Manipulation

► DOS File Storage Considerations

► Understanding Disk Clusters

► Summary

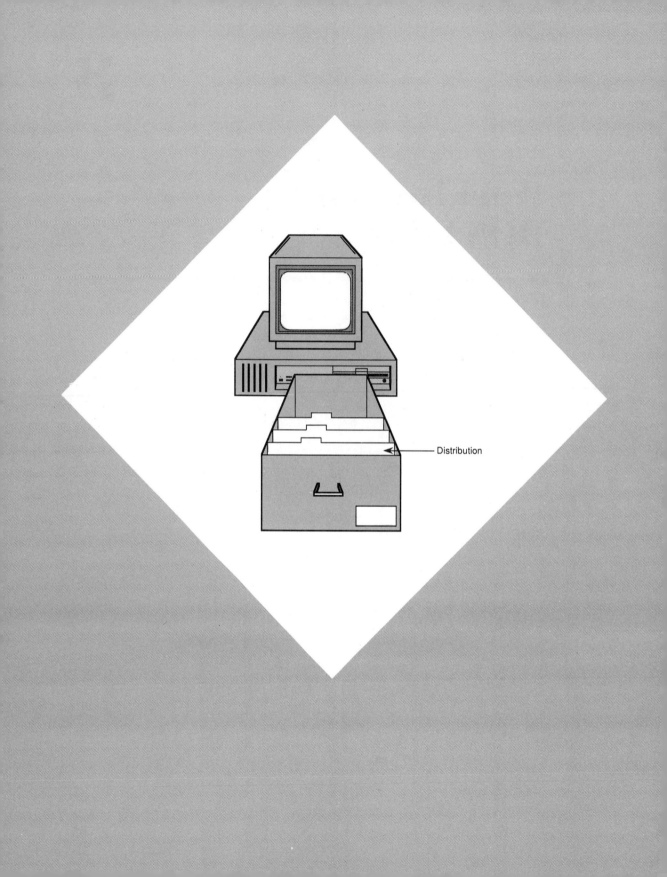

3

Working with
DOS Files

Although your computer's operating system performs many other tasks, its primary functions are program execution and file storage. Files exist to store information from one user session to the next. As discussed in Chapter 2, each operating system stores files differently. This chapter examines DOS files in detail. To begin, the chapter discusses the essential DOS file manipulation commands you will use on a daily basis. Next, it discusses the techniques DOS uses to store files on disk. If you are new to DOS, concentrate on the DOS file manipulation commands. After you are comfortable with DOS, spend time learning the DOS file storage techniques. Several of the commands we will discuss in later chapters use concepts and terms explained in detail in the second part of this chapter.

DOS File Manipulation

DOS files exist to store information. Just as you create, access, and later dispose of files in an office environment, the same is true of DOS files. To work with DOS files, you must know how to work with five key commands: DIR, COPY, TYPE, RENAME and DEL (short for delete). These five commands are the most commonly used DOS commands. By knowing how each command works, you can reduce the number of times you have to use third party file undelete and file locate programs.

Using the DIR Command

A directory is a list. A phone directory, for example, contains a list of phone numbers. A DOS directory is the list of files stored on your disk. As you will recall from Chapters 1 and 2, your disk stores information by magnetizing millions of molecules on your disk. To store files, the operating system must keep track of each file's size and location on disk. The operating system tracks files by placing an entry into the directory list each time you create a file. The directory entry contains the file's name, extension, size in bytes, and the date and time you created or last changed the file.

Learning DOS Commands

If you are new to DOS, the best way to understand the critical DOS file commands is to take time to execute each command as it is presented in the text. The examples in this chapter assume you have created the DOS subdirectory discussed in Chapter 2. If so, select the DOS subdirectory as the current directory by typing **CD** \ **DOS** and pressing Enter at the DOS prompt (C)):

```
C> CD \DOS
```

The DIR command displays each file in the directory list. When you issue the DIR command for your DOS files, for example, your screen displays the following output:

```
Volume in drive C is DOS
Directory of  C:\DOS

  .                <DIR>       01-19-90    2:10p
  ..               <DIR>       01-19-90    2:10p
  4201     CPI       17089 07-24-87   12:00a
  5202     CPI         459 07-24-87   12:00a
  ANSI     SYS        1647 07-24-87   12:00a
  APPEND   EXE        5794 07-24-87   12:00a
  ASSIGN   COM        1530 07-24-87   12:00a
  ATTRIB   EXE       10656 07-24-87   12:00a
    :        :         :       :         :
    :        :         :       :         :
```

```
RAMDRIVE SYS       6481 07-24-87   12:00a
REPLACE  EXE      13234 07-24-87   12:00a
RESTORE  COM      35650 07-24-87   12:00a
SHARE    EXE       8608 07-24-87   12:00a
TREE     COM       3540 07-24-87   12:00a
XCOPY    EXE      11216 07-24-87   12:00a
FC       EXE      15974 07-24-87   12:00a
        51 File(s)    46327808 bytes free
```

DIR displays the file name, extension, size, and date and time stamp in the order shown here.

Depending on your computer type, the directory listing of files may scroll past the top of your screen very quickly. By adding the /P switch at the end of your DIR command line, you direct DIR to display the directory listing one screen at a time.

```
C> DIR /P
```

The appendage (/P) is called a *switch* because it changes the way the DIR command behaves. In this case, the /P switch directs DIR to pause each time it displays a screenful of files, displaying the following message:

```
Strike a key when ready . . .
```

After you view the file entries on the screen, press any key to view the next screen of file entries.

Understanding the Directory Entry

Take a close look at the directory entries DIR displays. Every file has a unique file name and extension combination. The eight character file name and three character extension let you assign unique, meaningful names to your files. The eight character file name normally provides specifics about the file, whereas the three character extension describes the file's contents. For example, DOS commands have either the extension EXE (for executable program) or COM (for command). The file extension, in both cases, tells you that the file contains a DOS command. The eight character file name tells you the specific command, such as FDISK or FORMAT.

Filename.extension	File Contents
FDISK.COM	DOS FDISK command
FORMAT.COM	DOS FORMAT command
ATTRIB.EXE	DOS ATTRIB command
DISKCOPY.COM	DOS DISKCOPY command

DOS commands and programs use the COM and EXE extensions. The eight character file name is the actual command name. As you create files on your disk, take full advantage of the file name and extensions to create meaningful names. The file name should tell you specifics about the file. The extension should tell you the files contents. For example, many users commonly use the extension LTR for letters, the extension RPT for reports, and the extension BAK to indicate a backup copy of a file. As you create files, consider a category that best describes the file's contents. Use a three letter extension to abbreviate the category.

DOS provides up to eight characters for a file name. Use all eight characters as necessary to create descriptive file names. Table 3.1 contains several examples of meaningful file names and extensions. Although a period does not appear in the directory listing, you must use a period to separate your file name and extension when you create your files.

Table 3.1. *Descriptive file names and extensions.*

Filename.extension	File Contents
RJONES.RVW	Employee review for R. Jones
BUDGET90.DAT	Budget data for 1990
MAY-JUNE.SAL	Sales information for May and June
LAWYER.LTR	Personal letter to a lawyer
FISCAL.RPT	Annual fiscal report

DOS lets you use letters of the alphabet, numbers, and the following characters in your DOS file names:

~ !@#$^()&_-{}'

DOS automatically converts all lowercase letters in a file name to uppercase.

Following the file name and extension, DIR displays the file size. DOS tracks a file's size in bytes. As discussed in Chapter 1, a byte is a collection of eight binary digits. Each binary digit is a distinct magnetized domain on your disk.

The DIR command also displays a date and time for each file called the date and time *stamp*. This is the date and time that you created or last changed the file. It does not contain the date and time for the last time you used the file. For the date and time stamp to change, you must change the file's contents. Viewing a file's contents or executing a program stored in this file will not change the date and time stamp.

Changing the Date and Time Stamp

Normally, DOS only updates a file's date and time stamp when you create or alter a file. If you need to change a file's date and time stamp for a specific application, you will need to use the Jamsa Disk Utilities program called DATETIME. This program is included with the companion disk that accompanies this book. See Chapter 12 for more information on DATETIME.

The last piece of information the DIR command displays is the number of files in the directory. Many users make the mistake of ignoring this value. If you want to maximize your disk performance, you need to manage the number of files in the directory. Chapter 4 discusses DOS subdirectories, which are simply sublists of files that improve your disk organization. Using DOS subdirectories, you can reduce the number of files in any particular directory, which in turn improves disk performance.

Each time you invoke a DOS command that resides on disk, DOS must search through the directory entries one at a time until it locates the command. Each time you use a data file, for any purpose, DOS must search each directory entry. Simply put, the more directory entries DOS must examine, the longer the search takes. If you have an application that uses a considerable number of files (such as a data base program), the file search overhead may become considerable.

Searching Crowded Directories

A directory is a list of files. The longer the list, the more time DOS requires to locate a specific file. When DOS searches your directory, DOS starts with the first file and examines each successive file until it locates the desired file.

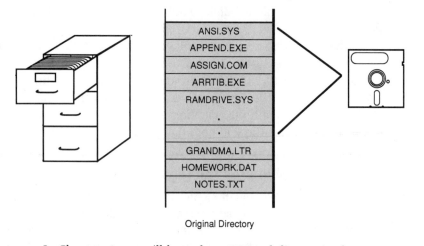

ANSI.SYS
APPEND.EXE
ASSIGN.COM
ARRTIB.EXE
RAMDRIVE.SYS
.
.
GRANDMA.LTR
HOMEWORK.DAT
NOTES.TXT

Original Directory

In Chapter 4 you will learn how DOS subdirectories let you organize your files, reducing the number of files in any directory to a manageable and efficient amount.

Locating a Specific File with DIR

Although the file size and date and time stamp are very important, you may find it easier to locate a specific file on your disk if you use DIR with the /W switch. The /W directs the DIR command to display a wide directory listing containing five file name and extension combinations per line. Again using the DOS files, a directory listing using the /W switch produces the following output:

```
Volume in drive C is DOS
Directory of  C:\DOS

  .                    ..             4201    CPI   5202    CPI   ANSI      SYS
APPEND    EXE   ASSIGN    COM   ATTRIB    EXE   CHKDSK    COM   COMMAND    COM
COMP      COM   COUNTRY   SYS   DISKCOMP  COM   DISKCOPY  COM   DISPLAY    SYS
DRIVER    SYS   EDLIN     COM   EXE2BIN   EXE   FASTOPEN  EXE   FDISK      COM
FIND      EXE   FORMAT    COM   GRAFTABL  COM   GRAPHICS  COM   JOIN       EXE
KEYB      COM   LABEL     COM   MODE      COM   MORE      COM   NLSFUNC    EXE
PRINT     COM   RECOVER   COM   SELECT    COM   SORT      EXE   SUBST      EXE
SYS       COM   BACKUP    COM   DEBUG     COM   EGA       CPI   GWBASIC    EXE
KEYBOARD  SYS   LCD       CPI   LINK      EXE   PRINTER   SYS   RAMDRIVE   SYS
REPLACE   EXE   RESTORE   COM   SHARE     EXE   TREE      COM   XCOPY      EXE
FC        EXE
         51 File(s)   46323712 bytes free
```

Many users find a printed, or *hard copy*, directory listing very convenient. Using the DOS output redirection operator (>), you can direct DOS to send the output of your directory listing to the printer as opposed to the screen display as shown here:

```
C> DIR > PRN
```

To get a printed copy of a wide directory listing, place the output redirection operator after the /W switch as shown here:

```
C> DIR /W > PRN
```

By default, the DIR command displays all of the files in the directory. To perform a directory listing of a specific file, simply include the file name in the DIR command line as shown here:

```
C> DIR FORMAT.COM
```

Using this technique, you can search a directory for a specific file. If the file exists, DIR will display the file's directory information.

```
Volume in drive C is DOS
Directory of  C:\DOS

FORMAT    COM    11671 07-24-87  12:00a
    1 File(s)   46319616 bytes free
```

If the file does not exist on disk, DIR will display the following error message:

```
File not found
```

Should this error message appear, one of three possible conditions may have occurred. First, you may have mistyped the file name. Check the spelling carefully. Second, the file may reside on the disk, but not in the current directory (see Chapter 4 for discussion on DOS subdirectories). Or, the file may simply not be on your disk.

Understanding Wildcard Characters

So far, the examples have used the DIR command to display one or all of the files on your disk. In many cases you will want to view a directory listing of a group of files. For example, at the end of the fiscal year you might want to identify each budget file with the extension BGT. Likewise, if you are searching your disk for a specific letter, you can perform a directory listing of all files with the extension LTR. DOS makes it easy for you to perform such directory operations using *wildcard* characters.

DOS defines two wildcard characters, the asterisk (*) and the question mark (?). Both wildcard characters exist to help you perform file operations on a group of files. The wildcards get their name from card games that let you substitute a "wildcard" for any card in the deck. On your computer, these wildcards direct DOS to substitute any valid file name character in the wildcard position. The difference between the two wildcards is the character substitution DOS performs for each.

The DOS question mark wildcard performs a single character substitution. For example, if you issue the following DIR command using the question mark wildcard character, DIR will display a directory listing for DISKCOPY.COM and DISKCOMP.COM.

```
C> DIR DISKCO??.COM

Volume in drive C is DOS
Directory of   C:\DOS3

DISKCOMP COM      5848 07-24-87  12:00a
DISKCOPY COM      6264 07-24-87  12:00a
      2 File(s)   46315520 bytes free
```

Think of the question mark wildcard character as an "I don't care" character. As such, the previous command told DIR to display directory listings for all files beginning with the characters DISKCO. The two question mark wildcard characters tell DOS that you don't care what that last two characters are, or for that matter, if the character positions are even in use. Just remember that each question mark represents a single replacement character.

The asterisk is the most powerful and the most commonly used wildcard character. Unlike the question mark which represents a single character, the asterisk wildcard tells DOS that you don't care about the character in the wildcard's position or any of the file name or extension characters that follow. To better understand the asterisk wildcard, consider the following examples.

If the asterisk appears at the beginning of the file name, DOS will use each file that matches the extension given. In this case, DOS will display a directory listing of all files with the extension COM.

```
C> DIR *.COM

Volume in drive C is DOS
Directory of   C:\DOS

ASSIGN   COM      1530 07-24-87  12:00a
CHKDSK   COM      9819 07-24-87  12:00a
COMMAND  COM     25276 07-24-87  12:00a
COMP     COM      4183 07-24-87  12:00a
DISKCOMP COM      5848 07-24-87  12:00a
DISKCOPY COM      6264 07-24-87  12:00a
EDLIN    COM      7495 07-24-87  12:00a
FDISK    COM     48919 07-24-87  12:00a
FORMAT   COM     11671 07-24-87  12:00a
GRAFTABL COM      6136 07-24-87  12:00a
```

```
GRAPHICS COM      13943 07-24-87   12:00a
KEYB      COM       9041 07-24-87   12:00a
LABEL     COM       2346 07-24-87   12:00a
MODE      COM      15440 07-24-87   12:00a
MORE      COM        282 07-24-87   12:00a
PRINT     COM       8995 07-24-87   12:00a
RECOVER   COM       4268 07-24-87   12:00a
SELECT    COM       4132 07-24-87   12:00a
SYS       COM       4725 07-24-87   12:00a
BACKUP    COM      29976 07-24-87   12:00a
DEBUG     COM      15866 07-24-87   12:00a
RESTORE   COM      35650 07-24-87   12:00a
TREE      COM       3540 07-24-87   12:00a
        23 File(s)    4615520 bytes free
```

Remember, the asterisk wildcard tells DOS you don't care about the character in the wildcard position or the characters that follow. In the previous example, the wildcard appeared in the first character position. As such, DOS ignored all eight file name characters.

By placing the asterisk wildcard after the letter D, the following command directs DOS to display a directory listing of all files that begin with the letter D and have the extension COM.

```
C> DIR D*.COM

Volume in drive C is DOS
Directory of  C:\DOS

DISKCOMP COM       5848 07-24-87   12:00a
DISKCOPY COM       6264 07-24-87   12:00a
DEBUG     COM     15866 07-24-87   12:00a
         3 File(s)    4615520 bytes free
```

If you change the previous command slightly to use the question mark wildcard, DIR displays the following output:

```
C> DIR D?.COM

Volume in drive C is DOS
Directory of  C:\DOS

File not found
```

Remember, the question mark wildcard only matches a single character at a time. The previous command would match only a two letter file name beginning with the letter D and having the extension COM.

Using the asterisk wildcard for the file name and extension, the following command directs DIR to perform a directory listing of all files on your disk.

```
C> DIR *.*
```

As you will recall, by default, placing the DIR command alone on the command line displays a listing of all files on your disk.

```
C> DIR
```

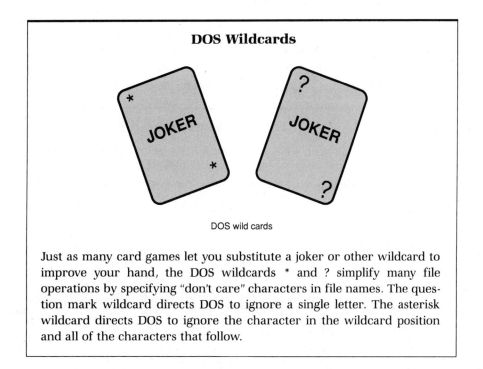

DOS Wildcards

DOS wild cards

Just as many card games let you substitute a joker or other wildcard to improve your hand, the DOS wildcards * and ? simplify many file operations by specifying "don't care" characters in file names. The question mark wildcard directs DOS to ignore a single letter. The asterisk wildcard directs DOS to ignore the character in the wildcard position and all of the characters that follow.

Table 3.2 contains several wildcard combinations and explanations of the files DIR will list. Experiment with each wildcard combination by using DIR to list the directory entries for your DOS files.

Table 3.2. *DOS wildcard character combinations and corresponding files.*

Wildcard Combination	Files Displayed
DIR *.*	All files
DIR ???????.???	All files
DIR DISK*.*	Files beginning with the letters DISK.
DIR *.EXE	All files with the EXE extension.
DIR *ISKCOPY.COM	All files with the COM extension. Once DOS encounters the asterisk wildcard, it ignores all characters that follow.
DIR ????COPY.*	Files with the characters COPY in the last four file name positions

Using the COPY Command

In Chapter 2, you used the DOS COPY command to create the files CONFIG.SYS and AUTOEXEC.BAT. The COPY command copies information from one file or device to another. Just as you make duplicate copies of important papers, you should do the same for key files.

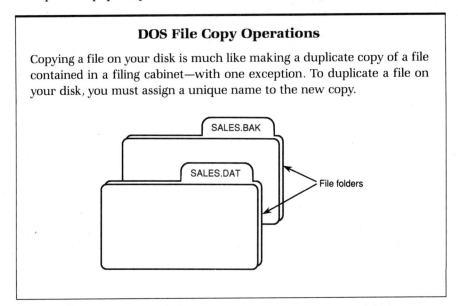

DOS File Copy Operations

Copying a file on your disk is much like making a duplicate copy of a file contained in a filing cabinet—with one exception. To duplicate a file on your disk, you must assign a unique name to the new copy.

SALES.BAK

SALES.DAT

File folders

The COPY command copies a file from a source to a destination. Using the following COPY command, create the file SAMPLE.TXT that contains the text shown:

```
C> COPY CON SAMPLE.TXT
The DOS COPY command copies a source
file to a target destination.
^Z
    1 File(s) copied
```

As you learned in Chapter 2, use the F6 function key to generate the end of file (^Z) character. All COPY commands use a source and destination. In the previous command, the keyboard or CON device was the source of the information and the file SAMPLE.TXT was the destination.

The following COPY command creates a backup copy of the SAMPLE.TXT file:

```
C> COPY SAMPLE.TXT SAMPLE.BAK
    File(s) copied
```

Every file name in a directory must be unique. As such, you must change either the file name or the extension when you create the duplicate copy of a file in the same directory of a disk. The previous COPY command created a file using the common backup file extension BAK.

The DOS COPY command fully supports wildcard characters. Using the asterisk wildcard, you can copy the file SAMPLE.TXT to the file SAMPLE.SAV, as shown here:

```
C> COPY SAMPLE.TXT *.SAV
    1 File(s) copied
```

When you use a wildcard character in the destination file name of a COPY operation, COPY creates the file using the same file name as the source, which in this case is SAMPLE. Likewise, if you use the asterisk wildcard in the destination file extension, COPY uses the extension of the source, as shown in the following figure.

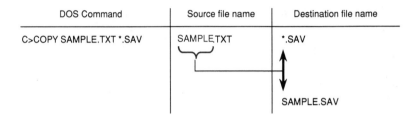

Using wildcard characters in file copy operations can reduce key strokes and save time. You need to understand exactly how DOS will interpret the wildcard character to prevent copy from overwriting existing files. COPY is a destructive command which means it has the ability to overwrite existing files. Once COPY overwrites a file, you have no way of retrieving the original file's contents. The original file contents no longer exist on disk. To reduce the possibility of file overwrite errors, many users first execute a DIR command using the wildcard characters they plan to use in the COPY operation. Using DIR, you can tell which files DOS will copy and which files COPY may overwrite.

Warning! COPY is a Destructive Command

When you issue the DOS COPY command, you must specify the name of the destination copy. If a file already exists on your disk with the name given, COPY will write over the existing file's contents. When a file is overwritten, the original contents are lost forever. Chapter 5 discusses the DOS ATTRIB command that allows you to prevent key files from being overwritten or inadvertently deleted.

Place a formatted disk in drive A and copy the contents of the file SAMPLE.TXT to it, as shown here:

```
C> COPY SAMPLE.TXT A:SAMPLE.TXT
    1 File(s) copied
```

When you copy a file from one disk to another, you must specify the source or destination disk drive if it is not the default drive. If you do not specify a drive, DOS assumes you want the operation to occur on the current drive.

Because the file name does not change in the previous file copy operation, you can reduce your keystrokes by using DOS wildcards. The following COPY command also copies the contents of the file SAMPLE.TXT to the disk in drive A:

```
C> COPY SAMPLE.TXT  A:*.*
    1 File(s) copied
```

In this case, COPY will create the file on drive A using the same file name and extension as the source.

You can minimize keystrokes even more for disk to disk file copy operations if you take advantage of the fact that, unless you specify otherwise, COPY creates the file on the disk specified using the same file name as the source file. The following COPY command shows the simplest way to copy the file SAMPLE.TXT to the disk in drive A:

```
C> COPY SAMPLE.TXT A:
```

Because the command only specifies drive A as the target, COPY creates the file on drive A using the file name SAMPLE.TXT. Table 3.3 describes several COPY commands in detail. Experiment with the commands shown.

Table 3.3. *DOS file copy operations.*

COPY Command	Action
C> COPY *.TXT *.OLD	Copies all files with the extension TXT to files with the same file name but having the extension OLD.
C> COPY A:*.*	Copies all files from the disk in drive A to the current directory using the source file names.
C> COPY SAMPLE.* A:	Copies all files with the file name SAMPLE, regardless of the file's extension, to drive A.
C> COPY SAMPLE.TXT PRN	Copies the contents of the file SAMPLE.TXT to the printer.
C> COPY CON PRN	Copies text typed at the keyboard directly to the printer. Use the F6 function key to end the file copy operation.

Using the RENAME Command

The RENAME command changes the name of an existing file on disk. The format of the RENAME command is RENAME *OldName NewName*. For example, the following command renames the file SAMPLE.TXT as SAMPLE.NEW:

```
C> RENAME SAMPLE.TXT SAMPLE.NEW
```

Like the COPY command, RENAME also uses the concept of a source and destination files as shown here.

C> RENAME   SAMPLE.TXT   SAMPLE.NEW

Source or original Destination or
file name   new file name

DOS File Rename Operation

Renaming a file on your disk is much like pulling a file from a filing cabinet, placing a new name on the file, and restoring the file to its original location.

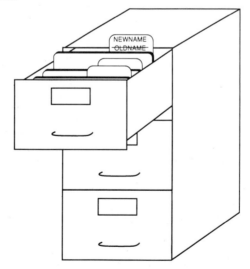

Renaming a file does not move the location of the file within the directory, nor does it move the file from one disk to another.

Because of its frequency of use, DOS lets users abbreviate RENAME as simply REN. With the abbreviation in mind, the following command renames the file SAMPLE.NEW to SAMPLE.TXT:

```
C> REN SAMPLE.NEW *.TXT
```

As you can see in the following figure, the command also uses the asterisk wildcard. Because the wildcard appears in the target file name position, RENAME uses the source file name, changing only the extension.

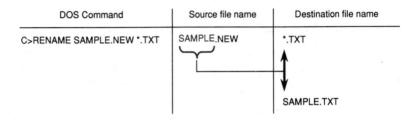

DOS Command	Source file name	Destination file name
C>RENAME SAMPLE.NEW *.TXT	SAMPLE.NEW	*.TXT
		SAMPLE.TXT

The DOS COPY command creates a second file containing the same contents as the source file. Because COPY creates a second file, DOS must also create a directory entry for the new file. The RENAME command, however, changes an existing directory entry; RENAME does not create a new directory entry. As a result, you cannot use RENAME to move a file from one disk to another, or one subdirectory to another. If you attempt to do so, RENAME displays the following error message:

```
C> RENAME SAMPLE.TXT A:SAMPLE.NEW
Invalid parameter
```

Because RENAME does not let you move a file, it displays the invalid parameter message anytime you include a DOS subdirectory path or disk drive letter before the destination file name. To rename a file that resides on a different disk, just specify the file name without a drive letter. RENAME determines the correct file location from the source file name. The following command, for example, renames the file SAMPLE.TXT on drive A to SAMPLE.NEW. Even though the destination file name does not include a disk drive specifier, the file remains on drive A.

```
C> REN A:SAMPLE.TXT SAMPLE.NEW
```

Remember, if you include a drive letter before the file name SAMPLE.NEW, an error will occur.

The RENAME command is not a destructive command. If a file already exists in the directory with the same name as the destination file, RENAME will display the following error message and the file name will remain unchanged:

```
Duplicate file name or File not found
```

Table 3.4 describes several different RENAME commands in detail.

Table 3.4. *DOS file rename operations.*

RENAME Command	Action
C⟩ REN *.TXT *.ASC	Renames all files with the extension TXT to files with the extension ASC.
C⟩ REN A:SAMPLE.TXT SAMPLE.NEW	Renames the file SAMPLE.TXT on drive A to SAMPLE.NEW. The file remains on drive A.
C⟩ RENAME *.ASC *.TXT	Renames all files with the extension ASC to files with the extension TXT. The command uses the complete RENAME command rather than the REN abbreviation.

Using the TYPE Command

The TYPE command displays a file's contents to your screen display. For example, using the file SAMPLE.TXT that you created earlier in this chapter, you can view the file's contents as follows:

```
C> TYPE SAMPLE.TXT
The DOS COPY command copies a source
file to a target destination.

C>
```

The TYPE command is very easy to use. To examine a file's contents, simply invoke TYPE with the file name. If the file resides on a different disk drive, place the disk drive letter and a colon immediately before the file name.

```
C> TYPE A:SAMPLE.NEW
```

If TYPE cannot find the file you specify on disk, TYPE will display the following error message:

```
C> TYPE A:SAMPLE.NEW
File not found

C>
```

If this error occurs, check the spelling of the file name. If necessary, use the DOS DIR command to help locate the file. The TYPE command does not support wildcards.

```
C> TYPE *.TXT
Invalid filename or file not found

C>
```

TYPE cannot display the contents of every file. Programs or other files that contain binary information are meaningless when you try to display them using TYPE.

For example, try to display the contents of the file FORMAT.COM using the following command.

```
C> TYPE FORMAT.COM
```

When you press Enter to execute the command, your screen will fill with uncommon characters and your computer's built in bell will sound. TYPE is attempting to display the binary digits as characters and can't.

Many users create files with a word processor and later try to display the file's contents using TYPE. When they do, the screen again contains many uncommon characters mixed within the recognizable text.

As you know, word processors let you format letters and reports, center text, and create flush margins. To perform these tasks, the word processor embeds special characters within your document. Although these characters are meaningful to your word processor, they are meaningless to DOS commands, such as TYPE. If you create a file with a word processor, the only way to read the file may be to use the word processing program.

Using the DEL Command

The DEL command deletes one or more files from your disk when you no longer need them. The format of the DEL command is DEL FILENAME.EXT. For example, the following command deletes the file SAMPLE.TXT:

```
C> DEL SAMPLE.TXT
```

When you press Enter to delete the file, the file is gone. DOS removes the file from the directory list. DOS does not provide you with a way to undelete a file.

To delete a file that resides on a different disk, precede the file name with the disk drive letter and a colon, as shown here:

```
C> DEL A:SAMPLE.NEW
```

If the DEL command locates the file, DEL will remove the file from disk. If DEL cannot locate the file, it will display the following error message:

```
File not found
```

If this message appears, double-check the spelling and, if necessary, use the DIR command to locate the file.

The DEL command fully supports DOS wildcards. Be very careful using DEL with wildcards. An errant command can inadvertently delete needed files. Most users should issue a DIR command using the same wildcard combinations they plan to use with DEL. If the files DIR displays match the files you want to delete, proceed with the DEL command. If DIR displays the names of unexpected files, examine your wildcard combination.

If you attempt to delete all of the files in your directory using the asterisk wildcard character for both the file name and extension, DEL will prompt you to ensure that you want to delete all of the files, as shown here:

```
C> DEL A:*.*
Are you sure (Y/N)?
```

Deleting a DOS File

Deleting a file from your disk is much like removing a file from a filing cabinet and throwing it in the trash.

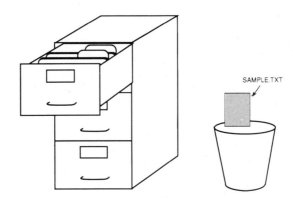

The Jamsa Disk Utilities include UNDELETE, a utility that allows you to recover a deleted file if you inadvertently delete a file. UNDELETE is included on the companion disk that accompanies this book. It is important that you do not save any other files after realizing you inadvertently deleted a file. When you delete a file, DOS reuses the disk space the file once occupied. As a result, if you create files on your disk after inadvertently deleting a file, DOS may very likely overwrite the deleted file making it impossible for UNDELETE to recover the file.

If you are sure you want to delete all of the files in the directory, type **Y** and press Enter. To cancel the command, leaving all of the files on disk, type **N** and press Enter.

Table 3.5 describes several DEL commands in detail.

Table 3.5. *DOS file deletion operations.*

DEL Command	Action
C〉 DEL *.TXT	Deletes files with the extension TXT.
C〉 DEL A:SAMPLE.NEW	Deletes SAMPLE.NEW from the disk in drive A.
C〉 DEL A:*.*	Deletes all files on the disk in drive A.

Using Wildcards with DELETE

Using DOS wildcards with the DEL command intimidates many new DOS users. The Jamsa Disk Utilities which accompany this book include a utility called SELDEL. This utility lets you select the specific files you want to delete using an on-screen menu. For more information on SELDEL, see Chapter 14.

DOS File Storage Considerations

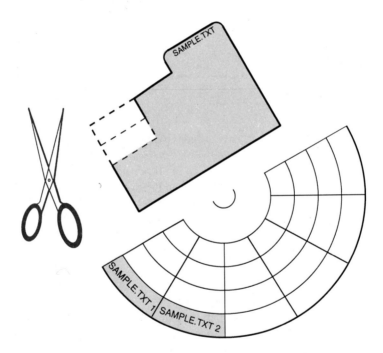

The previous section introduced key file manipulation commands to new DOS users and refreshed veteran users with several short cuts. In this section, we examine how DOS actually stores files on disk, keeping information for one file separate from the information in another file. If you are new to DOS, you might want to consider skipping ahead to Chapter 4 and the discussion of DOS subdirectories. You can return to this information later, after you feel more comfortable with DOS. If you have worked with DOS for some time and have encountered discussions of the FAT, this section explains the file allocation table's role in managing the files on your disk.

As discussed in Chapter 2, every DOS disk is divided into four parts: the boot record, *file allocation table*, the root directory, and the file/subdirectory data area, as illustrated in the following figure.

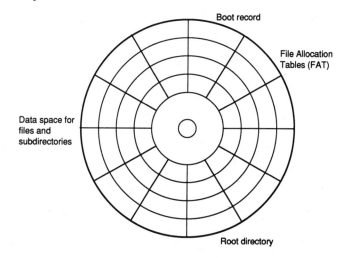

The file/subdirectory area holds the majority of your files. As discussed, DOS must keep each file's data separate. The difficulty in tracking files is that users constantly change or delete them. DOS must plan for events that increase or decrease a file's size.

To begin, DOS divides your disk into sectors. Depending upon the disk size, the number of sectors DOS creates will differ. As you create files on your disk, DOS assigns specific sectors to each.

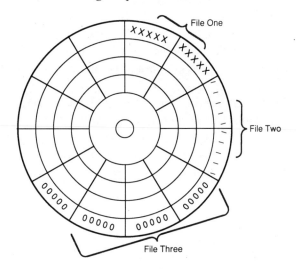

The file allocation table, or FAT, is a table of entries that tracks which sectors are in use, which are available, and the damaged sectors marked unusable during formatting.

To understand how the FAT works, let's take a look at a simplified example. Assume that your disk contains two files LARGE.DAT and SMALL.DAT using the sectors shown here.

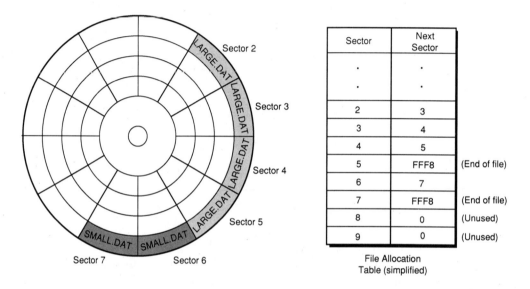

Sector	Next Sector	
.	.	
.	.	
2	3	
3	4	
4	5	
5	FFF8	(End of file)
6	7	
7	FFF8	(End of file)
8	0	(Unused)
9	0	(Unused)

File Allocation
Table (simplified)

The file allocation table creates a chain of values that points to each file sector. If you find the entry for sector 2, you'll see that it contains the value 3, which is the next sector in the file. Likewise, the entry for sector 3 points to sector 4, and sector 4 points to sector 5. The FAT uses the hexadecimal (base 16) value FFF8 to indicate the last sector in a file. In this case, sector 5 is the file's last sector. The file chain for the file SMALL.DAT begins with sector entry 6. If you follow the FAT entries until you encounter FFF8, you'll find that the file SMALL.DAT resides in sectors 6 and 7.

If you increase the size of the file LARGE.DAT, DOS searches the FAT for an available sector. The FAT uses the value 0 to indicate an available sector. Because the file SMALL.DAT uses sectors 6 and 7, the first available sector is sector 8. Assuming the file LARGE.DAT grows by two sectors, DOS would allocate sectors 8 and 9, as shown here.

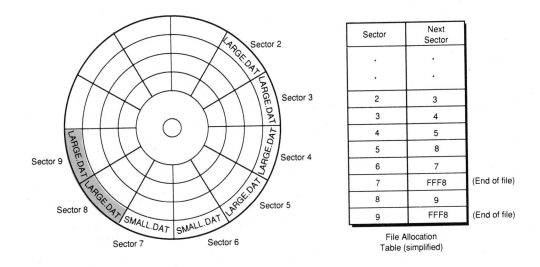

Sector	Next Sector	
.	.	
.	.	
2	3	
3	4	
4	5	
5	8	
6	7	
7	FFF8	(End of file)
8	9	
9	FFF8	(End of file)

File Allocation
Table (simplified)

Next, assume that you delete the file SMALL.DAT. To inform DOS that sectors 6 and 7 are no longer in use, the FAT entries are set to 0.

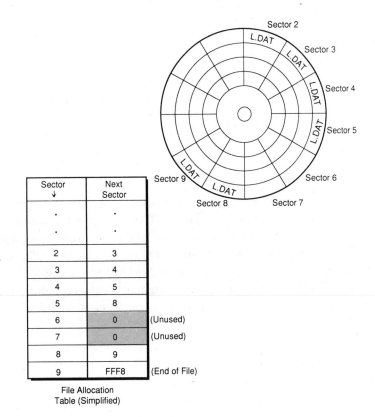

Sector ↓	Next Sector	
.	.	
.	.	
2	3	
3	4	
4	5	
5	8	
6	0	(Unused)
7	0	(Unused)
8	9	
9	FFF8	(End of File)

File Allocation
Table (Simplified)

If you create a single-sector file called THIRD.DAT, DOS will use one of the available sectors, as shown here.

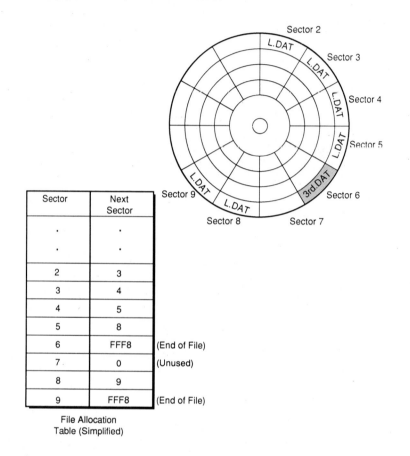

Sector	Next Sector	
.	.	
.	.	
2	3	
3	4	
4	5	
5	8	
6	FFF8	(End of File)
7	0	(Unused)
8	9	
9	FFF8	(End of File)

File Allocation
Table (Simplified)

The FAT truly is your file road map. When DOS accesses a file, DOS locates the file's first entry in the FAT and then follows the sector chain. The only question that remains is how DOS locates the first FAT entry.

As you'll recall, each time DOS creates a file, DOS creates a 32-byte directory entry for the file. In addition to the file name, extension, size, and date and time stamp, the directory entry contains the FAT entry to the file's first sector. The following figure shows a typical directory entry.

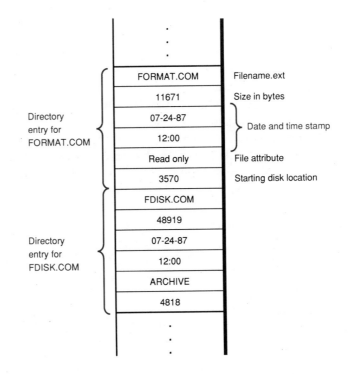

To locate a file on disk, DOS first locates the file's directory entry. Using the starting sector value, DOS can quickly follow the file's sector chain contained in the FAT.

Understanding Disk Clusters

The previous discussion was simplified because the FAT actually doesn't track sectors, but rather, a fixed-size group of sectors called a *cluster*. DOS uses clusters instead of sectors to reduce system overhead. A 30 megabyte hard disk, for example, uses about 60,000 512 byte sectors. If the FAT had to track each sector individually, not only would the FAT take up a considerable amount of disk space, the large FAT would also take DOS longer to traverse, which would decrease your system performance. To improve your system performance, DOS keeps a copy of the FAT in your computer's fast random-access memory. A FAT with 60,000 entries would simply be too large for DOS to store in RAM.

For hard disks, DOS normally uses a cluster size of four sectors. Each FAT entry, therefore, represents four sectors. As a result, the smallest amount of disk space that DOS can allocate to a file is four sectors or 2,048 bytes. Even if a file only contains one byte of information, DOS must still allocate a cluster of storage space. If a file is smaller than a cluster, the unused sectors in the cluster remain available for file growth. If the file never grows, the sectors are wasted. Most files, however, are large enough that the amount of wasted space is minimal. The wasted space is simply a fact of life.

Using clusters, consider a disk that again stores the files LARGE.DAT and SMALL.DAT. In this case, the file LARGE.DAT is 6,400 bytes in length, and SMALL.DAT is 1,024 bytes. To store the file LARGE.DAT, DOS must use four (4 sector) clusters.

```
Number of clusters = File size / cluster size
                   = 6,400 / 2,048
                   = 3.125
                   = 4 clusters
```

The file SMALL.DAT resides in a single cluster. In this case, the file allocation table entries become the following.

Assuming the file LARGE.DAT is 6400 bytes, the file requires 12.5 sectors. Because DOS allocates disk space by clusters, LARGE.DAT requires 4 clusters. Likewise, the 1024 byte file SMALL.DAT requires 1 cluster. Sectors marked with an (R) are allocated to the file for future growth but are not currently in use.

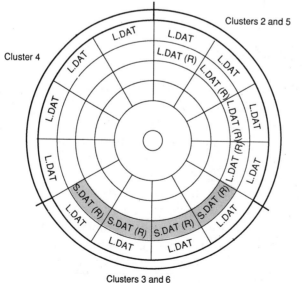

Cluster 4

Clusters 2 and 5

Clusters 3 and 6

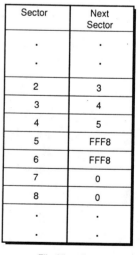

Sector	Next Sector
.	.
.	.
2	3
3	4
4	5
5	FFF8
6	FFF8
7	0
8	0
.	.
.	.

File Allocation Table

By knowing the file's first FAT entry, you can easily track the file's data on disk. For example, look at the following figure. Assuming the file LARGE.DAT is 6400 bytes, the file requires 12.5 sectors. Because DOS allocates disk space by clusters, LARGE.DAT requires four clusters. Likewise, the 1024-byte file SMALL.DAT requires one cluster. Sectors marked with an R in the figure are allocated to the file for future growth, but are not currently in use.

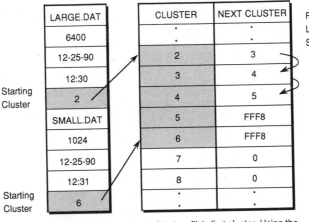

The DOS directory entry points to a file's first cluster. Using the File Allocation Table, DOS follows the chain of cluster numbers until it finds the last cluster.

Getting Disk Information

If you want more information on disk storage, the Jamsa Disk Utilities, included with this book, include a utility called DISKINFO. It not only displays your disk geometry (number of sides, tracks, and sectors), but also FAT information such as the number of sectors per cluster and bytes per sector for your disk. For more information on DISKINFO, refer to Chapter 11.

Summary

Files exist to store programs and data. To help organize your files, DOS lets you assign an eight character name and a three character extension to each file on your disk. When you reference a file, you must separate the file name and extension with a period (FILENAME.EXT). The three character extension lets you describe the content of each file (EXE for program, DAT for data, LTR for letter, and so on). Use all eight of the file name characters to make your filenames more meaningful.

A directory is a list of file names. The DOS DIR command displays the name of each file stored in a directory. In addition, DIR displays the file's size and the date and time the file was created or last modified.

As you perform file operations, it is often convenient to refer to a group of files with related names. DOS provides two wild cards you can place within your file names during specific operations. These wild cards let you apply a single command to a group of matching files. The asterisk wild card (*) directs DOS to ignore the characters in the position containing and following the asterisk. The question mark wild card (?) directs DOS to ignore only the characters in the position containing the question mark.

DOS provides commands that let you copy, rename, and erase files on your disk. The DOS COPY command copies the contents of one or more files to another file or disk. The DOS RENAME command renames an existing file. The DOS DEL command erases a file from your disk when the file is no longer needed.

You will use the COPY, RENAME, and DEL commands on a daily basis to manage your files. In Chapter 4, you will learn how to create and use DOS subdirectories to organize your files. The DOS subdirectories are the key to hard disk organization.

4

Organizing Your Files Using Subdirectories

- ► Understanding the Root Directory
- ► Creating Subdirectories Using MKDIR
- ► Selecting a Directory with CHDIR
- ► Removing Subdirectories with RMDIR
- ► Handling Multiple Directory Levels
- ► Understanding the Directory Abbreviations
- ► Executing Commands from Other Subdirectories
- ► Subdirectory Size Restrictions
- ► Summary

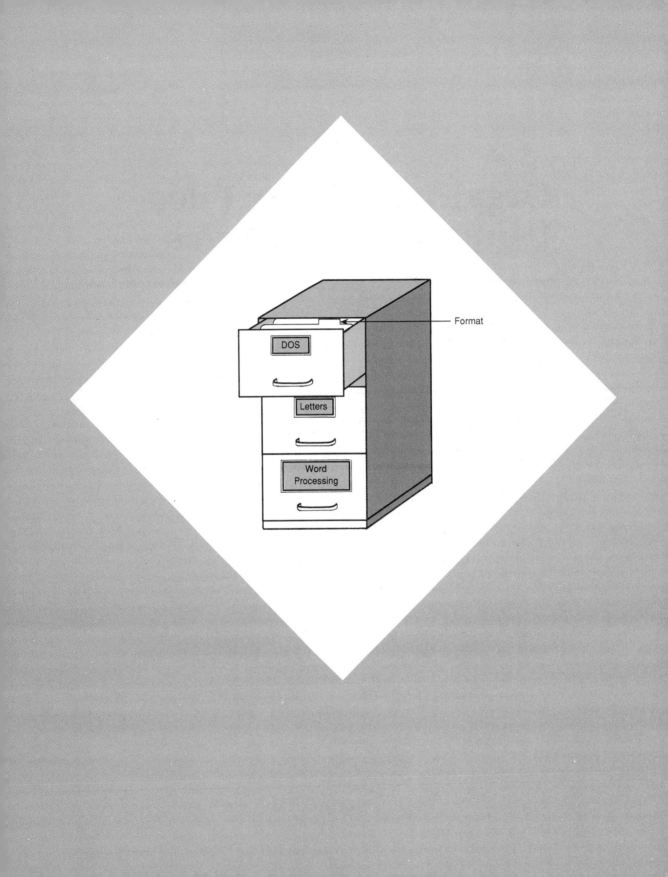

Organizing Your Files Using Subdirectories

Hard disk management is the art of organizing your disk and files to maximize performance while minimizing the possibility of data loss. Your primary tool for hard disk management is the *subdirectory*. As you know, a directory is simply a list of files. A subdirectory is a separate list of files created to group related files. Subdirectories organize your disk by letting you group files for business, personal, and school into unique locations. As a result, all of your files aren't intermixed, which makes locating specific files much easier.

To use your hard disk effectively, you must understand DOS subdirectories. This chapter contains many example commands. Take time to execute them to increase your understanding. Of all of the chapters in this book, this chapter contains the most essential information you'll need on a daily basis.

Understanding the Root Directory

When the FORMAT command completes, the only directory that exists on your disk is the root directory. As discussed in Chapter 2, the FORMAT command allocates a specific number of sectors to store the root directory. Because the root directory size is fixed, you can only store a fixed number of files in the root. For most hard disks, the root directory will store 512 files. After you use the last root directory file entry, you cannot create any more files on your fixed disk, regardless of the number of available megabytes of disk space. If you create DOS subdirectories, however, your disk is no longer restricted to a specific number of files.

The root directory is so named because the subdirectories are said to grow or branch from the root directory, much like a tree grows from its roots. Using this analogy, the subdirectories that you eventually create are said to make up your directory tree. In fact, DOS provides the TREE command that displays your disk's directory structure. The TREE command will be discussed in more depth in the next chapter.

DOS abbreviates the root directory using the back slash character (\). You can list the files in the root directory using the following DIR command:

```
C> DIR \
```

Make sure that you use a back slash character (\) for the root directory abbreviation and not a forward slash (/). If you use the forward slash, DOS will display the following error message:

```
C> DIR /
Invalid parameter
```

Using the back slash character, you can list files in the root directories of other disks by preceding the back slash with a disk drive letter and colon, as shown here:

```
C> DIR A:\
```

The Root Directory

Every formatted DOS disk starts with one directory called the root directory. Within this directory, you can store files or create other directories to group related files. As you create directories on your disk, the directories will grow out from the root, like branches from a tree.

If you were to store all of your files in the root, it would be very difficult to keep your files organized. To store files in directories other than the root, you must use the DOS subdirectory commands MKDIR, CHDIR, and RMDIR.

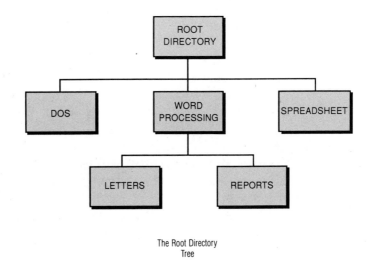

The Root Directory
Tree

Creating Subdirectories Using MKDIR

The MKDIR (short for *make directory*) command creates a subdirectory. The format of the MKDIR command is `MKDIR` *pathname.* The pathname is the name of the subdirectory MKDIR is to create. In Chapter 2, you created the subdirectory DOS using the following command:

```
C> MKDIR \DOS
```

Most DOS subdirectory pathnames begin with the root directory. In this case, the MKDIR command creates the subdirectory DOS immediately below the root directory.

Display the files in the DOS subdirectory by placing the DOS pathname in the DIR command line, as shown here:

```
C> DIR \DOS
```

The pathname ＼DOS tells the DIR command to begin at the root directory (＼) and locate the subdirectory DOS. By appending a file name to the ＼DOS subdirectory, you can list the directory entry for a specific file as shown here:

```
C> DIR  \DOS\FORMAT.COM

 Volume in drive C is DOS
 Directory of  C:\DOS

FORMAT    COM     11671 07-24-87  12:00a
        1 File(s)     43847680 bytes free
```

Many DOS manuals refer to a file's pathname. A pathname contains not only the file name (such as FORMAT.COM), but also the subdirectory that the file resides in. In the previous DIR command, the complete pathname to the FORMAT command was \DOS\FORMAT.COM. A file's pathname is so named because it tells DOS the path of subdirectories DOS must follow to locate the file.

DOS subdirectory names follow the same naming restrictions as DOS files. As you create your directories, assign meaningful names to them. Although DOS lets you assign extensions to subdirectory names, most users don't. Instead, most only use the eight character file name. By default, DIR displays the extension as ⟨DIR⟩ for subdirectories, as shown here:

```
C> DIR

 Volume in drive C is DOS
 Directory of  C:\

DOS          <DIR>     01-21-90  11:51a
AUTOEXEC BAT       128 12-13-89   8:52a
CONFIG   SYS       128 01-07-90   9:29a
DISKBOOK     <DIR>     01-21-90  11:51a
        4 File(s)   43839488 bytes free
```

Because MKDIR is frequently used, DOS lets you abbreviate MKDIR as simply MD. Using the MD abbreviation, create the subdirectory DISKBOOK.

```
C> MD \DISKBOOK
```

When the command completes, perform a directory listing of the DISKBOOK subdirectory.

```
C> DIR \DISKBOOK

 Volume in drive C is DOS
 Directory of  C:\DISKBOOK

 .            <DIR>      01-21-90  11:40a
 ..           <DIR>      01-21-90  11:40a
        2 File(s)   43845632 bytes free
```

Every DOS subdirectory you create will have the period and double period directory entries. As you will learn later in this chapter, these two entries are simply abbreviations that you can use to simplify DOS pathnames. For now, however, simply be aware that DOS places these two entries in every subdirectory.

Using the DOS COPY command (as discussed in Chapter 2), create the file NOTES.TXT in the subdirectory DISKBOOK, as shown here:

```
C> COPY CON \DISKBOOK\NOTES.TXT
The DOS MKDIR command creates subdirectories.
You can abbreviate MKDIR as MD.
^Z
    1 File(s) copied
```

To create a file within a specific DOS subdirectory, simply use the file's complete pathname. Using the file's pathname, the following DOS TYPE command displays the file's contents:

```
C> TYPE \DISKBOOK\NOTES.TXT
The DOS MKDIR command creates subdirectories.
You can abbreviate MKDIR as MD.

C>
```

All of the DOS file manipulation commands support DOS subdirectories. For example, the following COPY command copies the contents of the file NOTES.TXT to the file MKDIR.TXT. Because the COPY command uses complete pathnames, both files will reside in the DISKBOOK subdirectory.

```
C> COPY \DISKBOOK\NOTES.TXT  \DISKBOOK\MKDIR.TXT
    1 File(s) copied
```

A directory listing of the DISKBOOK subdirectory shows the directory entries for both files.

```
C> DIR \DISKBOOK

 Volume in drive C is DOS
 Directory of  C:\DISKBOOK

 .            <DIR>      01-21-90  11:40a
 ..           <DIR>      01-21-90  11:40a
 NOTES   TXT        80 01-21-90  11:43a
 MKDIR   TXT        80 01-21-90  11:47a
         4 File(s)   43841536 bytes free
```

Using RENAME, the following command renames the file MKDIR.TXT using the abbreviation MD.TXT:

```
C> REN \DISKBOOK\MKDIR.TXT   MD.TXT
```

As you will recall, the DOS RENAME command does not let you move a file from one disk to another, or from one DOS subdirectory to another. As such, the destination file name (MD.TXT) cannot have a subdirectory name before it. If you place a subdirectory name before the file name, RENAME assumes you are trying to move the file and the command fails, as shown here:

```
C> REN \DISKBOOK\MKDIR.TXT   \DISKBOOK\MD.TXT
Invalid parameter
```

Admittedly, if you always had to specify complete pathnames to files residing in DOS subdirectories, the additional keystrokes required for each file access would become time consuming and would make the use of the subdirectories less desirable. However, just as DOS defines the current disk drive as the disk it uses unless your command specifies otherwise (by using a drive letter: TYPE B:FILENAME.EXT), DOS also defines the current directory.

DOS MKDIR Command

The DOS MKDIR command creates a subdirectory. If you picture your hard disk as a large filing cabinet, creating a subdirectory is similar to placing a label on one of the cabinet drawers.

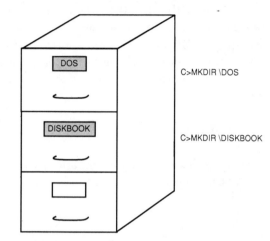

C>MKDIR \DOS

C>MKDIR \DISKBOOK

After you create a subdirectory, you can store related files in it, or even subdivide your files further by creating additional directories within it. In this case, creating a subdirectory within a directory is similar to placing labeled dividers within a filing cabinet drawer.

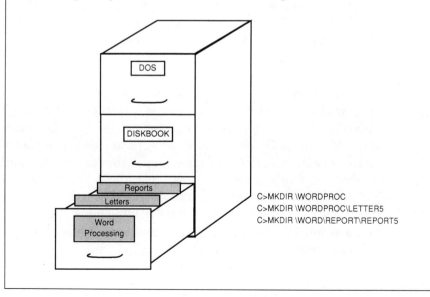

C>MKDIR \WORDPROC
C>MKDIR \WORDPROC\LETTER5
C>MKDIR \WORD\REPORT\REPORT5

Selecting a Directory with CHDIR

The current directory is the subdirectory DOS uses by default for file operations. Every time your system starts, the root directory is the current directory. If you use the DIR command to display directory entries, DIR displays the files that reside in the root. The CHDIR (short for change directory) command lets you select the current directory. The format of the CHDIR command is `CHDIR` *pathname*. As before, the pathname is the desired DOS subdirectory name. For example, the following command selects the subdirectory DISKBOOK as the current directory:

```
C> CHDIR \DISKBOOK
```

If you perform a directory command, DIR will display the contents of the DISKBOOK directory.

```
C> DIR

 Volume in drive C is DOS
 Directory of  C:\DISKBOOK

.              <DIR>      01-21-90  11:40a
..             <DIR>      01-21-90  11:40a
NOTES    TXT         80 01-21-90  11:43a
MD       TXT         80 01-21-90  11:47a
         4 File(s)    43841536 bytes free
```

In addition to helping you organize your files, DOS subdirectories also provide your files with a level of protection against accidental deletion. Unless you tell DOS to do otherwise, the file manipulation commands only affect files that reside in the current directory. If you issue an errant DEL command, for example, the only files DEL will delete are those in the current directory or a directory you specify. Files residing in other DOS subdirectories are not affected.

Due to its frequency of use, the CHDIR command may be abbreviated as simply CD. Using the CD abbreviation, the following command selects the directory DOS as the current directory:

```
C> CD \DOS
```

A directory listing of the current directory displays the DOS files.

```
C> DIR

Volume in drive C is DOS
Directory of  C:\DOS

.               <DIR>       01-19-90    2:10p
..              <DIR>       01-19-90    2:10p
4201    CPI     17089 07-24-87   12:00a
5202    CPI       459 07-24-87   12:00a
ANSI    SYS      1647 07-24-87   12:00a
APPEND  EXE      5794 07-24-87   12:00a
ASSIGN  COM      1530 07-24-87   12:00a
ATTRIB  EXE     10656 07-24-87   12:00a
CHKDSK  COM      9819 07-24-87   12:00a
COMMAND COM     25276 07-24-87   12:00a
  :       :         :       :         :
SHARE   EXE      8608 07-24-87   12:00a
TREE    COM      3540 07-24-87   12:00a
XCOPY   EXE     11216 07-24-87   12:00a
FC      EXE     15974 07-24-87   12:00a
        51 File(s)    43839488 bytes free
```

Note that each time you issue a DIR command, DIR not only displays a directory listing of the files on your disk, but also the name of the current directory.

```
C> DIR

Volume in drive C is DOS
Directory of  C:\DOS
```

Using the current directory, you can access files in one of two ways. First, you can simply specify a complete pathname to the file, as shown here:

```
C> TYPE \DISKBOOK\NOTES.TXT
```

Second, you can change the current directory to the subdirectory containing the desired file, and then issue the DOS command without the need for a complete pathname.

```
C> CD \DISKBOOK
C> TYPE NOTES.TXT
```

Displaying the Current Directory with CHDIR

If you invoke CHDIR without specifying a DOS subdirectory in the command line, CHDIR will display the current directory. If you don't set the DOS prompt to the current drive and directory as discussed, you can determine the current directory using CHDIR as follows:

```
C> CHDIR
C:\DISKBOOK
```

If you include only a drive specifier in the CHDIR command line, CHDIR will display the current directory for the drive specified.

```
C> CHDIR A:
A:\
```

The CHDIR Command

The DOS CHDIR command selects a subdirectory as the current directory. Using the filing cabinet analogy, selecting a subdirectory with CHDIR is equivalent to opening a specific drawer of the cabinet to access the files contained within.

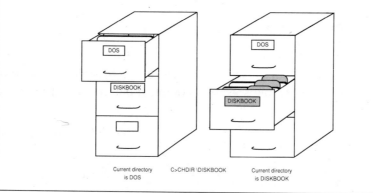

Current directory   C>CHDIR \DISKBOOK   Current directory
is DOS   is DISKBOOK

Displaying the Current Directory
as Part of the DOS Prompt

It can get tiring to always use the CHDIR command to find out where you are in the subdirectory organization. There is a handy DOS command you can use to instruct DOS to always let you know where you are.

By default, the DOS prompt contains the current disk drive letter followed by a greater than sign (A)). Each time you change current disk drives, DOS changes its prompt to indicate the current drive.

```
A> C:
C>
```

Most hard disk users find it very helpful if DOS also displays the name of the current directory within the prompt. To direct DOS to do so, issue the following PROMPT command:

```
C> PROMPT $p$g
C:\>
```

The PROMPT command supports several character combinations that begin with the dollar sign character. In this case, the $p directs PROMPT to display the current disk drive and subdirectory name. The $g directs PROMPT to display the greater than character. When you execute the PROMPT command, the DOS prompt changes to the current drive letter followed by the current directory name. Watch how the prompt changes with the current directory, as shown here:

```
C:\> CD \DOS
C:\DOS> CD \DISKBOOK
C:\DISKBOOK> CD \
C:\>
```

Place the PROMPT pg command in the file AUTOEXEC.BAT so your prompt always contains the current directory.

Removing Subdirectories with RMDIR

Just as DOS lets you delete files from your disk when you no longer need them, the same is true for DOS subdirectories. The RMDIR command (short for remove directory) lets you remove a subdirectory from your disk when it is no longer needed. For example, assume that you are storing files for the annual budget report in the directory BUDGET. After your report is complete and you no longer need the files on your hard disk, you can delete the files using DEL and then remove the subdirectory using RMDIR. The format of the RMDIR command is `RMDIR` *pathname*.

Using the DOS MKDIR command, create the subdirectory 12345678, as shown here:

```
C:\> MKDIR \12345678
```

A directory listing of the new subdirectory shows that it exists on disk.

```
C:\> DIR
 Volume in drive C is DOS
 Directory of  C:\

DOS           <DIR>      01-21-90  11:51a
AUTOEXEC BAT       128 12-13-89   8:52a
CONFIG    SYS       128 01-07-90   9:29a
DISKBOOK      <DIR>      01-21-90  11:51a
12345678      <DIR>      01-21-90  12:01a

      5 File(s)   43839488 bytes free
```

Next, using RMDIR, remove the directory as follows:

```
C> RMDIR \12345678
```

A second directory listing shows that RMDIR has successfully removed the subdirectory.

```
C:\> DIR

 Volume in drive C is DOS
 Directory of  C:\

DOS          <DIR>       01-21-90  11:51a
AUTOEXEC BAT         128 12-13-89   8:52a
CONFIG   SYS         128 01-07-90   9:29a
DISKBOOK     <DIR>       01-21-90  11:51a

     4 File(s)   43839488 bytes free
```

Because the command is frequently used, DOS lets you abbreviate RMDIR as RD. To reduce the possibility of inadvertent file deletion, RMDIR will not remove a subdirectory that contains files. If you attempt to remove the subdirectory that contains files (DISKBOOK, for example), RMDIR will display the following error message:

```
Invalid path, not directory,
or directory not empty
```

The RMDIR Command

The DOS RMDIR command removes a subdirectory from your disk when the directory is no longer needed. Just as an office cleans out file drawers when they are no longer needed, you will erase directories of files on your disk. Using RMDIR to remove a DOS subdirectory is similar to removing the label from a drawer of the filing cabinet when the drawer no longer has any files in it.

To prevent you from inadvertently losing files, RMDIR does not let you remove a directory that still contains files. To remove a directory, you must delete all of a directory's files using DEL, and then issue the RMDIR command.

Handling Multiple Directory Levels

As you add more files to your DOS subdirectories, you can improve your disk organization by creating additional DOS subdirectories within your existing subdirectories. For example, assume that you have created the subdirectory INVEST that stores your investment files. To improve your file organization, you may want to create subdirectories within INVEST to store bonds, stocks, and real estate, as shown here.

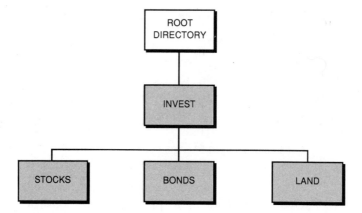

To better understand several levels of subdirectories, place a blank formatted disk in drive A, and select drive A as the default drive.

```
C:\> A:
A:\>
```

Next, create the subdirectory INVEST using MKDIR.

```
A:\> MKDIR \INVEST
```

To create the subdirectory BONDS, you have two choices. First, you can specify a complete subdirectory pathname, as shown here:

```
A:\> MKDIR \INVEST\BONDS
```

Second, you can use CHDIR to select INVEST as the current directory, and then create the subdirectory BONDS without specifying a complete pathname.

```
A:\> CHDIR \INVEST
A:\INVEST> MKDIR BONDS
```

The previous MKDIR command did not specify a complete pathname, only the subdirectory to create. By default, if you reference a subdirectory name without a complete path, DOS assumes the subdirectory resides in the current directory. In this case, the subdirectory BONDS should reside in the current directory INVEST so you can omit the complete pathname.

Using this same technique, you can create the subdirectories STOCKS and LAND, as shown here:

```
A:\INVEST> MKDIR STOCKS
A:\INVEST> MKDIR LAND
```

You can omit the complete pathname for these directories because you are creating them in the current directory.

Using the CHDIR command, select the root as the current directory.

```
A:\INVEST> CHDIR\
A:\>
```

Next, try to select the subdirectory BONDS as the current directory without specifying a complete pathname.

```
A:\> CHDIR BONDS
Invalid directory
```

If the requested directory is not available from the current directory, use the complete pathname to access the directory. In this case, the subdirectory BONDS does not reside in the root directory, but rather, the directory INVEST. To select BONDS as the current directory, you must use a complete pathname, as shown here:

```
A:\> CHDIR \INVEST\BONDS
A:\INVEST\BONDS>
```

To change from the subdirectory BONDS to STOCKS, again specify a complete pathname.

```
A:\INVEST\BONDS> CHDIR \INVEST\STOCKS
A:\INVEST\STOCKS>
```

To remove the subdirectory land, for example, you can simply specify a complete pathname, as shown here:

```
A:\INVEST\STOCKS> RMDIR \INVEST\LAND
```

If you instead select INVEST as the current directory, you can remove the directory without a complete pathname.

```
A:\INVEST\STOCKS> CHDIR \INVEST
A:\INVEST> RMDIR LAND
```

When your disk contains multiple subdirectories, using the DOS prompt to display the current directory helps to remind you where you're at.

Understanding the Directory Abbreviations

Each time you create a DOS subdirectory, DOS automatically creates two entries as shown here.

```
.              <DIR>      01-21-90   11:40a
..             <DIR>      01-21-90   11:40a
```

These directory entries are abbreviations used to reduce the length of subdirectory pathnames. The period is an abbreviation for the current directory. Assuming that the current directory is DISKBOOK, a directory listing using the period abbreviation displays the files in the same directory.

```
C> DIR .

 Volume in drive C is DOS
 Directory of  C:\DISKBOOK

.              <DIR>      01-21-90   11:40a
..             <DIR>      01-21-90   11:40a
NOTES    TXT         80 01-21-90   11:43a
MD       TXT         80 01-21-90   11:47a
        4 File(s)     43835392 bytes free
```

The double period is an abbreviation for the subdirectory that resides immediately above the current directory, which in this case is the root. Using DISKBOOK as the current directory, a directory listing using the double period displays the root directory.

```
C> DIR ..

 Volume in drive C is DOS
 Directory of  C:\

DOS          <DIR>      01-21-90  11:51a
AUTOEXEC BAT       128 12-13-89   8:52a
CONFIG   SYS       128 01-07-90   9:29a
DISKBOOK     <DIR>      01-21-90  11:51a
        4 File(s)   43839488 bytes free
```

In a directory structure with only one level of directories, the subdirectory abbreviations aren't very useful. However, if your directory structure contains several levels, as does the floppy disk in drive A, the subdirectory abbreviations become more convenient. Again select drive A as the current drive.

```
C:\DISKBOOK> A:
A:\INVEST>
```

Next, select the subdirectory BONDS as the current directory.

```
A:\INVEST> CHDIR BONDS
A:\INVEST\BONDS>
```

A directory listing using the double period displays the subdirectory INVEST which resides immediately above the current directory. To select the subdirectory STOCKS as the current directory, use a complete pathname, or use the double period abbreviation shown here:

```
A:\INVEST\BONDS> CHDIR ..\STOCKS
A:\INVEST\STOCKS>
```

The pathname in this case directs CHDIR to start at the directory immediately above the current directory and then to select the subdirectory STOCKS from that directory. Because the subdirectory INVEST resides immediately above the current directory, the command succeeds.

Using the double period abbreviation again, you can select the subdirectory INVEST from the directory STOCKS as follows:

```
A:\INVEST\STOCKS> CHDIR ..
A:\INVEST>
```

In this case, the command directs CHDIR to select the directory that resides immediately above the current directory.

Executing Commands from Other Subdirectories

You should create individual subdirectories to store each software program you place on your hard disk. Most users place all of the DOS external commands in a subdirectory named DOS. To execute commands that reside in the DOS subdirectory, such as FORMAT, you have several choices. First, you can invoke the command using a complete pathname. For example, the following command invokes FORMAT to format the floppy disk in drive A:

```
C:\> \DOS\FORMAT A:
```

To locate the file FORMAT.COM, DOS follows the pathname, beginning at the root, and searches the subdirectory DOS.

You can also invoke the FORMAT command by first selecting the subdirectory DOS as the current directory, and then invoking FORMAT without a pathname, as shown here:

```
C:\> CHDIR DOS
C:\DOS> FORMAT A:
```

In Chapter 2, you created the file AUTOEXEC.BAT which contained the following PATH entry:

```
PATH C:\DOS
```

The PATH command defines a list of subdirectories that DOS should search for external commands, such as FORMAT. Each time you invoke a command at the DOS prompt, DOS searches its list of internal commands such as CLS, DATE, and TIME to see if your command is an internal command. If the command is an internal command, DOS executes it. If the command is not internal, DOS searches either the current directory or the path specified for the command. If DOS locates your command or disk as an EXE, COM, or BAT file, DOS executes the command. If DOS still has not found the command, DOS checks to see if you have defined a command path using PATH. If a command path exists, DOS searches each of the directories listed for the command. If DOS locates the command in one of the directories, DOS executes it; otherwise, after it has searched all the directories without locating the command, DOS will display the following message telling you it could not locate the command:

```
Bad command or file name
```

In this case, if DOS fails to locate a command as an internal command in memory or an external command on disk, DOS will search the subdirectory DOS for the command. By supporting the command path, DOS makes it easier for you to execute your most commonly used commands.

The command path is not restricted to only one subdirectory. If you have two or more directories that are likely to contain commands, separate the directory names with a semicolon when you issue the PATH command. The following PATH command directs DOS to search the subdirectories DOS and UTIL for external commands:

```
PATH C:\DOS;C:\UTIL
```

DOS searches the subdirectories in the same order the subdirectory names appear in the PATH command. In this case, DOS will first search the directory DOS, and then, if necessary, search the directory UTIL. The disk drive letters that appear in the directory path are very important. Should you change default drives, DOS will look for the subdirectories on the correct disk.

Improving the Performance of Your Command Path

Although the PATH command simplifies command execution, it can also impact your system performance. First, if your command path contains several different directory names, DOS may waste time searching directories that are unlikely to contain files. To reduce wasted search time, limit the directories in the command path to those likely to contain commonly used commands. Next, order those directories that appear in the command path so the directories most likely to contain commonly used commands come first.

Each time DOS searches a subdirectory for a command, DOS must examine each file in the directory, one file at a time. If a subdirectory in the path contains an excessive number of files, DOS will take longer to search the subdirectory.

Subdirectory Size Restrictions

Each time you format a disk using the DOS FORMAT command, DOS sets aside a specific number of sectors to store the root directory. Depending on your disk type, the number of sectors that DOS reserves for the root directory will vary. To determine the number of directory entries the root can store, use the following equation:

```
Root Entries = (Root Sectors) * (Sector Size) / (Entry Size)
```

For most hard disk partitions, DOS sets aside thirty-two 512 byte sectors. Knowing that each directory entry requires 32 bytes, you can determine the number of files the root directory can store, as shown here:

```
Root Entries = 32 * 512 / 32
             = 512
```

Once you use up the root directory entries, you cannot create any more files or subdirectories in the root.

DOS subdirectories, however, can store an unlimited number of entries. Here's why. DOS treats a subdirectory as a file. Like all DOS files, a subdirectory can grow to store more information. The subdirectory file contains one or more 32-byte directory entries. Each time you create a new file within a subdirectory, DOS simply stores another 32-byte entry in the subdirectory file. As long as your disk has available space, DOS can create files in subdirectories. However, if you have too many

---

Root Directory Size

DOS sets aside a fixed number of sectors to store files and subdirectories in the root directory. If you use up all of the root directory entries, you cannot create any other files or subdirectories in the root. Visualize the root directory as a large filing cabinet with a fixed number of drawers. Once you have labelled each of the drawers, you cannot store a new file in its own drawer. Instead, you must share one of the existing drawers using a divider.

The same concept holds true for DOS subdirectories. Although the size of the root is fixed (like the number of drawers), you can always create more files and directories within existing subdirectories.

Most users will never have to worry about filling up their hard disk root directory if they use subdirectories to properly organize their files.

---

files in a subdirectory, your system performance will suffer for file operations. Each time DOS accesses a file, DOS must search each entry in the directory until it finds the file, or determines that the file does not exist. If a directory contains a large number of files, you will experience slow directory searches for every file operation.

Summary

A directory is a list of files. Each time a file is created on your disk, DOS creates an entry for the file. The DOS DIR command displays specifics about each file in the directory list. When you format a disk, DOS creates a directory called the root, which DOS abbreviates with the back slash character (\ ).

To help organize related files, DOS lets you create subdirectories. Creating a subdirectory is conceptually similar to placing a divider in a filing cabinet drawer. When you add new software packages to your disk, each package should reside in its own subdirectory. As a result, your disk may contain a subdirectory called DOS that contains your DOS commands, a subdirectory for a word processor, or other application programs, and a subdirectory named DISKUTIL that contains the programs provided on the Jamsa Disk Utilities.

As you organize your files into subdirectories, you will need to create, select, and possibly later remove a directory. The DOS MKDIR command lets you create a directory. Because MKDIR is frequently used, DOS lets you abbreviate it as MD.

The DOS CHDIR command (abbreviated as CD) lets you select the current directory. Conceptually, selecting a current directory is equivalent to opening a specific drawer of the filing cabinet. Unless told to do otherwise, DOS commands only effect files in the current directory.

The DOS RMDIR command (abbreviated as RD) removes an empty directory from your disk when it is no longer needed. As stated, DOS commands only effect files in the current directory. To access a file in a different directory, specify the complete path name to the file. The path name includes the subdirectories DOS must traverse to locate the file. To simplify the execution of commonly used commands, define a command path using the PATH command. By default, when you type in a command name, DOS first checks to see if the command resides in the current directory. If not, DOS checks to see if a command path has been defined. If a command path exists, DOS automatically searches the files in each subdirectory contained in the path. If DOS locates the command, DOS will execute it. If the command PATH = C: \ DOS has been placed in the file AUTOEXEC.BAT, DOS will always check to see if the command entered resides in the DOS subdirectory.

The MKDIR, CHDIR, RMDIR, and PATH commands provide the tools needed to organize your files with DOS subdirectories. In Chapter 5, you will learn the key DOS file and disk commands needed to get the most from DOS.

5

Hard Disk Commands

- ► Assigning and Displaying Disk Labels
- ► Displaying the Directory Structure with TREE
- ► Changing Attributes with ATTRIB
- ► Abbreviating Long Directory Names with SUBST
- ► Defining a Data File Search Path with APPEND
- ► Improving File Access Performance with FASTOPEN
- ► Replacing Specific Files on Your Disk with REPLACE
- ► Salvaging Damaged Files with RECOVER
- ► Optimizing the PRINT Command
- ► Comparing Two Files with COMP
- ► Displaying a File with MORE
- ► Sorting a File's Contents with SORT
- ► Locating Key Text with FIND
- ► Summary

Hard Disk Commands

Chapter 3 presented the DOS file manipulation commands you will need on a daily basis. Likewise, Chapter 4 discussed the essential DOS subdirectory commands that help you organize your disk. This chapter examines several different DOS commands that you may not use every day, but are still very useful. With almost 70 different DOS commands, this chapter restricts its discussion to commands specific to disks and files.

Assigning and Displaying Disk Labels

Each time you perform a directory listing, the DIR command displays either the disk volume name, or the message:

```
Volume in drive C has no label
```

A disk volume name, or label, is an optional 11-character name you can assign to your disk. Disk labels help you organize floppy disks that may contain files with the same name, but for a different period of time. For example, assume that a stock broker tracks stock prices in three files: HIGHTECH.DAT, LOCAL.DAT, and FORT500.DAT. A directory listing of the broker's floppy disk reveals the following:

```
A:\> DIR

Volume in drive A has no label
Directory of   A:\

HIGHTECH DAT     23424 01-23-90    3:05p
LOCAL    DAT     23424 01-23-90    3:05p
FORT500  DAT     34816 01-23-90    3:05p
          3 File(s)      280576 bytes free
```

Assuming that with each new fiscal year the broker creates a new floppy disk to store the stock trends, the broker could quickly accumulate several disks with different files having the same name. Should the broker inadvertently put the wrong floppy disk in the disk drive, it could be difficult for the broker to recognize the error. If the broker performs a directory listing of the files, the broker might notice that the file's date and time stamp don't match the current date. By assigning a unique volume label to the disk, the broker is more likely to notice an incorrect disk in the drive.

A volume label can contain up to 11 characters. For most DOS versions, these characters must be the same as the characters allowed in DOS file names. Some versions of DOS do, however, let you use the space character in volume names. For the stock broker scenario, the broker may want to assign the disk label STOCKS-1990 to the disk. After the broker does so, a directory listing of the floppy disk displays the following:

```
A:\> DIR

Volume in drive A is STOCKS-1990
Directory of   A:\

HIGHTECH DAT     23424 01-23-90    3:05p
LOCAL    DAT     23424 01-23-90    3:05p
FORT500  DAT     34816 01-23-90    3:05p
          3 File(s)      280576 bytes free
```

Each year, when the broker creates a new floppy disk to store files, the broker can assign a different volume label to the new disk.

Although volume labels exist primarily to increase your floppy disk organization, DOS lets you assign a volume label to your hard disk. Most users use the volume label to "customize" their disk. If the computer has a specific office function, you might assign a corresponding label such as DESKTOP__PUB for a desktop publishing system, or NET__SERVER for a local area network server. For systems that don't have a specific use, many users assign a label containing the current DOS version number, such as DOS__3__3.

The file LABEL.COM contains DOS's LABEL command. When you invoke LABEL, it prompts you to enter the disk volume name as follows:

```
Volume label (11 characters, ENTER for none)?
```

For example, the following LABEL command assigns the label name DOSDISK to the current disk:

```
C:\> LABEL
Volume label (11 characters, ENTER for none)? DOSDISK
```

After the label is assigned, a directory listing of the disk displays the label name, as shown here:

```
C:\> DIR

 Volume in drive C is DOSDISK
 Directory of  C:\

AUTOEXEC BAT       128 12-13-89    8:52a
CONFIG   SYS       128 01-07-90    9:29a
DISKBOOK       <DIR>     01-21-90  11:40a
DOS            <DIR>     11-19-89   5:23p
        4 File(s)   43689984 bytes free
```

The LABEL command lets you specify the desired label name in the command line, as shown here:

```
C:\> LABEL DOSDISK
```

In this case, because the command line contains the desired label name, LABEL will not prompt you to enter one. If the specified label name contains invalid characters, LABEL will beep and display the following error message:

```
Invalid characters in volume label
```

Should this error message occur, make sure you are using characters that are valid in DOS file names. Remember, your version of DOS
may not allow a space or period within a file name. If your version of
DOS does support spaces in volume names, you can change the previous
volume label for DOSDISK to DOS DISK. Using spaces may substantially
improve the clarity of your volume labels.

To change an existing disk label, simply invoke LABEL as if a label
name does not exist. To delete an existing label, invoke LABEL and you
will see the following:

```
Delete current volume label (Y/N)?
```

If you type **Y** and press Enter, LABEL will delete the disk label. If
you type **N** and press Enter, LABEL will leave the existing label
unchanged.

Before continuing, assign your desired label to your hard disk.

The FORMAT command also lets you assign a volume label to your
disks as soon as they are formatted. To do so, include the /V switch, as
shown here:

```
C:\> FORMAT A: /V
```

When FORMAT has prepared your disk for use, FORMAT will
prompt you do enter the disk volume name, as follows:

```
Volume label (11 characters, ENTER for none)?
```

If you simply press Enter, FORMAT leaves the disk unlabeled.

The VOL command displays the disk volume label. At the DOS
prompt, type VOL and press Enter. Your screen will display the current
disk label, as shown here:

```
C:\> VOL

 Volume in drive C is DOS 4

C:\>
```

To display the disk volume label for a disk other than the default
drive, simply place the disk drive letter followed by a colon in the VOL
command line, as shown here:

```
C:\> VOL A:

Volume in drive A is STOCKS-1990

C:\>
```

Where DOS Stores the Volume Label

When you assign a disk volume label, DOS creates a directory entry in the root to hold the volume label name. DOS makes this file entry a hidden file so the file does not appear when you use the DIR command. When you remove the volume label, DOS removes the directory entry containing the volume label name. To prevent you from deleting this directory entry, DOS marks the entry as hidden. As such, the volume label directory entry does not appear in a DIR command.

Displaying the Directory Structure with TREE

As discussed in Chapter 4, your disk directory structure is often compared to the branches of a tree because both start at the root and can grow over time. The DOS program TREE.COM contains the TREE command that displays your disk's directory structure and, optionally, the files residing in each directory.

Assume, for example, that your directory structure contains the following subdirectories.

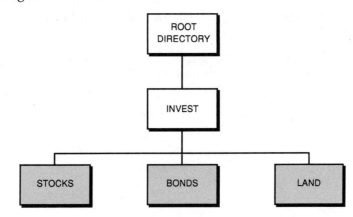

The DOS TREE command lists each subdirectory on your disk as follows.

```
Directory PATH listing
Volume Serial Number is 2D52-10D8
A:
    └───INVEST
            ├──STOCKS
            ├── BONDS
            └── LAND
```

In this case, the directory structure is still fairly simple. As the number of directories on your disk increases, you can use TREE to quickly locate subdirectories and even files residing within subdirectories. The /F switch directs TREE to display the subdirectories on your disk and the files each directory contains. Assume that your directory structure contains the following files.

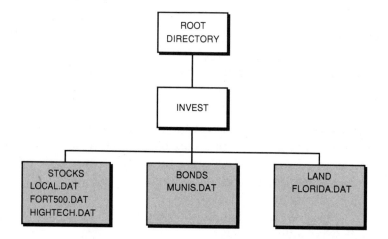

Using the /F switch, the output of the TREE command becomes the following.

```
Directory PATH listing
Volume Serial Number is 2D52-10D8
A:
    └───INVEST
            ├──STOCKS
            │       LOCAL.DAT
            │       FORT500.DAT
            │       HIGHTECH.DAT
            │
            ├──BONDS
            │       MUNIS.DAT
            └──LAND
                    FLORIDA.DAT
```

Many people use the DOS output redirection operator (>) to redirect TREE's output from the screen display to the printer, as shown here:

```
C:\> TREE /F > PRN
```

By redirecting TREE's output to the printer, you obtain a hard copy listing of the files on your disk.

Changing Attributes with ATTRIB

If you examine the 32-byte directory entry DOS creates for each file, you will find that each file has an attribute byte, as shown here.

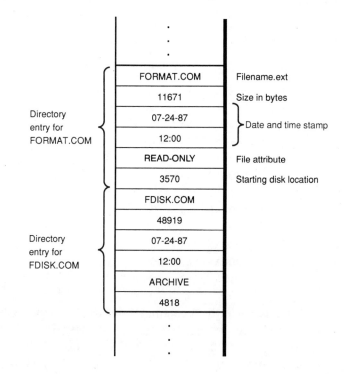

DOS uses the attribute byte to determine which files are hidden, which directory entries are subdirectories, which entry contains the disk volume label, which files have been backed up to another disk, as well as which files a program can change or delete. Table 5.1 lists the possible attributes DOS can assign to a directory entry.

Table 5.1.   *File attribute values.*

Value	Meaning
0	Normal file
1	Read-only file
2	Hidden file
4	System file
8	Volume label
16	DOS subdirectory
32	File archive needed (back up to another disk)

The DOS file ATTRIB.EXE contains the DOS ATTRIB command that lets you set or display a file's read-only and archive attributes. To display the file attributes for each file on your disk, issue the following command:

```
C:\> ATTRIB \*.* /S
```

ATTRIB will display each file's attribute followed by a complete pathname to the file, as shown here:

```
A          C:\DISKBOOK\NOTES.TXT
A          C:\DISKBOOK\MD.TXT
A          C:\DOS\COMMAND.COM
A          C:\DOS\COUNTRY.SYS
A          C:\DOS\SORT.EXE
A          C:\DOS\SUBST.EXE
A          C:\DOS\TREE.COM
A          C:\DOS\XCOPY.EXE
A          C:\DOS\CHKDSK.COM
A          C:\DOS\PRINT.COM
```

The uppercase letter A that precedes the file name tells you that the file has been created or modified since the last disk backup operation (discussed in Chapter 8). The DOS BACKUP and XCOPY commands use the archive-required attribute to let you copy to floppy only those files on your hard disk that require archiving.

The ATTRIB /S switch directs ATTRIB to access files that reside in directories below the directory specified. In this case, the current directory is the root, so the /S directs ATTRIB to access every subdirectory on the disk.

If ATTRIB displays the uppercase R before a file name, the file is a read-only file that cannot be changed or deleted. By setting your important files that don't change regularly to read-only, you reduce the possibility of an inadvertent file deletion. The DOS commands are an excellent candidate for read-only files. The only time these commands change is when you upgrade from one version of DOS to another. By setting these files to read-only, you can't accidentally delete them using DEL. Should you later need to delete the files for a DOS upgrade, simply remove the read-only attribute value using ATTRIB, and DOS is free to delete the files. To set the files in your DOS subdirectory to read-only, issue the following command:

```
C:\> ATTRIB +R \DOS\*.*
```

The +R option directs ATTRIB to set the files to read-only. To verify that ATTRIB has set the file's read-only attribute, issue the following ATTRIB command and note the uppercase R indicating a read-only file:

```
A    R    C:\DOS\COMMAND.COM
A    R    C:\DOS\COUNTRY.SYS
A    R    C:\DOS\DISKCOPY.COM
A    R    C:\DOS\FORMAT.COM
A    R    C:\DOS\SORT.EXE
A    R    C:\DOS\SUBST.EXE
```

To better understand read-only files, create the file READONLY.TXT that contains the following:

```
C:\> COPY CON READONLY.TXT
DOS cannot delete a read-only file using DEL.
^Z
    1 File(s) copied
```

Next, set the file's read-only attribute using the following command:

```
C:\> ATTRIB +R READONLY.TXT
```

Next, try to delete the file using DEL.

```
C:\> DEL READONLY.TXT
Access denied
```

The Access denied message tells you DOS does not have access to delete or modify the file. DOS can change the file's name using RENAME, but DOS cannot change or delete the file's contents. Using the −R option, remove the file's read-only attribute, as shown:

```
C:\>  ATTRIB -R READONLY.TXT
```

Next, using DEL, delete the file.

```
C:\> DEL READONLY.TXT
```

A directory listing of the disk reveals that DOS has successfully deleted the file.

```
C:\> DIR READONLY.TXT
File not found
```

Setting a file to read-only is an important step you can take to reduce the possibility of accidental file deletion.

Each time you create or change a file, DOS sets the file's archive attribute to indicate the file should be backed up to another disk. In Chapter 8, you will use the archive attribute to control which files the DOS BACKUP command copies from your disk. For now, however, you can use the archive attribute with the DOS XCOPY command to simplify the process of copying files from a DOS subdirectory to a floppy disk.

Assume, for example, that you have a subdirectory on your hard disk that contains 100 very large files. If you use the DOS COPY command as discussed in Chapter 3, you may be able to copy the files to the floppy disk in drive A using the following command:

```
C:\> COPY *.* A:
```

Depending upon the size of your files, the floppy disk may not have room to store all of them. As a result, DOS will display the following error message:

```
Insufficient disk space
```

Should this message occur, the file copy operation is incomplete. By performing a directory listing of the files on drive A, you can determine the last file successfully copied to the floppy disk and begin copying files one at a time to a new floppy disk from that point. Depending upon the number of uncopied files, you may spend considerable time and effort to complete the operation.

Luckily, using the ATTRIB and XCOPY commands, you can simplify this task greatly. To understand this process, copy all of the files in your DOS subdirectory to floppy disks in drive A. First, add the +A option to the ATTRIB command to set each file's archive attribute for the files in the DOS subdirectory.

```
C:\> ATTRIB +A \DOS\*.*
```

Setting the archive attribute does not change a file's read-only attribute setting. Next, invoke the DOS XCOPY command, as follows:

```
C:\> XCOPY \DOS\*.* A: /M
```

The /M switch directs XCOPY to only copy those files whose archive attribute is set. Each time XCOPY successfully copies a file, the /M switch directs XCOPY to successfully copy a file, the /M switch also directs XCOPY to remove or clear the archive attribute for that file. If your floppy disk fills up, XCOPY will display the following message:

```
Insufficient disk space
```

If this message occurs, place a formatted disk in drive A and repeat the previous XCOPY command. Because XCOPY has removed the archive attribute for each file it successfully copied to floppy, XCOPY can begin the file copy with the file that follows the last file successfully backed up. In essence, the archive attribute lets XCOPY place a book mark at the last file successfully copied. Table 5.2 describes the ATTRIB options.

Table 5.2.   *Summary of ATTRIB command line options.*

Option	Meaning
+R	Sets a file's read-only attribute
⊥R	Removes a file's read-only attribute
+A	Sets a file's archive attribute
−A	Removes a file's archive attribute

Changing Other File Attributes

ATTRIB lets you change only a limited number of file attributes. If you want to change the other file attributes, you need a special utility program such as FILEATTR, which is included as part of the Jamsa Utilities. FILEATTR lets you display and set a file's read-only, archive, hidden, and system attributes. FILEATTR has a menu driven interface that is very easy to use—there are no special switches or commands to remember.

Abbreviating Long Directory Names with SUBST

Several software packages written for early versions of DOS did not understand the notion of subdirectories. If you tried to open a file using a complete pathname, these older programs would generate an error message and the file access would fail. As a result, beginning with version 3.1, DOS provided the SUBST command which lets you abbreviate a pathname with an unused disk drive letter. The DOS file SUBST.EXE contains the DOS SUBST command. The format of the SUBST command is `SUBST` *drive__letter: pathname*. The drive__letter is an unused disk drive letter, such as E. The pathname is the DOS subdirectory path to abbreviate. The following SUBST command, for example, abbreviates the pathname C: \ DOS as drive E:

```
C:\> SUBST E: C:\DOS
```

After you substitute a path with a drive letter, DOS automatically translates all references to the drive letter. For example, the following DIR command displays a directory listing of the DOS commands:

```
C:\> DIR E:

Volume in drive C is DOS
Directory of  C:\DOS

.                <DIR>      01-19-90    2:10p
..               <DIR>      01-19-90    2:10p
4201     CPI      17089 07-24-87   12:00a
5202     CPI        459 07-24-87   12:00a
ANSI     SYS       1647 07-24-87   12:00a
APPEND   EXE       5794 07-24-87   12:00a
ASSIGN   COM       1530 07-24-87   12:00a
ATTRIB   EXE      10656 07-24-87   12:00a
CHKDSK   COM       9819 07-24-87   12:00a
COMMAND  COM      25276 07-24-87   12:00a
  :        :         :       :          :
SHARE    EXE       8608 07-24-87   12:00a
TREE     COM       3540 07-24-87   12:00a
XCOPY    EXE      11216 07-24-87   12:00a
FC       EXE      15974 07-24-87   12:00a
        51 File(s)    44550144 bytes free
```

If you invoke SUBST without specifying a command line, SUBST displays the current disk substitutions.

```
C:\> SUBST
E: => C:\DOS
```

Because drive E does not physically exist as a separate disk drive, DOS refers to the drive as a logical drive. By default, DOS only supports the drive letters A-E. If you specify a drive letter greater than E, DOS will display an error message.

```
C:\> SUBST F: C:\UTIL
Invalid parameter
```

As discussed in Chapter 6, the CONFIG.SYS command LASTDRIVE = *entry* lets you specify the drive letter of the last logical disk drive DOS will support. If you are abbreviating several pathnames with logical drive letters, you will need to place a LASTDRIVE = *entry* in CONFIG.SYS and reboot.

Although DOS provided the SUBST command to support older software programs, most users use SUBST to abbreviate long, commonly used directory names. Assume your disk has the following directory structure.

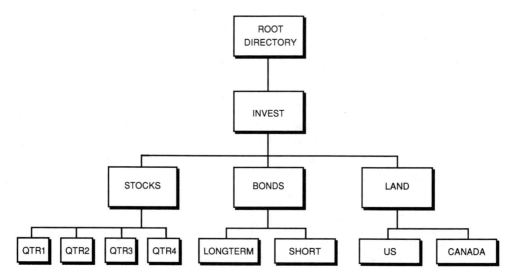

Using the DOS SUBST command, you can abbreviate a long pathname in drive E as follows:

```
C:\> SUBST E: C:\INVEST\STOCKS\QTR1
```

After you abbreviate the directory name, you can access files in the directory using the drive letter, as shown here:

```
C:\> TYPE E:FILENAME.EXT
```

If the abbreviated directory contains additional subdirectories, you can access the directories by placing their names after the logical drive letter, as shown here:

```
C:\> DIR E:\SUBDIR
```

When you no longer need a directory substitution, remove the abbreviation by placing the SUBST /D immediately after the logical drive letter.

```
C:\> SUBST E: /D
```

After you remove the pathname abbreviation, an attempt to access the logical drive letter results in the following error message:

```
C:\> DIR E:
Invalid drive specification
```

If you commonly use a long pathname, consider abbreviating the pathname with logical disk drive letter by placing a SUBST command in AUTOEXEC.BAT.

Defining a Data File Search Path with APPEND

In Chapter 4, you learned that the DOS PATH command lets you define a list of subdirectories that DOS searches to locate external commands. In a similar manner, the DOS APPEND command defines a list of directories DOS will use to locate all types of files. The basic format of the APPEND command is APPEND *pathname*.

Assume, for example, several of the programs you execute everyday use files that reside in the subdirectory BUDGET. Rather than having to specify a complete pathname for the files each time you access them, you can define a data file search path. In this case, your APPEND command becomes the following:

```
C:\> APPEND C:\BUDGET
```

Each time DOS fails to locate a data file, DOS will search the directory BUDGET for the file. If DOS locates the file, DOS will use the file as desired.

Select the subdirectory DISKBOOK that you created in Chapter 4.

```
C:\> CHDIR \DISKBOOK
```

Next, create the file APPEND.TXT, as shown here:

```
C:\DISKBOOK> COPY CON APPEND.TXT
The DOS APPEND command defines a data file search path.

^Z
    1 File(s) copied
```

Next, select the root directory as the current directory.

```
C:\DISKBOOK>CHDIR \
C:\>
```

If you try to use the DOS TYPE command to display the file's contents without specifying a complete pathname to the file, the command will fail.

```
C:\> TYPE APPEND.TXT
File not found
```

Next, use the APPEND command to include the subdirectory DISKBOOK in the data file search path, as shown here:

```
C:\> APPEND C:\DISKBOOK
```

Repeat the previous TYPE command.

```
C:\> TYPE APPEND.TXT
The DOS APPEND command defines a data file search path.
```

This time, because DOS searches the data file search path, TYPE locates the file.

Like the PATH command, DOS lets you specify several subdirectories in the APPEND data file search path. To do so, simply separate each subdirectory name with semicolons. The DOS file APPEND.EXE contains the APPEND command. The first time you invoke it APPEND loads software that remains in memory to manage the data file search path. As such, the first time you invoke APPEND, you can add the following switches:

/E   directs APPEND to place an entry in the DOS environment

/X   assists APPEND in file search operations. Requires DOS 3.3

The /E switch directs APPEND to place an entry in the DOS environment containing the current data file search path. You can only specify this switch the first time you invoke APPEND. To view the environment entry, issue the DOS SET command.

```
C:\> SET
COMSPEC=C:\DOS\COMMAND.COM
PATH=C:\DOS
PROMPT=$P$G
APPEND=C:\DATA
```

By default, not all of the DOS commands support the data file search path. Under DOS version 3.3, you can use the /X switch the first time you invoke APPEND to increase the number of commands that support the data file search path.

Many users are concerned that DOS may inadvertently delete the wrong file if DOS locates a matching file name in the data file search path. To prevent such an accidental file deletion, DOS will not delete or rename files it matches by using the data file search path. If, for example, you try to delete the file APPEND.TXT using the data file search path, the DEL command will fail and DOS will display either the error message `File not found` or `Access denied`.

If you invoke APPEND without a command line, APPEND will display the current data file search path, as shown here:

```
C:\>APPEND
APPEND=C:\DISKBOOK
```

When you no longer need the data file search path, you can delete the path by placing a semicolon in the APPEND command line, as shown here:

```
C:\>APPEND ;
```

Most users don't need to define a data file search path. If, however, you repeatedly use the same subdirectory to access data files, you may consider placing a corresponding APPEND command in AUTOEXEC.BAT.

Improving File Access Performance with FASTOPEN

As discussed in Chapter 3, DOS locates a specific file on disk by using the file's directory entry to determine the file's first cluster entry in the file allocation table. To improve performance, DOS keeps a copy of file allocation table in the computer's fast random-access memory. In doing so, DOS does not have to read the FAT from disk each time it performs a file operation.

By default, each time you access a file, DOS reads the directory from disk and then sequentially searches each directory entry for the file. Depending upon your disk type, computer speed, and file organization, the amount of time DOS spends searching a directory can become considerable.

Starting with DOS 3.3, the FASTOPEN command can decrease the amount of time DOS spends searching for files on your hard disk. FASTOPEN directs DOS to keep track of the starting cluster entry for each file DOS opens on your hard disk. The first time DOS opens a hard disk file, DOS must perform the slow disk read and directory search. If you open the same file a second time, DOS remembers where the file begins and the directory search is not necessary.

By default, FASTOPEN remembers the last 10 files you opened. The following command directs FASTOPEN to remember 50 files for drive C:

```
C:\> FASTOPEN C:=50
```

The FASTOPEN command supports only hard disks. If you have two or more hard disk partitions, you can track files on both disk, as shown here:

```
C:\> FASTOPEN C:=50 D:=30
```

FASTOPEN can track up to 999 entries. This is a total for all disk combined. Like all system performance "tuning" commands, you will need to experiment with FASTOPEN to determine the setting that gives you the best performance. If you direct FASTOPEN to track too many files, you can consume considerable memory (each entry requires 35 bytes of RAM) and create processing overhead as DOS searches the FASTOPEN list for files.

Many users allocate FASTOPEN buffers based upon their disk size. A better guide line is to track the number of files you access more than once. FASTOPEN only improves disk access time for files you open two or more times. DOS only lets you invoke FASTOPEN once. If you need to change the FASTOPEN setting, you must reboot. Once you determine a proper FASTOPEN setting, place a corresponding entry in AUTOEXEC.BAT.

Using FASTOPEN with Defragmenters.

If you install FASTOPEN to track files on your hard disk and later run a third party disk defragmenter (see Chapter 9), you must reboot DOS immediately after the defragmenter completes its work. The defragmenter does its job by moving files around on your disk. The new file locations may not correspond to the values FASTOPEN has recorded. If DOS uses FASTOPEN's values, you may damage your files.

Replacing Specific Files on Your Disk with REPLACE

To simplify the process of updating software programs stored on hard disks, DOS version 3.2 introduced the REPLACE command. REPLACE reads a source directory of files and then searches a target disk for matching files. If REPLACE finds a matching file, REPLACE updates the file using the file residing on the source disk. For example, the following command updates each file on your hard disk that resides on the source disk in drive A:

```
C:\> REPLACE A:\*.* C:\ /S
```

The /S switch directs REPLACE to search every subdirectory on the target disk for matching files. If multiple copies of a file exist in different directories on your disk, using the /S switch, REPLACE will update every occurrence of the file.

The REPLACE command supports several switches in addition to /S.

/A   Directs REPLACE to add files that exist on the source disk but not in the target. Files existing in the target directory are not replaced.

/P   Directs REPLACE to prompt you to enter Y or N to selectively replace every file.

/R   Directs REPLACE to update files marked as read-only. Without /R, REPLACE stops at the first read-only file it encounters.

/W   Directs REPLACE to pause for the user to press Enter before starting the file replacement. The pause lets you insert the desired floppy disk in drive A.

To understand how REPLACE works, place a DOS system disk in drive A. Next, issue the following command:

```
C:\> REPLACE A:*.* C:\ /S /R
```

In this case, REPLACE will begin searching your hard disk for each DOS command file it reads from drive A. Each time REPLACE encounters a matching file, it updates the file and displays the message:

```
Replacing C:\FILENAME.EXT
```

A Caution on Using REPLACE

The REPLACE command only matches files by name. REPLACE does not compare date and time stamps. As such, it is possible for REPLACE to overwrite a newer version of a file, or an unrelated file that happens to have the same name as a file on source disk. Although REPLACE provides a convenient means of updating files, it has the potential to overwrite files you may not want replaced. If you are not sure which files on your disk REPLACE will update, invoke REPLACE with the /P switch and respond with Y or N to selectively update files.

Salvaging Damaged Files with RECOVER

The low-level format locates and identifies the areas of your disk that are initially damaged. Unfortunately, the everyday use of a disk will eventually take its toll on disk sectors, and eventually the sectors are unusable. When a disk sector becomes damaged, DOS will display an error reading or writing drive C: message, followed by the familiar Abort, Retry, or Ignore message.

If a file sector becomes damaged, you may be able to recover a portion of the file using the DOS RECOVER command. If the file is an executable program, recovering a portion of the file is of little use. In fact, executing a portion of a once complete executable program is very dangerous to your system. However, if the file contains critical data, a portion of the file may be better than none. In such cases, the RECOVER command may be helpful.

The DOS RECOVER command should be your **last resort** for recovering a damaged file or disk! Do not rely on RECOVER. Instead, perform regular system backup operations, as discussed in Chapter 8. Never, never use RECOVER on a disk that is not damaged!

Should a file become damaged, use RECOVER as follows to salvage as much of the file as possible:

```
C:\> RECOVER FILENAME.EXT
```

When RECOVER completes, edit the file to begin the file restoration. RECOVER does not undelete files, it only recovers portions of damaged files. To undelete a file, use the UNDELETE utility provided on the companion disk that accompanies this book.

If a disk containing important files becomes damaged and DOS can no longer read it, you may be able to recover several files on the disk. The following command, for example, recovers a damaged floppy disk in drive A:

```
C:\> RECOVER A:
```

As RECOVER salvages files, RECOVER creates files in the disk's root directory with names in the form FILEnnnn.REC. Using the floppy disk example, the root directory may contain the following files:

```
C:\> DIR A:

Volume in drive A has no label
Directory of  A:\

FILE0001 REC      512 01-23-90    3:43p
FILE0002 REC     4608 01-23-90    3:43p
FILE0003 REC     1024 01-23-90    3:43p
FILE0004 REC      512 01-23-90    3:43p
FILE0005 REC     1024 01-23-90    3:43p
FILE0006 REC     2048 01-23-90    3:43p
FILE0007 REC     2048 01-23-90    3:43p
FILE0008 REC     1536 01-23-90    3:43p
FILE0009 REC     4608 01-23-90    3:43p
FILE0010 REC      512 01-23-90    3:43p
        10 File(s)       161280 bytes free
```

Using an editor, you can examine the files and copy them to a new disk with the proper name.

RECOVER will begin salvaging files, placing the files in the root directory with the file name FILEnnnn.REC. To restore your disk to its operational status, you will have several hours of file and directory manipulation. Because RECOVER is used so seldom, many users remove RECOVER.COM from their hard disk.

Optimizing the PRINT Command

The PRINT command lets you send one or more files to the printer while continuing to execute another program at the DOS prompt. To print the file APPEND.TXT that you created earlier in this chapter, invoke PRINT as follows:

```
C:\> PRINT \DISKBOOK\APPEND.TXT
```

The first time you invoke the PRINT command, PRINT will prompt you to enter the printer device name, as shown here:

```
Name of list device [PRN]:
```

Most users have a parallel computer attached to the printer port LPT1. DOS uses the name PRN (that PRINT displays within brackets) as another name for the default parallel printer port. If you are using a parallel printer, simply press Enter, and the file will begin printing. If you are using a serial printer, it is probably connected to the serial port COM1. As such, type COM1 at PRINT's prompt and press Enter. PRINT only displays this prompt the first time you invoke it.

The PRINT command lets you specify several files for printing on the same command line. For example, the following command prints the files AUTOEXEC.BAT and CONFIG.SYS, both of which reside in the root directory:

```
C:\> PRINT \AUTOEXEC.BAT \CONFIG.SYS
```

When you execute this command, PRINT informs you that it is printing the file AUTOEXEC.BAT and that the file CONFIG.SYS is in a *queue*.

```
C:\AUTOEXEC.BAT is currently being printed
C:\CONFIG.SYS is in queue
```

A queue is a waiting line. In this case, the queue is a line of files waiting to be printed. Because your printer can print only one file at a time, CONFIG.SYS must wait. By default, PRINT can queue up to 10 files.

The PRINT command supports DOS wild cards. The following PRINT command prints all of the files residing in the DISKBOOK subdirectory:

```
C:\> PRINT \DISKBOOK\*.*
```

Although most users invoke the PRINT command on a regular basis, most don't take advantage of several switches that boost PRINT's performance. The first time you invoke the PRINT command, PRINT installs memory resident software that controls the printer and the print queue. PRINT supports several switches that can only be specified the first time you invoke PRINT.

/B:BufferSize	Defines the size of the memory buffer PRINT uses for file read operations. The larger the buffer, the fewer slow disk reads required. The buffer size must be in the range 512 to 32,767.
/D:DeviceName	Specifies the printer device name. Normally PRN or COM1.
/M:ClockTicks	Specifies the maximum number of CPU clock ticks over which PRINT can retain control The value must be in the range 1 through 255.
/Q:QueueEntries	Specifies the number of files PRINT can queue. The value must be in the range 1 through 32.
/S:TimeSlices	Specifies the number of PRINT time slices in each second. The value must be in the range 1 through 255.
/U:ClockTicks	Specifies the number of CPU clockticks PRINT can wait for the printer to become ready for the next set of characters. The value must be in the range 1 through 255.

The /B:BufferSize switch specifies the size of the memory buffer PRINT uses to print a file. By default, PRINT uses a 512 byte buffer. Each time PRINT prints a file, PRINT reads a portion of the file from disk into the print buffer.

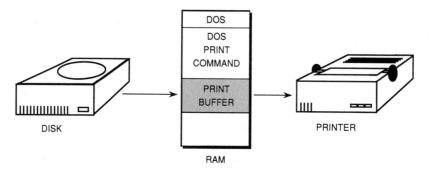

If the file contains 4,096 bytes, PRINT must perform eight disk read operations to print the file.

```
Disk read operations = (File Size) / (Buffer Size)
                     = 4096 / 512
                     = 8
```

A disk's mechanical nature makes disk read operations slow in comparison to the computer's fast electronic operations. The golden performance rule remains: To improve performance, reduce disk read or write operations. In this case, you can increase PRINT's buffer size and reduce the number of disk read operations required to read a file. A single-spaced page of typed text contains about 4,000 characters. If you increase the PRINT buffer size to 4,096 bytes, you will reduce the number of disk read operations required to print the previous file to one. If your system has 640K of memory, you might even consider a buffer as large as 8,192 bytes. The PRINT buffer size you select should always be a multiple of 512 bytes (the DOS disk sector size).

As discussed, the first time you invoke the PRINT command, PRINT displays the following prompt to determine the printer device name:

```
Name of list device [PRN]:
```

The /D:DeviceName switch directs PRINT to use the device name specified for the printer, suppressing the previous printer name prompt.

A print queue is a list of files waiting to be printed. By default, PRINT can queue up to ten files. The /Q:QueueEntries switch lets you specify a queue size from 1 through 32. If you print a large number of files at the same time, you may want to increase the size of the print queue.

The /M, /S, and /U switches control the amount of CPU time the PRINT command can "borrow" from DOS. PRINT is called a background command because it allows you to execute other DOS commands while it works behind the scenes (in the background) to print your files. PRINT and DOS cooperate by sharing CPU time. DOS will execute a command for several CPU clock ticks and then pass control of the CPU to PRINT in order to print files for several clock ticks. A CPU clock tick occurs every 0.0549 seconds. The CPU switching occurs so rapidly that DOS and PRINT appear to be working simultaneously.

The /M:ClockTicks switch determines the length of time (number of CPU clock ticks) that PRINT controls the CPU when PRINT's turn at control occurs. The value must be in the range 1 through 255. Again, this is a system performance value with which you need to experiment. Most users find the value 64 a good starting point. If the value is too large, your keyboard response may be slow.

The /S switch specifies the number of times PRINT and DOS can exchange control of the CPU each second. The value must be in the range 1 through 255. Again, experiment with this value. Most users keep the default setting of 8.

Compared to your computer's other devices, the printer is very slow. In many cases, PRINT is ready to send the next series of characters to the printer, but the printer is still busy printing the previous characters. The /U switch specifies the number of CPU clock ticks PRINT can wait for the printer to become available, before returning control to DOS. The value must be in the range 1 through 255. Most users find that the value 16 is a good starting point for older mechanical printers.

Because these switches can only be used the first time PRINT is invoked, you should determine the settings best suited for your system and then place a corresponding entry in AUTOEXEC.BAT, as shown here:

```
PRINT /B:8096 /D:PRN /M:64 /U:16
```

In addition to the switches just discussed, PRINT supports three switches that let you add and remove files from the print queue.

/C   Removes the file name specified immediately before the switch, as well as those that follow the switch from the queue.

/P   Adds the file name specified immediately before the switch, as well as those that follow the switch from queue.

/T   Removes all files from the queue, canceling the printing of the current file.

To display the files that are currently in the print queue, invoke PRINT without a command line, as shown here:

```
C:\> PRINT
```

Assume that the print queue contains the following files:

```
C:\> PRINT

  C:\DISKBOOK\APPEND.TXT is currently being printed
  C:\AUTOEXEC.BAT is in queue
  C:\CONFIG.SYS is in queue
```

To remove the file AUTOEXEC.BAT from the queue, you can use the /C qualifier, as shown here:

```
C:\> PRINT AUTOEXEC.BAT /C
```

To cancel all of the files in the queue, you can use the /T switch, as shown here:

```
C:\> PRINT /T
```

PRINT will cancel the current print task, removing all files from the queue. Next, PRINT will print a page containing the message:

```
All files canceled by operator
```

If your printer has its own built-in memory, the printer may print several pages before the termination message appears and the print job stops.

The /P switch lets users cancel and add files to the print queue in one command. The following PRINT command, for example, removes the file OLD.DAT using /C while adding the file NEW.DAT:

```
C:\> PRINT OLD.DAT /C NEW.DAT /P
```

Comparing Two Files with COMP

Although two similarly named files may appear identical in size in a directory listing, the actual contents of the files may differ.

The DOS COMP command compares the contents of two files and reports any differences it encounters. The format of the DOS COMP command is **COMP** *first__file second__file.* To understand how the COMP command works, create the files COMPARE.ONE and COMPARE.TWO, as shown here:

```
C:\> COPY CON \DISKBOOK\COMPARE.ONE
11111
22222
33333
44444
^Z
    1 File(s) copied

C:\> COPY CON \DISKBOOK\COMPARE.TWO
11121
22232
33343
44454
^Z

    1 File(s) copied
```

Next, issue the following COMP command:

```
C:\> COMP \DISKBOOK\COMPARE.ONE \DISKBOOK\COMPARE.TWO
```

When COMP compares the files, COMP locates and displays the following differences:

```
C:\> COMP \DISKBOOK\COMPARE.ONE   \DISKBOOK\COMPARE.TWO

C:\DISKBOOK\COMPARE.ONE and C:\DISKBOOK\COMPARE.TWO
Compare error at OFFSET 3
File 1 = 31
File 2 = 32
Compare error at OFFSET A
File 1 = 32
File 2 = 33
Compare error at OFFSET 11
File 1 = 33
File 2 = 34
Compare error at OFFSET 18
File 1 = 34
File 2 = 35
EOF mark not found


Compare more files (Y/N) ?
```

Users have difficulty understanding COMP because COMP displays its output in hexadecimal, the base 16 numbering system. If you look at the first offset and count characters beginning with the value 0, the offset of 3 for the first difference makes sense. The hexadecimal value A is the value 10 in decimal. Although they don't appear on your screen, each line of the file contains a carriage-return and linefeed character, as shown here:

```
11121<CR><LF>
22232<CR><LF>
33343<CR><LF>
44454<CR><LF>
```

By counting, starting at offset 0, the offset value of 10 for the second difference again makes sense. The decimal equivalent of the hexadecimal values 11 and 18 are 17 and 24, which are the offsets of the last two differences in the file.

COMP will only display the first ten differences between two files. After ten differences, COMP ends the comparison and displays the following message:

```
10 Mismatches - ending compare
```

If the two files are identical, COMP displays the following message:

```
Files compare OK
```

If you don't specify the files to compare in the COMP command line, COMP will prompt you to enter the file names, as shown here:

```
C:\> COMP
Enter primary file name
\DISKBOOK\COMPARE.ONE

Enter 2nd file name or drive id
\DISKBOOK\COMPARE.TWO
```

Note the prompt for the second file name. If you specify a drive letter instead of a file name, COMP will search the current directory on the drive specified for a file with the same name as the primary file. The DOS COMP command supports wildcard characters.

Many users invoke COMP to verify that an important file copy operation was successful. The following commands copy the file COMPARE.ONE to drive A and then compare both copies of the file to ensure they are identical:

```
C:\> COPY \DISKBOOK\COMPARE.ONE A:
C:\> COMP \DISKBOOK\COMPARE.ONE A:
```

If COMP encounters differences between the files, an error occurred during the file copy operation.

Displaying a File with MORE

In Chapter 3, you learned that the TYPE command displays a file's contents. If your file is smaller than a screen in length, the TYPE command is very easy to use. However, if your file is long, the file's contents may scroll past you very quickly on the screen.

The DOS MORE command lets you display long files a screenful at a time. To display a file with MORE, you must use the DOS input redirection operator (⟨), as shown here:

```
C:\> MORE < FILENAME.EXT
```

Each time MORE displays a screenful of information, MORE suspends output and displays the following message:

```
-- More --
```

To view the next screen of information, simply press any key. To cancel the command, use the Ctrl + C keyboard combination. Using the DOS TREE command discussed earlier in this chapter, create the file FILES.DAT that contains the name of every file on your disk, as shown here:

```
C:\> TREE /F > \DISKBOOK\FILES.DAT
```

Next, using the MORE command, display the contents of FILES.DAT a screenful at a time.

```
C:\> MORE < \DISKBOOK\FILES.DAT
```

In addition to displaying files a screenful at a time using MORE, many users view the output of DOS commands with MORE using the DOS *pipe operator* (¦). The pipe operator directs DOS to make the output of one program the input of another. For example, the following command displays the files in the DOS subdirectory a screenful at a time:

```
C:\> DIR \DOS ¦ MORE
```

In a similar manner, the following command displays the attributes of each file on your disk a screenful at a time:

```
C:\> ATTRIB C:\*.* /S ¦ MORE
```

The next two commands, SORT and FIND, also fully support DOS input redirection using the input redirection operator and the DOS pipe.

Sorting a File's Contents with SORT

Just as the DOS MORE command displays redirected input one screen at a time, the DOS SORT command sorts redirected input in either ascending (lowest to highest) or descending order. The following command displays a sorted directory listing of the files in the DOS subdirectory:

```
C:\> DIR \DOS ¦ SORT
```

In this case, the DOS pipe operator redirects the output of the DIR command to become the input to the SORT command.

The SORT command will also sort files. Create the following file SORTDATA.DAT:

```
C:\> COPY CON \DISKBOOK\SORTDATA.DAT
44444
33333
11111
55555
22222
^Z
    1 File(s) copied
```

Next, sort the file using the DOS input redirection operator, as shown here:

```
C:\> SORT < \DISKBOOK\SORTDATA.DAT
11111
22222
33333
44444
55555
```

The /R switch directs SORT to sort its input in descending order (highest to lowest). The following command uses the /R switch to sort the file SORTDATA.DAT in descending order:

```
C:\> SORT /R < \DISKBOOK\SORTDATA.DAT
55555
44444
33333
22222
11111
```

SORT also lets you sort input based on a specific column value. The following command sorts a directory listing by size beginning at column 13:

```
C:\> DIR \DOS | SORT /+13 /R
```

The command uses column 13 because it is the first column following the file name and extension. If the sorted directory listing scrolls past you too quickly, redirect the output of the SORT command to MORE, as shown here:

```
C:\> DIR \DOS | SORT /R /+13 | MORE
```

In this case, MORE will display the sorted directory listing a screenful at a time.

Permanently Sorting Directories

Using the SORT command, you can obtain sorted listings of the files in your directory. This will help you view your directories in an organized manner, but this method can be frustrating because SORT must then be used every time you wish to view the organized directory. To permanently place the file names in sorted order, you must use the a utility program, such as SORTDIR (included with the Jamsa Disk Utilities which are bound with this book).

Locating Key Text with FIND

As the number of files on your disk increases, there may be times when you need to search files for a specific word or phrase. The DOS FIND command provides a way to do so. To begin, create the file FINDTEXT.DAT, as shown here:

```
C:\> COPY CON \DISKBOOK\FINDTEXT.DAT
The DOS FIND command searches a file for
a key word or text. Like the DOS SORT and
MORE commands, FIND supports input
redirection and the DOS pipe.
^Z
    1 File(s) copied
```

Next, you can use FIND to display each line in the file that contains the word DOS, as shown here:

```
C:\> FIND "DOS" \DISKBOOK\FINDTEXT.DAT

---------- \DISKBOOK\FINDTEXT.DAT
The DOS FIND command searches a file for
a key word or text. Like the DOS SORT and
redirection and the DOS pipe.

C:\>
```

Note that you must place the word or phrase you are searching for within double quotes. The FIND command supports several switches that increase its flexibility.

/C	Directs FIND to display only a count of the number of lines containing the word or phrase specified.
/N	Directs FIND to precede each line containing the word or phrase with its line number.
/V	Directs FIND to display each line that does not contain the word or phrase.

Using the /C switch, the following FIND command displays a count of the number of lines in the file FINDTEXT.DAT that contains the word DOS:

```
C:\> FIND /C "DOS" \DISKBOOK\FINDTEXT.DAT

---------- \DISKBOOK\FINDTEXT.DAT: 3
C:\>
```

Likewise, the following FIND command precedes each line containing the word DOS with its line number:

```
C:\> FIND /NC "DOS" \DISKBOOK\FINDTEXT.DAT

---------- \DISKBOOK\FINDTEXT.DAT:
[1]The DOS FIND command searches a file for
[2]a key word or text. Like the DOS SORT and
[4]redirection and the DOS pipe.

C:\>
```

FIND is case sensitive, which means it will not match an uppercase string to the same string in lowercase. The following FIND command finds no occurrences of the lowercase word *dos*:

```
C:\> FIND "dos" \DISKBOOK\FINDTEXT.DAT

---------- \DISKBOOK\FINDTEXT.DAT:

C:\>
```

Using the /V switch, the following FIND command displays each line in the file FINDTEXT.DAT that does not contain the word DOS:

```
C:\> FIND /V "DOS" \DISKBOOK\FINDTEXT.DAT

---------- \DISKBOOK\FINDTEXT.DAT:
MORE commands, FIND supports input

C:\>
```

The DOS FIND command supports input redirection using either the DOS input redirection operator (⟨) or the DOS pipe. If the FIND command line does not contain a file name, FIND assumes redirected input. The following command redirects the output of the DIR command to become the input of the FIND command. FIND searches the input for each occurrence of the characters ⟨DIR⟩, which lets it display each subdirectory that resides in the root.

```
C:\> DIR \ ¦ FIND "<DIR>"
DISKBOOK      <DIR>      01-21-90   11:40a
DOS           <DIR>      11-19-89    5:23p

C:\>
```

Admittedly, this chapter has presented a considerable number of DOS commands. Take time now to review each command. It's not important to memorize each command's format or switches, but you do need to understand each command's function and how it performs. You can always review a command's format when you need to issue the command.

These commands, combined with the file manipulation commands in Chapter 3 and the subdirectory commands from Chapter 4, make up almost all of the hard disk commands. In fact, the only DOS commands left to discuss are CHKDSK (discussed in Chapter 7), BACKUP, and RESTORE (discussed in Chapter 8).

Summary

In this chapter, you learned the DOS commands that help you work with your hard disk files. With DOS you can assign a name to your disk using the LABEL command and use the DIR and VOL commands to display the disk (volume) name.

The DOS TREE command displays your subdirectory structure on the screen, optionally listing the files in each directory. As the number of subdirectories on your disk grows, the DOS TREE command will be helpful when you locate specific directories.

DOS assigns an attribute value to every file on your disk. The attribute value may tell DOS the file needs to be backed up to floppy disk or that the file cannot be changed or deleted. The DOS ATTRIB command lets you set or display a file's read-only and archive attributes. By setting a file to read-only, you prevent DOS from overwriting or deleting the file if you issue an event command.

The DOS SUBST command lets you substitute an unused drive letter for a long path name. When you substitute a directory, DOS automatically routes each reference to the drive letter to the correct directory.

The DOS APPEND command lets you define a data file search path that tells DOS where to locate your commonly used data files. When you establish a data file search path, you no longer have to specify complete path names for data files that reside in the path.

The DOS FASTOPEN command provides one of the easiest and least expensive methods of improving your disk performance. It lets you direct DOS to renumber the last *n* files for which you have referenced locations. By using FASTOPEN, DOS doesn't have to search the disk each time you access a frequently used file, DOS remembers where the file exists. Everyone should place a FASTOPEN entry in AUTOEXEC.BAT.

The DOS REPLACE command helps you update all of the files on your disk when a new version of a software program is released. REPLACE will optionally search every directory on your disk, replacing each file on the new source disk.

In this chapter, you learned how to maximize PRINT's performance. Experiment with the recommended PRINT settings and place the PRINT command that provides you with the best performance in AUTOEXEC.BAT.

DOS stores information on disk using sectors. If your disk becomes damaged, DOS may not be able to read one or more of the sectors containing your file's information. If the damaged sector appears in the middle or at the end of your file, the DOS RECOVER command can recover the contents of your file that preceded the damaged sector. Depending on the state of your backups, recovering a partial file may be better than no file at all.

The DOS COMP command lets you compare the contents of two files. Because COMP displays its output using hexadecimal, most users only invoke COMP to ensure COPY operations are successful. If you copy a file to a different disk and then invoke COMP to compare the original to the copy, you can ensure the operation was indeed successful.

In Chapter 3, you used the DOS TYPE command to display a file's contents. Depending on the size of the file, its contents may have scrolled past very quickly on the screen. The DOS MORE command lets you view a file's contents a screenful at a time.

The DOS SORT command lets you sort a file or redirected input. Many users invoke SORT to display a sorted directory listing. SORT does not actually sort a directory. Instead, SORT displays the file's contents in sorted order. To actually sort the directory, use the Jamsa Disk Utilities SORTDIR command.

The DOS FIND command searches a file or redirected input for a specific word or phrase. FIND will display each line of the file containing the desired word. Optionally, FIND will precede each line with its line number and display a count of the total number of occurrences.

As you can see, DOS provides a very powerful set of file manipulation commands, many of which may be used to improve your disk's performance. In Chapter 6, you will examine the DOS startup process and learn several additional techniques to improve your system's performance.

6

DOS System Start-Up and Your Hard Disk

- ► System Start-Up
- ► Using CONFIG.SYS to Customize Your System
- ► Using AUTOEXEC.BAT
- ► Summary

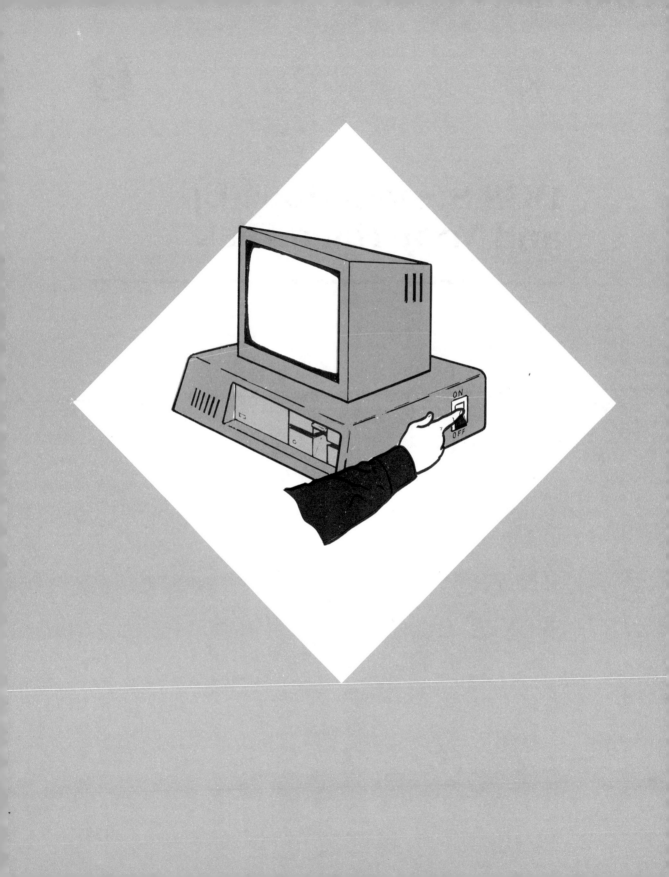

6

DOS System Start-Up and Your Hard Disk

Although most users take the DOS start-up procedure for granted, it performs several very important steps, many of which affect your system's performance. Knowledge of the start-up process helps you better understand disk partitioning, assists you in recognizing hardware errors, and lets you improve your system performance by placing correct entries in the AUTOEXEC.BAT and CONFIG.SYS files.

This chapter begins by taking a detailed look at the steps your computer performs to load DOS each time you turn your computer on or reboot your system. The discussion includes steps you can take to troubleshoot hardware errors that may prevent your system from booting. Next, the chapter examines the file CONFIG.SYS, which lets you customize your system. The majority of the CONFIG.SYS entries are disk related, and several of the entries can improve your system performance. Pay close attention to the recommended settings. Finally, the chapter briefly discusses the AUTOEXEC.BAT file, recommending several DOS commands you should place in that file.

System Start-Up

Each time you turn on your computer's power, a program built into your computer begins a power on self test (POST). The test examines several key hardware components and then examines your computer's random-access memory. In most cases, the POST displays a count of the working memory on your screen, similar to

```
00640 KB OK
```

If your computer does not display the working memory and later fails to boot DOS, you can tell the computer repairman that your computer has failed its power on self test.

If the POST is successful, the PC first checks drive A for a bootable floppy disk. If drive A contains a floppy disk that can start DOS, the system begins loading DOS into memory from the floppy disk. If drive A contains a floppy disk, but it is not bootable, your system will display the following error message:

```
Non-system disk or disk error
Replace and strike any key when ready
```

Should this error occur, either place a bootable floppy disk in drive A and press any key or open the disk drive latch on drive A and press a key. This last procedure allows the system to start DOS from your hard disk.

Your system always tests for a bootable disk in drive A first to prevent a hard disk error from leaving your system unbootable. Several of the utilities provided on the companion Jamsa Disk Utilities disk help you recover from hard disk errors. When such errors occur, you can restart your system from drive A if necessary and then run the appropriate Jamsa Disk Utilities program to correct the error.

If your computer does not turn on drive A's disk activation light in search of DOS, your computer failed its power on self test.

If drive A does not contain a disk or if it contains a disk and the drive latch is open, your computer's start-up program searches for a hard disk. If a hard disk exists, your computer will read the disk's master boot record, which contains the disk partitioning information. The computer uses this information to determine which partition to boot. The start-up program then reads the boot record from the first sector of the desired partition. If the boot record exists, your computer begins to load DOS.

The following figure is a flowchart that shows the computer's start-up procedures to this point.

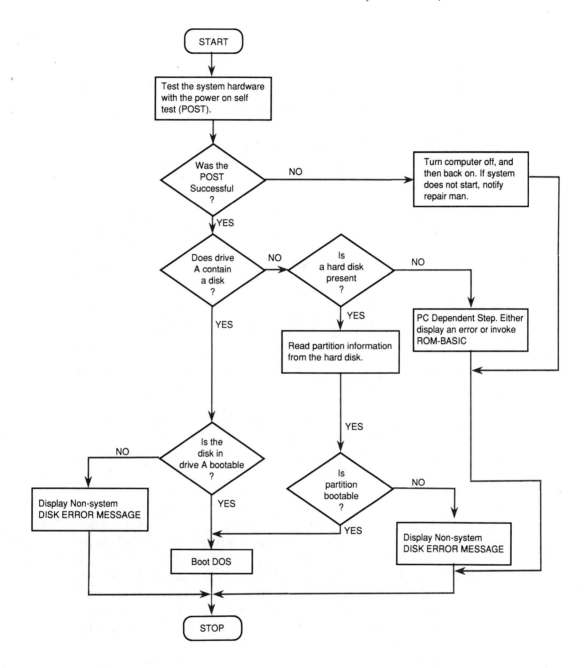

If you have a hard disk but your computer ignores it during start-up, check the following.

▶ Was the hard disk partitioned using FDISK as discussed in Chapter 2?

▶ Was the hard disk formatted using FORMAT /S as discussed in Chapter 2?

▶ Does the hard disk require a special device driver in CONFIG.SYS? See your hardware manual.

If your computer successfully reads the partition's boot record and the disk contains the necessary DOS system files, the DOS start-up actually begins. Until this point, your computer has been executing the start-up program built into your computer. The DOS boot record, however, contains a small program that takes over the process of loading DOS from disk into memory.

To begin, DOS locates the hidden system files in the root directory. If you are using MS-DOS, the files are IO.SYS and MSDOS.SYS. If you are using PC-DOS, the files are IBMBIO.COM and IBMDOS.COM. If your version of MS-DOS is from another vendor, then these files may have a different name. Regardless of the names of these files, the booting procedure is the same. For simplicity, the following discussion assumes that you are using MS-DOS.

First, DOS loads the file IO.SYS into memory. This file contains software that lets DOS perform basic input and output operations. In addition, the file contains a small program named SYSINIT (short for system initialization) that takes over the start-up process and reads the file MSDOS.SYS into memory. The file MSDOS.SYS contains the DOS system services that let DOS create files and directories, execute programs, and maintain the system date and time. After MSDOS.SYS is present in memory, the SYSINIT program opens the file CONFIG.SYS for processing. As we will discuss in detail next, the file CONFIG.SYS exists to let you customize your system. After DOS has processed the CONFIG.SYS entries, SYSINIT invokes the DOS command line processor, COMMAND.COM. The first time DOS invokes COMMAND.COM, it searches your root directory for the batch file AUTOEXEC.BAT, which is briefly discussed at the end of this chapter.

The following figure shows the last half of the DOS start-up procedure.

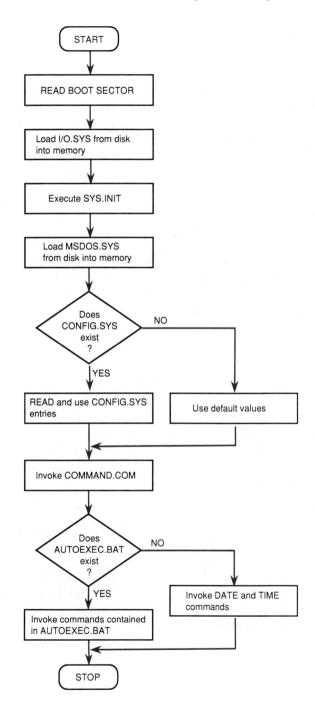

Using CONFIG.SYS to Customize Your System

Each time DOS starts, the DOS start-up procedures search the root directory for the file CONFIG.SYS. The CONFIG.SYS file is a text file you can create with an editor or word processor or by simply copying its contents from the keyboard as shown in Chapter 2. CONFIG.SYS contains one or more single-line entries. In Chapter 2, for example, you created a two-line CONFIG.SYS that contained the following.

```
BUFFERS=25
FILES=20
```

This chapter examines each of the CONFIG.SYS entries in detail, beginning with the entries that affect your hard disk. This chapter also provides recommended settings for each CONFIG.SYS entry. Each time you change or add an entry to CONFIG.SYS, you must reboot DOS for the change to take effect.

Defining Disk Transfer Buffers

Each time DOS reads information from a disk, DOS tells the disk controller the desired sector number. The controller then reads the sector and places the data into a section of RAM reserved by DOS called a *disk buffer*. After the data resides in the disk buffer, DOS can transfer the data to the application's data buffer as shown here.

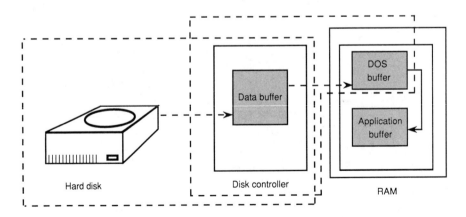

Each time DOS reads or writes information to a disk, DOS transfers a sector, or 512 bytes of data. If an application wants only the first 10 bytes of a file, for example, DOS must read the file's first sector. DOS places the sector into a disk buffer. Should the application later need the next 10 bytes of the file, the information already exists in the disk buffer. DOS doesn't need to read the data from disk. Because even the fastest disk drives are slow in comparison to your computer's fast electronic RAM, any steps you can take to reduce disk operations will increase your system performance. Disk buffers reduce the number of disk operations DOS must perform by increasing the likelihood of DOS locating file information in memory.

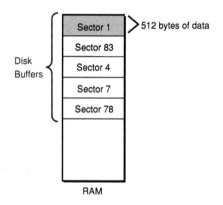

Assume, for example, that you are using a database program that tracks family birthdays and anniversaries. Each record in the database requires 64 bytes as shown in this figure.

Name	Birthday
Kevin	October 18
Stephanie	February 23
Kellie	January 29
Aunt Sandie	April 2
Grandma	December 7
Debbie	December 8

44 bytes   20 bytes

64 bytes

Assume that the database program reads the first record from disk. Because DOS must read an entire sector from disk, DOS buffers the first 8 records of the database as shown in the following figure.

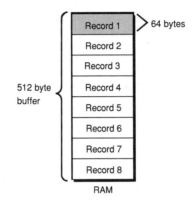

Should the database program need records 2 through 8, they already reside in the computer's memory, which means DOS does not have to read the information from disk.

Each time DOS must read a sector from disk, it first checks its disk buffers to see if the sector is present. If so, it uses the information without having to perform a slow disk operation. If the sector is not in a buffer, DOS must read the information from disk. The CONFIG.SYS BUFFERS= entry lets you define the number of disk buffers DOS keeps in memory. By default, DOS uses two buffers for the IBM PC and three buffers for the PC AT. If you increase the number of disk buffers, you also increase the likelihood that DOS will locate file information in RAM, which means fewer slow disk operations.

The format of the BUFFERS= entry is

BUFFERS=*value*

where the value ranges from 2 through 255. If you make the value too small, you decrease the likelihood of DOS locating sectors in RAM. However, if you make the value too large, your system performance can also suffer. First, each disk buffer consumes 528 bytes of memory. If you use 255 disk buffers, you will consume over 130K of memory. Second, each time DOS must perform a disk read operation, DOS may spend a considerable amount of time searching the disk buffers for the sector. Most systems should get best performance from about 25 disk buffers. If you are running disk-intensive database programs or using a fast 386-based system, experiment with increasing the number of buffers by 5 at a time until you find a value that gives you optimal performance.

Defining the Number of Files DOS Can Open at One Time

The second entry you added to the CONFIG.SYS file created in Chapter 2 was `FILES = 20`. By default, DOS lets your programs open up to eight different files at one time. Although eight files sounds sufficient, DOS actually assigns five of the files to its standard devices. The standard devices, which result in reserved files, are detailed in Table 6.1.

Table 6.1. *Files reserved by DOS.*

File Name	Device	Operation Type
Stdin	CON	Keyboard/redirected input
Stdout	CON	Screen/redirected output
Stderr	CON	Screen
Stdaux	AUX	Serial communications
Stdprn	PRN	Parallel printer

Because of these five standard files, DOS effectively restricts your applications to opening only three files at any one time. Most database programs cannot execute if you don't increase the number of files DOS can open. The CONFIG.SYS `FILES=` entry lets you increase the number of files DOS can open at one time. The format of this entry is

`FILES=value`

where *value* specifies the number of files DOS can open at one time from 8 through 255. Most users will find that 20 files is more than sufficient. The value 20 supports the 5 reserved files and allows for 15 additional files.

Increasing the Number of Logical Disk Drives

In Chapter 5 you learned that DOS lets you abbreviate long or commonly used subdirectory names with a disk drive letter using the SUBST

command. For example, the following command abbreviates the subdirectory DOS as drive E.

```
C:\> SUBST E: C:\DOS
```

   After you perform a directory substitution, you can access the
subdirectory using the drive letter. In this case, because drive E does not
actually exist as a physical drive that you can touch, it is referred to as a
logical drive. By default, DOS supports logical drives A through E. If you
refer to a drive letter greater than E, DOS displays the following error
message:

```
C:\> SUBST F: C:\SOMEDIR
Invalid parameter
```

   If you want to substitute several drive letters, you must increase
the number of logical drives DOS supports using the CONFIG.SYS
LASTDRIVE= entry. The entry's format is

```
LASTDRIVE=drive_letter
```

where *drive_letter* is a letter of the alphabet from E through Z. The
following entry directs DOS to support the logical disk drive letters A
through K.

```
LASTDRIVE=K
```

   Many users ask, "Why not simply use LASTDRIVE = Z and not
worry about the entry?" The answer is: Most users don't use logical drive
substitutions. Those users who do, normally use only a few logical
drives. Each logical drive CONFIG.SYS reserves space for consumes 80
bytes of memory. If you reserve space for a logical drive and then fail to
use it, the memory space is wasted.

Supporting Older Applications
That Use File Control Blocks

Software programs written for the earliest 1.x versions of DOS accessed
files using a buffer called a *file control block* (FCB). With DOS version 2.0,

DOS changed its file access methods to use a structure called a *file handle*. The CONFIG.SYS `FILES=` entry discussed earlier sets aside memory to store file handles.

In some cases, users who are still running very old software programs under newer versions of DOS experience errors when the program tries to open a file. In such cases, increasing the number of FCBs that DOS supports may correct the problem. The CONFIG.SYS `FCBS=` entry defines the number of file control blocks DOS will support. The entry's format is

`FCBS=MaximumFCBS,OpenFCBS`

where *MaxnimumFCBS* specifies the maximum number of file control blocks DOS can have open at one time and *OpenFCBS* specifies the number of FCBs DOS must leave open at the same time. The value for *MaximumFCBS* must be in the range 1 through 255. By default, DOS uses the value 4. The value for *OpenFCBS* must be in the range 0 through 255. By default, DOS uses the value 0.

Most DOS users don't need to use the `FCBS=` entry. If you experience file open errors with very old DOS programs, experiment with the following setting:

`FCBS=20,4`

Moving COMMAND.COM from the Root Directory

Chapter 4 discussed DOS subdirectory manipulation in great detail. You learned that only the files CONFIG.SYS, AUTOEXEC.BAT, and COMMAND.COM normally reside in the root directory. Most users keep a copy of the file COMMAND.COM in the root directory as well as in the DOS subdirectory. The CONFIG.SYS `SHELL=` entry lets you eliminate the need for the second copy of COMMAND.COM in the root directory. The following CONFIG.SYS entry directs DOS to locate COMMAND.COM in the subdirectory DOS in drive C.

`SHELL=C:\DOS\COMMAND.COM /P`

As discussed earlier in this chapter, the last step of the DOS start-up procedure is to load COMMAND.COM into memory. Because DOS has processed the CONFIG.SYS entries prior to this, the SHELL= entry tells DOS where to locate COMMAND.COM. By default, DOS assumes COMMAND.COM will reside in the root directory. The /P switch must be present for DOS to execute the batch file AUTOEXEC.BAT. If the /P switch is missing, DOS ignores AUTOEXEC.BAT, displaying only the DOS prompt.

Once you change the CONFIG.SYS SHELL= entry, you must also change the file AUTOEXEC.BAT. Place the following command in AUTOEXEC.BAT:

```
SET COMSPEC=C:\DOS\COMMAND.COM
```

Some programs are so large that they overwrite a portion of COMMAND.COM in memory as they execute. When the program ends, DOS must reload a portion of COMMAND.COM from disk back into memory. To reload COMMAND.COM, DOS uses the COMSPEC environment entry.

After you change both CONFIG.SYS and AUTOEXEC.BAT, you can delete COMMAND.COM from the root directory, provided a copy of the file exists in the DOS subdirectory. Next, reboot your system. If you have performed the steps correctly, your system will restart. If DOS displays the message

```
Bad or missing Command Interpreter
```

restart your system using a bootable floppy disk in drive A. Make sure CONFIG.SYS contains a correct SHELL= entry. Next, make sure the file COMMAND.COM resides in the DOS subdirectory.

```
C:\> DIR \DOS\COMMAND.COM

 Volume in drive C is DOS
 Directory of  C:\DOS

COMMAND  COM     25276 07-24-87  12:00a
        1 File(s)   43694080 bytes free
```

Finally, make sure that the AUTOEXEC.BAT SET COMSPEC entry is correct.

Using SHELL= to Increase the Environment Size

The DOS environment is a region in memory that DOS sets aside to store information such as the current prompt, the command path, and the `COMSPEC` entry just discussed. If you invoke the DOS SET command, DOS will display the current environment entries.

```
C:\> SET
COMSPEC=C:\DOS\COMMAND.COM
PATH=C:\DOS
PROMPT=$P$G
```

The SET command also lets you add entries to the environment. For example, the following command assigns the file name CONFIG.SYS to the entry `SYSFILE`.

```
C:\> SET SYSFILE=CONFIG.SYS
```

If you invoke SET again, without a command line, SET will display the new entry as shown here.

```
C:\> SET
COMSPEC=C:\DOS\COMMAND.COM
PATH=C:\DOS
PROMPT=$P$G
SYSFILE=CONFIG.SYS
```

Several DOS commands create environment entries. Also many complex batch files use environment entries for named parameter processing. As a result, the number of entries in the environment can become quite large. Unfortunately, if you load a memory-resident software program or a DOS command such as FASTOPEN, APPEND, or PRINT, the environment size cannot grow as your needs require.

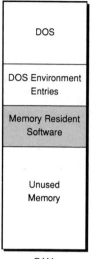

RAM

Eventually, you may use up the entire environment space and DOS will display the following error message:

```
Out of environment space
```

Should this error message occur, you can increase the environment size DOS starts with by using the /E switch with SHELL= as shown here.

```
SHELL=C:\DOS\COMMAND.COM /P /E:1024
```

In this case, DOS will allocate 1,024 bytes of memory for the environment. DOS lets you specify an environment size up to 32,767 bytes. The default size is 127 bytes.

Loading Software Device Drivers

By default, DOS knows how to access the standard devices that accompany your computer such as the keyboard, the printer, the screen display, and most disk drives (see Table 6.1). If you have purchased unique third-party devices such as a mouse, scanner, FAX, or even a high storage disk, you may have to install special software that helps DOS access the device. Such software is normally provided to you by the hardware manufacturer and is called a *device driver*.

DOS must load the device driver into memory during system start-up for DOS to have access to the device. The CONFIG.SYS `DEVICE=` entry specifies the complete path name to a driver as shown here.

```
DEVICE=C:\DOS\ANSI.SYS
```

In this case, DOS will load the device driver ANSI.SYS into memory when the system starts. ANSI.SYS is a device driver provided by DOS that increases your screen and keyboard capabilities. For specifics on the ANSI.SYS driver, refer to your DOS manual.

Most device drivers use the extension SYS to indicate they are system files. If you perform a directory listing of your DOS files, you will find several device driver files:

```
C:\> DIR \DOS\*.SYS

 Volume in drive C is DOS
 Directory of  C:\DOS

ANSI     SYS     1647 07-24-87  12:00a
COUNTRY  SYS    11254 07-24-87  12:00a
DISPLAY  SYS    11259 07-24-87  12:00a
DRIVER   SYS     1165 07-24-87  12:00a
KEYBOARD SYS    19735 07-24-87  12:00a
PRINTER  SYS    13559 07-24-87  12:00a
RAMDRIVE SYS     6481 07-24-87  12:00a
       7 File(s)      43694080 bytes free
```

The actual directory listing for your version of DOS may differ from the one shown here. Table 6.2 briefly describes the functions of these drivers. For specifics on each driver, refer to your DOS manual.

If you are not using the international capabilities built into DOS, you won't need to worry about the device drivers COUNTRY.SYS, DISPLAY.SYS, KEYBOARD.SYS, and PRINTER.SYS. Because they are related to disks, this chapter discusses the device drivers DRIVER.SYS and RAMDRIVE.SYS.

Table 6.2. *Summary of DOS device drivers.*

Driver	Function
ANSI.SYS	Enhances screen and keyboard capabilities.
COUNTRY.SYS	Installs country-specific symbols for international users.
DISPLAY.SYS	Provides screen support for code page (character set) switching for international users.
DRIVER.SYS	Provides support for external floppy drives.
KEYBOARD.SYS	Installs a country-specific keyboard template for international users.
PRINTER.SYS	Provides printer support for code page (character set) switching for international users.
RAMDRIVE.SYS	Installs a fast, temporary storage disk in the computer's random-access memory.

Using DRIVER.SYS to Support External Disks

Although DRIVER.SYS is used most often to support external floppy disk drives, periodically, a third party external hard disk requires you to install the DRIVER.SYS device driver. If you must install DRIVER.SYS, the documentation that accompanies your disk should contain the correct CONFIG.SYS entry. The DRIVER.SYS device driver supports several switches discussed here.

/D:DriveNumber Specifies the physical disk drive number for the external disk drive. Physical drive numbers begin with drive A = 0, B = 1, C = 2, etc.

/C Directs DOS to perform a latch closed check before attempting to access the disk. For floppy drives, specify /C.

/F:FormFactor Specifies the device type:

0	160/180K or 320/360K floppy
1	1.2M floppy
2	720K floppy
3	8-inch single density floppy disk
4	8-inch double density floppy disk
5	Hard disk
6	Tape drive
7	1.44M floppy disk

/H:MaxHeadNumber	Specifies the number of heads per disk. The default value is 2.
/N	Specifies the number of sectors per track from 1 through 99. The default value is 9.
/T:Tracks	Specifies the number of tracks per side from 1 through 999. The default value is 80.

The following example provides support for an external 1.2M floppy disk.

```
DEVICE=C:\DOS\DRIVER.SYS /F:1 /C /S:15
```

Remember, you need to use only DRIVER.SYS if the manual that accompanies your disk directs you to do so. In some cases, the disk may require its own unique device driver.

Using RAMDRIVE.SYS to Install a RAM Drive

As discussed in Chapter 1, your computer provides two types of storage: primary and secondary storage. Your computer's RAM makes up your computer's primary storage. As DOS executes your programs, the programs and the storage locations they use to store intermediate values reside in RAM. The contents of RAM is only temporary. Each time you turn your computer off or reboot DOS, the values stored in RAM are lost.

Hard and floppy disks provide your computer's secondary storage. These devices let you save and retrieve information from one user session to the next.

RAMDRIVE.SYS lets you reserve a portion of the computer's memory to serve as a temporary disk drive. Because the drive resides in memory, it is called a *RAM drive*. As you will recall, your computer's electronic components such as RAM are much faster than mechanical disk drives. Many users create RAM drives to store temporary files. Using a RAM drive for temporary files can improve your system's performance. However, you must keep in mind that if you turn off your computer or reboot DOS or if your system hangs due to an error in a program you are running, the contents of your RAM disk are lost. The information a RAM disk stores resides only in the computer's electronic memory; it is never actually magnetized on disk.

With the exception that it stores information only temporarily, a RAM drive behaves like any other disk drive. A RAM drive has a disk drive letter, in many cases, the drive letter E. You access files on the RAM drive using the drive letter as shown here.

```
C:\> DIR E:
```

The RAMDRIVE.SYS device driver supports several options and switches discussed here.

DiskSize	Specifies the size of the RAM drive in kilobytes. The default size is 64K. The minimum value allowed is 16K.
SectorSize	Specifies the sector size in bytes. The size must be 128, 256, 512, or 1,024. The default size is 128 bytes.
RootEntries	Specifies the number of root directory entries the drive supports. The value must be in the range 4 through 1,024. The default size is 64.
/A	Directs DOS to place the RAM drive in extended memory using the Lotus/Intel/Microsoft (LIM) Expanded Memory Specification (EMS).
/E	Directs DOS to place the RAM drive in extended memory.

If your computer has only 640K of RAM, you don't need to worry about the /A and /E switches. If you are using either extended or expanded memory, installing the RAM drive in those areas will leave more conventional DOS memory readily available to your applications.

The following CONFIG.SYS entry creates a 64K RAM drive using the RAMDRIVE.SYS default values.

```
DEVICE=C:\DOS\RAMDRIVE.SYS
```

If you need a larger RAM disk, you can specify a disk, sector, and directory entry size as shown here.

```
DEVICE=C:\DOS\RAMDRIVE.SYS 256 512 128
```

In this case as shown in the following figure, DOS will create a 256K RAM drive using 512-byte sectors. The RAM drive will support 128 entries in the root directory.

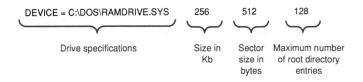

DEVICE = C:\DOS\RAMDRIVE.SYS   256   512   128

Drive specifications   Size in Kb   Sector size in bytes   Maximum number of root directory entries

If you specify values for the RAM drive options, you must specify the entries in the order shown.

Controlling Extended Ctrl + Break Checking

Most DOS commands let you cancel the command by pressing either the Ctrl + Break or Ctrl + C keyboard combination. For example, invoke the DATE command. At the prompt for a new system date, hold down the Ctrl key and press C. DOS will end the command as shown.

```
C:\> DATE
Current date is Tue 01-23-1990
Enter new date (mm-dd-yy): ^C

C:\>
```

By default, DOS tests for a Ctrl + C or Ctrl + Break keyboard combination each time it reads a character from the keyboard or writes a character to the screen or printer. If you have a program that performs much processing but rarely performs input or output to the devices specified, DOS may take a considerable amount of time to recognize the Ctrl + Break and end the program. The BREAK command lets you increase the number of times DOS checks for a Ctrl + Break. The following command, for example, directs DOS to perform the extended Ctrl + Break checking.

```
C:\> BREAK ON
```

To disable extended Ctrl + Break checking, enter the following command:

```
C:\> BREAK OFF
```

If you invoke BREAK without specifying ON or OFF, BREAK will display the current state of Ctrl + Break extended checking.

```
C:\> BREAK
BREAK is off
```

Extended Ctrl + Break checking is a mixed blessing. Although it allows DOS to possibly recognize a user-entered Ctrl + Break sooner than standard Ctrl + Break checking, it places more overhead on your system, which decreases your overall performance. With extended Ctrl + Break checking enabled, DOS spends a considerable amount of time simply testing for a Ctrl + Break. The additional testing decreases the amount of time DOS can spend on your application. In turn, the application executes more slowly.

Most users disable extended Ctrl + Break checking due to its additional processing overhead. Programmers who are testing newly written programs, however, often enable extended Ctrl + Break checking to increase their ability to end programs containing errors.

By default, DOS disables extended Ctrl + Break checking. The CONFIG.SYS `BREAK=` entry lets programmers and other system developers enable extended Ctrl + Break checking during system start-up. The following entry enables extended Ctrl + Break checking during system start-up and leaves it enabled until you turn it off using the DOS BREAK command.

```
BREAK=ON
```

Most users don't want the overhead of extended Ctrl + Break checking. If DOS does not find a `BREAK=` entry in CONFIG.SYS, the default setting is off.

Selecting an International Symbol and Character Set

The CONFIG.SYS COUNTRY= entry lets international DOS users select their own symbol set for currency, dates, and times, as well as their own character set. Under DOS 3.3, the format of the entry is

```
COUNTRY=CountryCode[,[CodePage][,CountryFile]]
```

where the items within brackets are optional. Table 6.3 defines the values for CountryCode. Table 6.4 contains the CodePage values. The CountryFile is the file COUNTRY.SYS, which resides in the DOS subdirectory.

Table 6.3. *DOS country code values.*

Country	CountryCode
United States	001
French-Canadian	002
Latin America	003
Netherlands	031
Belgium	032
France	033
Spain	034
Italy	039
Switzerland	041
United Kingdom	044
Denmark	045
Sweden	046
Norway	047
Germany	049
Australia	061
Portugal	351
Finland	358
Arabic Nations	785
Israel	972

Table 6.4. *DOS codepage values.*

Country	CountryCode
United States	437
Multilingual	850
Portuguese	860
French-Canadian	863
Nordic	865

The following entry, for example, selects the symbol set and CodePage for Norway.

```
COUNTRY = 047,865,C:\DOS\COUNTRY.SYS
```

Supporting Excessive Hardware Interrupts

Many of the hardware devices in your computer, such as the disk controller, perform a specific task and then interrupt DOS when they are done. The disk controller, for example, may begin reading a 512-byte sector. When it is done, it can interrupt DOS and transfer the disk information to a DOS buffer.

Each time a device interrupts DOS, it must temporarily suspend the task it is performing to handle the interrupt. To do so, DOS makes a note of where it is stopping so it can start there later. Although DOS could receive so many interrupts at one time that it doesn't have enough memory to record its current state, such an event is unlikely. For such an event to occur, DOS must receive many interrupts, one right after another. If DOS cannot handle the interrupts, it will display the following message and you must restart your computer.

```
Fatal: Internal Stack Failure, System Halted
```

If this message occurs, you need to place a STACKS= entry in CONFIG.SYS.

The format of the entry is

```
STACKS=NumberOfStacks, StackSize
```

A *stack* is the region of memory in which DOS records its current state when an interrupt occurs. By increasing the number and size of available stacks, you decrease the likelihood of the fatal stack error. The *NumberOfStacks* option specifies how many stacks to support from 0 through 64. The *StackSize* option specifies the size of each stack in bytes from 0 through 512.

The following entry selects eight stacks of 512 bytes each.

```
STACKS=8,512
```

The only time you need to use the STACKS= entry is when your system experiences a fatal stack error.

Using AUTOEXEC.BAT

The last step DOS performs during system start-up is to search the root directory for a file named AUTOEXEC.BAT. If DOS locates the file, DOS executes each of the commands the file contains. If the file does not exist, DOS executes the DATE and TIME commands.

AUTOEXEC.BAT is a DOS batch file that contains a list of commands you want DOS to execute automatically each time your system starts. Although you may very likely add other DOS commands and third-party software programs to AUTOEXEC.BAT, most hard disk users should place the DOS PATH, PROMPT, and PRINT commands in AUTOEXEC.BAT. If you are using DOS 3.3, placing a FASTOPEN command in AUTOEXEC.BAT will improve your disk performance. The following batch file illustrates a sample AUTOEXEC.BAT under DOS 3.3.

```
PATH C:\DOS
PROMPT $p$g
PRINT /B:8096 /D:PRN /M:64 /U:16
FASTOPEN C:=75
```

Summary

You can use CONFIG.SYS and AUTOEXEC.BAT to customize how DOS behaves and to control your environment while using your computer.

While it is possible to do many things within your CONFIG.SYS file (this chapter covered many of the possibilities), it is necessary to do only a few things. In most cases, you need to use only the BUFFERS=, FILES=, and possibly DEVICE= entries. Remember that the only time DOS examines CONFIG.SYS is during system start-up; if you add or change the file, you must reboot your system for the changes to take effect.

It is possible to do even more things with your AUTOEXEC.BAT file. First, you need to examine what you do on a daily basis and to look at the programs you use and how you use them, then you must decide what your AUTOEXEC.BAT file should contain.

In the next chapter you will begin to learn how to detect and correct errors on your hard disk.

CHKDSK—The First Line of Defense

7

- ► Getting Started with CHKDSK
- ► Displaying File Names with CHKDSK
- ► Understanding and Correcting Disk Errors
- ► Summary

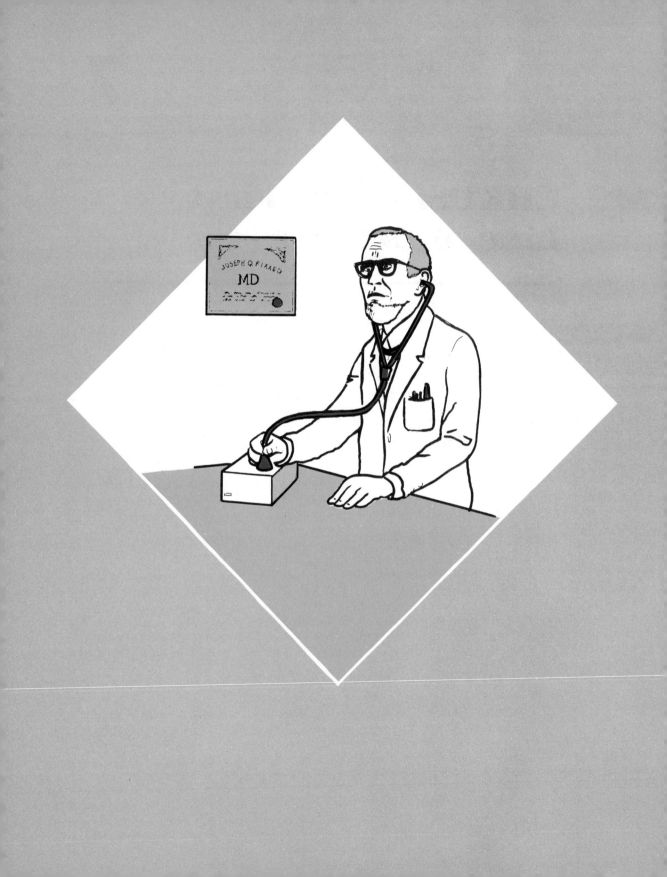

7

CHKDSK—The First Line of Defense

As with all mechanical devices, the normal wear and tear of everyday use may eventually damage your hard disk. Depending upon the severity of the error, you may lose the contents of a single file, or possibly your entire disk. Several third-party software packages thoroughly test each sector on your disk to ensure that the sector can still correctly record data. In many cases, these third-party programs can salvage the data that reside on questionable sectors.

Even if you have third-party programs that test your disk's "health," your first line of defense is the CHKDSK command. CHKDSK examines the file allocation table and each directory entry to ensure consistency. CHKDSK can locate and possibly correct damaged files. In addition, CHKDSK provides information on disk fragmentation that can impact disk performance (see Chapter 9).

As you will learn in this chapter, CHKDSK can correct and detect several FAT and directory entry errors. You need to invoke CHKDSK on a regular basis. In fact, many users running disk-intensive applications, such as a database program, place the CHKDSK command in AUTOEXEC.BAT to ensure that CHKDSK runs each time their system starts.

Getting Started with CHKDSK

CHKDSK is an external DOS command, stored in the file CHKDSK.COM. From the DOS prompt, invoke CHKDSK as follows:

```
C:\> CHKDSK
```

Depending on the condition of your disk's FAT and directories (and your version of DOS), CHKDSK will display the following information and possibly error messages, which we will discuss throughout this chapter.

```
C:\> CHKDSK

61607936 bytes total disk space
   75776 bytes in 2 hidden files
   59392 bytes in 23 directories
17127424 bytes in 749 user files
44345344 bytes available on disk

    2048 bytes in each allocation unit
   30082 total allocation units on disk
   21653 available allocation units on disk

  655360 total bytes memory
  501472 bytes free
```

CHKDSK's first line of output tells you the total disk space in this partition. The second line tells you the number of hidden files on your disk. As you will recall, every DOS disk contains two hidden files that DOS uses to boot. They are hidden to prevent you from inadvertently deleting or renaming them. A hidden file exists on disk but is not accessible by the DOS file manipulation commands. If you have assigned a volume label to your disk as discussed in Chapter 5, DOS will store the volume label in a hidden file. As a result, your disk may have three hidden DOS files.

The third line CHKDSK displays reports the number of bytes DOS is using to store directory entries. As you know, each file on your disk requires a 32-bit directory entry. The space CHKDSK reports for sub-directory use corresponds to the directory entries. The fourth line contains the amount of disk space currently in use for storing files, as well as the number of files on your disk. The fifth line contains the amount of space still available on your disk.

Finally, CHKDSK displays the amount of conventional memory in your system. In the previous output, the value 655,360 corresponds to 640K (640 x 1,024 bytes). CHKDSK will not display information on expanded or extended memory. The bottom value labeled *"bytes free"* tells you the amount of memory unused by DOS and other memory-resident programs you may have installed.

If you assigned a disk volume label as discussed in Chapter 5, CHKDSK displays the volume label and the date you assigned the label.

```
C:\> CHKDSK

Volume DOS        created 01-26-1990 9:11p

  61607936 bytes total disk space
     75776 bytes in 3 hidden files
     59392 bytes in 23 directories
  17127424 bytes in 749 user files
  44345344 bytes available on disk

      2048 bytes in each allocation unit
     30082 total allocation units on disk
     21653 available allocation units on disk

    655360 total bytes memory
    501472 bytes free
```

Note that once you assign a volume label, CHKDSK reports a third hidden file. DOS stores the volume label name and date and time you assigned the disk volume in a directory entry. To prevent you from inadvertently deleting this directory entry, DOS sets the entry's hidden attribute.

If your disk contains bad sectors that have been marked unusable by FORMAT, CHKDSK will report the bad sectors as shown here:

```
C:\> CHKDSK

Volume DOS        created 01-26-1990 9:11p

  61607936 bytes total disk space
     75776 bytes in 4 hidden files
     59392 bytes in 23 directories
  17127424 bytes in 749 user files
  nnnnnnnn bytes in bad sectors
  44345344 bytes available on disk
```

```
 2048 bytes in each allocation unit
30082 total allocation units on disk
21653 available allocation units on disk

655360 total bytes memory
501472 bytes free
```

If CHKDSK encounters errors, it will display a prompt such as the following:

```
nnn lost clusters found in n chains
Convert lost chains to files (Y/N)?
```

Should this error message occur, type **N**. Even if you answer **Y**, CHKDSK will not make corrections. The next section covers how to instruct CHKDSK to make corrections.

By default, CHKDSK examines the current disk. To examine a disk other than the default drive, place the drive identifier in the CHKDSK command line. The following command, for example, examines drive A.

```
C:\> CHKDSK A:
```

Displaying File Names with CHKDSK

To perform its consistency check, CHKDSK reads the directory entry for every file on your disk. Using the /V switch, you can direct CHKDSK to display each file's complete path name. The following CHKDSK command displays the files on the current disk.

```
C:\> CHKDSK /V
```

You may find a hard copy listing of your disk's files to be helpful in locating files. The following command redirects the output of the CHKDSK command to your system printer.

```
C:\> CHKDSK /V > PRN
```

If CHKDSK previously displayed an error message and prompt to correct the error, do not redirect CHKDSK's output to the printer until you correct the error as discussed in the next section.

Understanding and Correcting Disk Errors

Before we examine the steps you should take to correct the errors that CHKDSK reports, you need to understand that, by default, CHKDSK only detects errors—CHKDSK does not correct them. Several of the error messages discussed here display a prompt asking you if CHKDSK should correct the error. By default, even if you respond to such as prompt with **Y** to correct the error, CHKDSK will not perform the correction.

To direct CHKDSK to correct errors it encounters, you must invoke CHKDSK using the /F switch.

```
C:\> CHKDSK /F
```

The /F switch directs CHKDSK not only to report errors, but also to correct the errors if so directed. If you don't include the /F switch and CHKDSK encounters errors, CHKDSK will display the following message telling you that it will not correct the errors on your disk.

```
Errors found, F parameter not specified.
Corrections will not be written to disk.
```

Even if you type **Y** to a prompt to correct the errors, CHKDSK will not record the corrections on disk until you include /F.

The following explains several of the most common error messages CHKDSK may encounter.

Lost Clusters

In Chapter 3, we examined several files and traced the corresponding FAT chains to identify the file's sectors. To access a file, DOS uses the directory entry to determine the file's first FAT entry and then follows the chain of FAT entries until DOS encounters the end-of-file marker. During its consistency test, CHKDSK examines each cluster entry. If a cluster is marked "in use" but is not a member of a file's cluster chain, the cluster is called a *lost cluster*.

Consider the following disk and file allocation table.

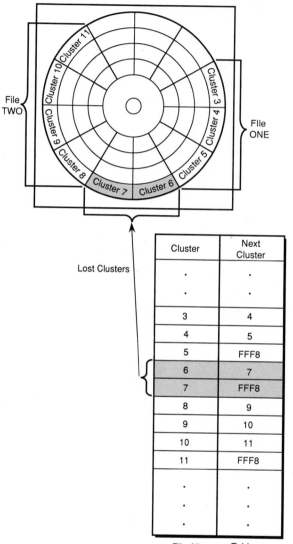

File Allocaton Table

File ONE uses clusters 3, 4, and 5. File TWO uses clusters 8, 9, 10, and 11. If you look closely at the FAT, you'll find that clusters 6 and 7 are marked as in use. However, no files on the disk are using the clusters. CHKDSK reports these two clusters as lost clusters.

Lost clusters can occur as a result of an unexpected disk error or when a user turns off the computer or reboots DOS when the program has files open. In many cases, lost clusters correspond to cross-linked files, which are discussed in the next section.

When CHKDSK encounters lost clusters, CHKDSK displays the following message:

```
nnnn  Lost cluster found in n chains
Convert lost chains to files  (Y/N)?
```

CHKDSK lets you copy the information in each chain of lost clusters to a file. CHKDSK creates the files in the root directory using the file name FILE*nnnn*.CHK. The CHK extension tells you CHKDSK created the files. The *nnnn* is a value from 0001 to 9999, which produces a file name such as FILE0001.CHK.

The number of files CHKDSK will create depends upon the number of lost chains. Once the files exist, you can view them with your editor or the TYPE command to determine if the files contain useful information. If the file is useful, rename it and place it in the correct subdirectory. If the file is not useful, delete it with DEL.

Depending on the number of files in your root directory and the number of files CHKDSK must convert, your root directory may fill up, and CHKDSK cannot create additional files. If your root directory fills, CHKDSK will display the following error message:

```
Insufficient space in root directory
```

Should this error occur, examine the file CHKDSK has created. Move useful files to the correct subdirectories and delete unnecessary FILE*nnnn*.CHK files. After you make available disk space in the root directory, repeat the CHKDSK command to convert the remaining lost chains.

Cross-Linked Files

Just as a disk error can result in lost clusters, disk errors can also result in two files pointing to the same cluster. When CHKDSK encounters cross-linked files, it will display the names of the two files involved in a format similar to:

```
FILENAME.EXT is cross linked on Cluster n
```

In most cases, one of the files is still valid while the second file is damaged. Consider the disks and file allocation tables shown here.

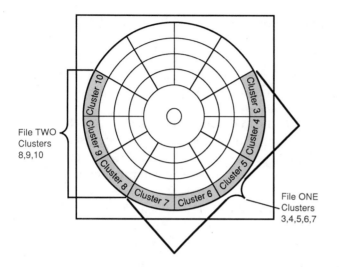

File TWO
Clusters
8,9,10

File ONE
Clusters
3,4,5,6,7

Cluster	Next Cluster
.	.
.	.
3	4
4	5
5	6
6	7
7	FFF8
8	9
9	10
10	FFF8
.	.
.	.
.	.

File Allocaton
Table
Before cross link

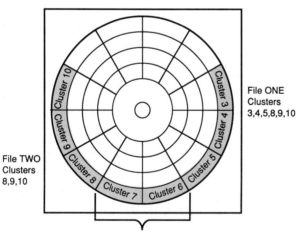

File ONE
Clusters
3,4,5,8,9,10

File TWO
Clusters
8,9,10

Low clusters

Cluster	Next Cluster
.	.
.	.
3	4
4	5
5	8
6	7
7	FFF8
8	9
9	10
10	FFF8
.	.
.	.
.	.

File Allocaton
Table
After cross link

In this case, according to the disk, file ONE uses clusters 3, 4, 5, 6, and 7 while file TWO uses clusters 8, 9, and 10. If you examine the FAT, however, file ONE uses clusters 3, 4, 5, 8, 9, and 10. The files have become cross-linked on cluster 8. If you issue the TYPE command to display file ONE's contents, TYPE displays part of file ONE and all of file TWO. If you use TYPE to display file TWO, the file's contents are correct.

Cross-linked files are often accompanied by lost clusters. In this case, clusters 6 and 7 are not associated with a file. To correct cross-linked files, you must perform the following steps:

1. Copy both files to a new directory or disk.

2. Delete the original files.

3. Using CHKDSK, recover lost clusters into file names.

4. If the corrupted file is a text file you can edit, remove any data in the file copied from the cross link. If DOS recovered the lost clusters to a file, insert the file at the correct location.

5. Copy the files back to their original directories.

Using the files ONE and TWO shown previously, the recovery process can be seen more clearly in the following example.

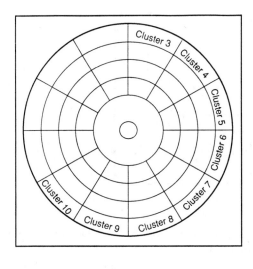

Cluster	Next Cluster	
.	.	
.	.	
3	4	
4	5	
5	8	
6	7	} Lost
7	FFF8	} Clusters
8	9	
9	10	
10	FFF8	
.	.	
.	.	

File Allocation
Table

To copy both files to a new disk, create files THREE and FOUR. As shown in the next figure, file THREE contains a copy of the information contained in Clusters 3, 4, 5, 8, 9, and 10. Likewise, file FOUR contains a copy of the information contained in Clusters 8, 9, and 10.

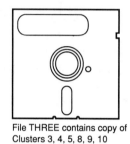

File THREE contains copy of
Clusters 3, 4, 5, 8, 9, 10

File FOUR contains copy of
Clusters 8, 9, 10

To delete the original files, set the file allocation table entries for clusters 3, 4, 5, 8, 9, and 10 to 0. Note in the following figure that the lost clusters still remain.

Cluster	Next Cluster
.	.
.	.
3	0
4	0
5	0
6	7
7	FFF8
8	0
9	0
10	0
.	.
.	.

File Allocation Table

Recover the lost clusters using CHKDSK. It will create a file on disk named FILE0001.CHK that contains the lost clusters 6 and 7. The disk now contains the files THREE, FOUR, and FILE0001.CHK as shown in the following figure. All of the original data is available for editing.

THREE contains copy of clusters 8, 9, 10
FOUR contains copy of clusters 8, 9, 10
FILE0001.CHK contains clusters 6, 7

Next, delete the data in file THREE that resulted from copying clusters 8, 9, and 10. The file will contain a copy of the data that was in clusters 3, 4, and 5 as shown here.

THREE contains copy of clusters 3, 4, 5
FOUR contains copy of clusters 8, 9, 10
FILE0001.CHK contains clusters 6, 7

After this, append the data in the file FILE0001.CHK to file THREE. As shown in the next figure, this file now contains the original information. It is safe to delete FILE0001.CHK.

THREE contains copy of clusters 3, 4, 5, 6, 7
FOUR contains copy of clusters 8, 9, 10

Finally, copy the files back to their original directories. The files contain their original data and reside in their original directory as shown here.

FILE ONE
FILE TWO

Allocation Errors

If CHKDSK displays the following message:

```
Allocation error, size adjusted
```

the file size in a directory listing did not correspond with the number of clusters in use for the file according to the FAT. CHKDSK will change the file's directory entry to match the size corresponding to the FAT.

Consider the disk and FAT shown in the following figure. In this case files ONE and TWO are cross linked.

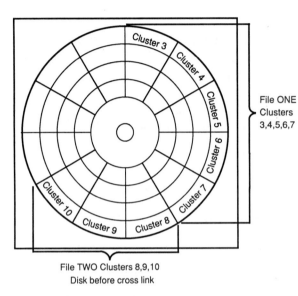

File ONE Clusters 3,4,5,6,7

Cluster	Next Cluster
.	.
.	.
3	4
4	5
5	6
6	7
7	8
8	9
9	10
10	FFF8
.	.
.	.

File Allocation Table

File TWO Clusters 8,9,10
Disk before cross link

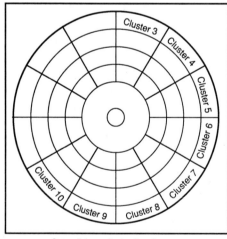

Cross link on cluster 8 makes
file ONE appear to have 4 clusters.

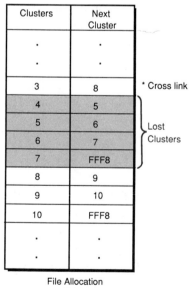

Clusters	Next Cluster
.	.
.	.
3	8	* Cross link
4	5
5	6	Lost
6	7	Clusters
7	FFF8
8	9
9	10
10	FFF8
.	.
.	.

File Allocation Table

The directory entry for file ONE is 10,000 bytes (requires five clusters). When CHKDSK examines file ONE's cluster chain, CHKDSK realizes the file has only four clusters or 8,192 bytes (4 ∗ 2,048). As a result, CHKDSK reduces the file size of the file's directory entry. In most cases, this error accompanies cross-linked files or lost clusters.

FAT Reading and Writing Errors

DOS keeps two identical copies of the file allocation table on your disk to prevent a sector error in the FAT from rendering your disk unreadable. If CHKDSK encounters an error reading from or writing to a FAT, it will use the remaining FAT. If both FAT's are corrupted, you will need good backup copies of your files (see Chapter 8). If only FAT goes bad, back up your disk immediately.

To correct the error, try reformatting your disk with FORMAT. Remember, FORMAT destroys the contents of your disk so you will need backup copies of your files first. If FORMAT is successful, you can restore the backup files to your disk and continue. If FORMAT encounters errors, your disk may require a low-level format as discussed in Chapter 1.

In some cases, CHKDSK cannot even begin to access a disk's file allocation table. As a result, CHKDSK will display the following message:

```
File allocation table bad drive n:
```

If this message appears, the cluster chains in the FAT are severely corrupted, or the disk was never correctly formatted by DOS. Begin recovery by issuing the FORMAT command.

Another FAT Recovery Method

The Jamsa Utilities, included with this book, contain two utilities, DISKSAVE and UNFORMAT, which may help you recover your FAT. If you used the DISKSAVE program before the FAT was corrupted, then UNFORMAT may restore it to a good condition. For more information on these utilities, see Chapter 22.

Invalid Cluster Numbers

DOS locates a file's first cluster using the file's directory entry. If CHKDSK displays the following message:

```
First cluster number is invalid, entry truncated
```

the file's directory entry points to a FAT entry containing the value 0, telling DOS the first cluster is available. Because the FAT does not have a cluster chain for the file, CHKDSK assigns the size field in the file's directory entry to 0.

In most cases, this error is associated with lost clusters that contain the file's data. If lost clusters exist, recover them as previously discussed. If not, restore the file from your backup disk.

Non-DOS Disk Errors

Each disk you format using FORMAT has a DOS boot record. One of the fields in the boot record is called the *media descriptor byte*. DOS uses the media descriptor byte to determine the disk's type. If CHKDSK cannot identify the media descriptor byte, it assumes the disk is not a DOS disk and informs you with the following message:

```
Probable non-DOS disk
```

Should this error occur, use the DISKINFO utility provided as part of the Jamsa Disk Utilities to display the specifics DOS stores in the boot record. Using this information, you can view the current media descriptor byte and cross reference it to the disk types discussed in Chapter 11.

Invalid Drive Errors

If the disk drive specified in a CHKDSK command line is unknown to DOS, it cannot access the disk and will display the invalid drive error message. If you have not partitioned the disk with FDISK as discussed in Chapter 2, do so now. If the disk was previously accessible, but you can no longer access it, make sure you have not inadvertently removed from CONFIG.SYS a device driver that DOS needs if it is to see the disk.

Finally, the master boot record on your hard disk may have become corrupted. Invoke FDISK to display the current partition information. If the master boot record is damaged, back up all accessible partitions on your disk. Next, try to redefine the partitions using FDISK. If successful, you will need to format the partitions and then restore your data from your backups. If FDISK is not successful, your disk may require a low-level format. With luck, you can successfully partition your disk, using your backup files to restore the disk to its original condition.

Unrecoverable Directory Errors

A *directory* is a file containing individual 32-byte directory entries. When CHKDSK reads a directory, it examines the entries one entry at a time. If CHKDSK cannot understand an entry or encounters an error reading the directory, CHKDSK displays the following error message:

```
Unrecoverable error in directory.
Convert directory to a file (Y/N)?
```

Should this message occur, respond with the letter **N** to leave the directory in place. If possible, back up the files that reside in the directory. Next, delete the files and remove the directory. Create a new copy of the directory and restore the files.

If you cannot access the subdirectory to back up and restore the files, repeat the CHKDSK command and convert the subdirectory to a file. Using the DEL command, you can delete the file, thereby removing it from your disk. Your disk will very likely contain lost clusters that you can recover with CHKDSK.

Current Directory Does Not Exist

Every DOS subdirectory contains single periods (.) and double periods (..) as shown in this sample directory:

```
C:\> DIR \DISKBOOK

 Volume in drive C is DOS
 Directory of  C:\DISKBOOK
```

```
.              <DIR>     01-21-90   11:40a
..             <DIR>     01-21-90   11:40a
NOTES    TXT        80 01-21-90   11:43a
MD       TXT        80 01-21-90   11:47a
COMPARE  ONE        28 01-23-90    3:56p
COMPARE  TWO        28 01-23-90    3:59p
FINDTEXT DAT       152 01-23-90    4:01p
        7 File(s)   44343296 bytes free
```

The single-period entry is an abbreviation for the current directory. The double periods abbreviate the parent directory.

If the subdirectory is corrupted, CHKDSK may not be able to locate one of these entries, and CHKDSK will display the following message:

```
. Does not exist
```

Should such an error occur, invoke CHKDSK with the /F switch. If the directory error persists, create a new directory, copying to it the files from the damaged directory. After you have successfully copied the files, delete the damaged directory and the files it contains. Use the RENDIR utility provided on the disk that accompanies this book to rename the new directory to the previous directory name.

If CHKDSK cannot access the parent directory, it will display the following message.

```
..Does not exist
```

Follow the steps just discussed to recover the directory.

Cannot Use CHDIR

CHKDSK examines each of the subdirectories on your disk. If it cannot select a specific directory as the current directory, CHKDSK will display this error message:

```
Cannot CHDIR to pathname
tree past this point not processed
```

As you know, the directory structure is often called the *directory tree*. In this case, CHKDSK tells you that it could not process subdirectories below the directory in the directory tree because it could not access the directory specified.

If this error occurs, perform a disk backup. If possible, copy the files contained in the damaged directory and those below it. Next, delete the files, the directory, and the backup copies of the files.

If you cannot access the directory, try to remove it, restoring the files it contained from your last backup operation.

Summary

The DOS CHKDSK command is your first line of defense against fatal disk errors. Get into the habit of invoking CHKDSK regularly. If CHKDSK provides a clean bill of health for your disk, your files are relatively safe from disk errors. If your disk is beginning to experience problems, CHKDSK will be the first to identify and possibly correct them.

8

Minimizing Data Loss

Minimizing Data Loss

Hard disk management requires you to consider disk performance utilization, data security, and convenience. Chapter 10 discusses several steps you can use to improve your disk's performance. *Disk utilization* measures how effectively you are using your disk storage. By creating DOS subdirectories and eliminating duplicate copies of files, you can improve your disk utilization. *Data security* includes protection from fire, theft, unauthorized access, power failures, viruses, and inadvertent file deletions. Depending on the nature of your data, the levels of protection you take will differ. Whether your data resides in a vaulted room or your family room, you need to make duplicate copies of your critical files. Once you have these duplicate files, place them in a safe place in a room other than the room with the computer. Placing the disks in a different room protects them from the same smoke, spills, or theft that might damage your hard disk. It is unfortunate that most users don't back up their systems because they feel backups are too time consuming and inconvenient. As you strive to increase disk performance and protect your files, your system must still be convenient to use.

This chapter examines the BACKUP and RESTORE commands and their use in minimizing your data loss. No backup policy can guarantee that you won't ever lose a file. However, if you make backups regularly, you may lose only a day's work. Compared to losing all the files on your hard disk, a few hours of lost work is acceptable.

Admittedly, if you had to back up every file on your disk each day, the backups would become very time consuming and you would soon quit doing them. Most of the files on your disk don't change everyday. As such, you need to back up only those files that do change. Most users can back up all the files they have changed in a day in a manner of minutes. Whether you back up your files at the end of the day or at the start of the day, the few minutes you spend making backups is time spent wisely. Hopefully, you will never need your backups. However, if you do, I hope you have them prepared.

Knowing the Threats

The files on your disk have many different threats, some obvious and some covert. By knowing the threats to your files, you can eliminate several. Your only defense against the other threats are current backups.

First, because your hard disk is a mechanical device, it will eventually wear out. In fact, all hard disks will fail eventually. If your disk head crashes, the information on your disk will very likely be completely destroyed. Your only defense against hard disk failure and head crashes is current backups.

Next, fire and theft are two very real threats to your computer's data. Homeowners insurance may cover your computer's replacement cost provided you have purchase receipts. Take pictures of your computer and software library and record serial numbers. Store the pictures in a safe location with your receipts. Reimbursement for lost data is very difficult. You need backups of your critical data. Do not store the backups in the same room as your computer.

Many innocent-looking items on your desk can cause harm to your disks. Your telephone, for example, gives off a strong magnetic flux when it rings. The flux is powerful enough to change the data magnetized on your disk. Many pencil sharpeners can have this same effect. Also, many users now stand their computer vertically next to or under their desks. Although this arrangement frees up much-needed desk space, the computer is now much closer to the static electricity in the carpet and the electronic flux generated by a vacuum cleaner. Keep any office device such as a copier that uses a powerful motor away from your disks. In most cases, floppy disks fall victim to these devices since users often leave floppy disks on their desk. However, if your computer shares a desk with many such devices, it is not impossible for one to damage your hard disk. Eliminate the possibility of electronic devices damaging your data by moving the devices to a different location.

Because we in our society have put a computer on every office desk, the computer is often treated like a piece of furniture. People set drinks, snacks, and newspapers on top of the computer. Drinks and snacks can obviously spill and cause the computer to short. When this occurs, the computer's circuitry burns up. The disk may or may not be damaged; however, the computer will not be usable. Because the computer's electronics create heat, the computer and monitor have vents to disperse the hot air. Many people inadvertently cover these vents with newspapers or printouts. If the computer gets too hot, it can burn up chips and the disk circuitry and possibly start a fire. Luckily, you can easily avoid these threats by keeping the computer clean and keeping food and drinks away from the computer.

Dust and smoke are disk killers. Since the disk head rests very close to the surface of your disk, any contaminant, no matter how small, is likely to cause damage as shown here (see chapter 1).

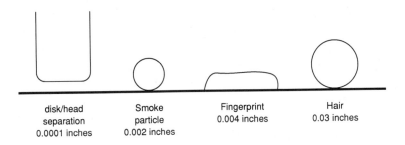

disk/head
separation
0.0001 inches

Smoke
particle
0.002 inches

Fingerprint
0.004 inches

Hair
0.03 inches

If smoke or dust gets into your disk drive, it will very likely cause a head crash. Keep your computer dust free. If you smoke, keep backups in a safe smoke-free environment.

A *power spike* occurs when a large surge of power travels down your power line into devices that are plugged in and turned on. These spikes are often caused by heavy machinery on the line or lightning. Depending on the size of the surge, it can destroy the electronics of the devices it passes through. Destruction from power surges isn't restricted to computers. A surge can destroy a television, stereo, or any other electronic device. The best defense against power spikes is to purchase a surge suppressor. A *surge suppressor* sits between your hardware and the wall outlet. The suppressor plugs into the wall and then your devices plug into the suppressor as shown in the following figure.

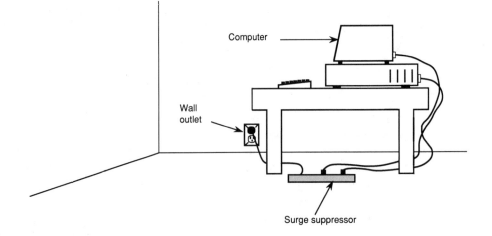

Surge suppressor

The surge suppressor prevents power spikes from reaching your computer. Suppressors range in price from $29.95 to $129.95. In most cases, the cost difference is not due to increased protection but rather added capabilities such as individual power on and off switches for each device plugged into the suppressor. Do not confuse power strips with surge suppressors. A power strip is an electrical cord that lets you plug several devices into the same outlet. Power strips do not perform surge suppression and often create fire hazards. If you don't have a surge suppressor, buy one. In fact, consider one each for your TV and other expensive electronic devices.

Although a surge suppressor prevents too much power from reaching your computer, it does nothing for a power loss. Depending upon the application's importance, you might consider an *uninterruptable power supply* (UPS). A UPS is much more expensive than a surge suppressor, ranging in price from several hundred to several thousand dollars. A UPS provides the computer with adequate power when power temporarily drops or goes off. Most UPSs provide up to 15 minutes of use when power is lost. The 15 minutes gives you more than enough time to save critical files and end applications in an orderly fashion. Assume, for example, that DOS is updating the file allocation table when you lose power. Without a UPS, the FAT update is incomplete, files may be cross linked, and lost clusters may exist. If you cannot correct the disk errors using CHKDSK as discussed in Chapter 7, you will need to use your backups. Although a UPS is an excellent protection device, its cost forces most users to rely on current backups.

Finally, several disk errors are directly related to errant DOS commands. If you inadvertently delete files, you may be able to recover the files using the UNDELETE utility provided with the Jamsa Disk Utilities that accompany this book. If your disk is fragmented, however, third-party undelete utilities can't guarantee 100% recovery. Likewise, if you accidentally format your hard disk, the Jamsa UNFORMAT utility may be able to recover the disk. If a third-party program cannot recover files from an errant DOS command, you must rely on current backups.

Although you can reduce the number of threats to your data, you can't eliminate them. If you can't afford loss of data, you must perform regular backups.

Using Time-Saving Steps

Most users will agree that good backups are essential. Even so, most users will tell you that they don't make backups regularly because they take too much time. When you back up files, you must copy them from a slow mechanical hard disk to a much slower floppy disk. As a result, the more files you have to back up, the longer the backup operation takes. The key to quick backup operations lies in backing up only those files that have been created or changed since the previous backup.

In addition, many third-party backup utilities claim tremendous backup speeds that reduce the amount of time you must spend performing backups. In most cases, these backup utilities slow down tremendously when the target floppy disks are not formatted. Whether you are using the DOS BACKUP command or a third-party backup utility, the backup will take much less time if you use formatted floppy disks.

To determine the maximum number of floppy disks a backup operation will require, invoke the DOS CHKDSK command.

```
C:\> CHKDSK

 21309440 bytes total disk space
    53248 bytes in 2 hidden files
    22528 bytes in 5 directories
 11323392 bytes in 466 user files
    20480 bytes in bad sectors
  9889792 bytes available on disk

   655360 bytes total memory
   594032 bytes free
```

If you subtract the amount of available disk space from the total disk space, you can determine the number of bytes as follows:

```
Disk Space in Use = (Total Disk Space) - (Bytes Available on Disk)
                  = 21,309,440 - 9,889,792
                  = 11,419,648 bytes
```

Additional Disk Information

The Jamsa Disk Utilities include DISKINFO, a program that provides you with additional information about your disk. Rather than manually determining the amount of disk space in use, you can use DISKINFO. For more information on this utility, see Chapter 11.

Table 8.1 contains the number of bytes of storage for common floppy disks. Using the values in this table, you can determine the number of floppy disks required to back up your hard disk.

Table 8.1. *Common floppy disk storage capabilities.*

Disk Type	Bytes of Storage
360K	368,640 bytes
720K	737,280 bytes
1.2M	1,213,952 bytes
1.44M	1,457,664 bytes

Using the amount of used disk space already calculated, and a 1.2M floppy disk, the maximum number of floppy disks required to back up the disk becomes the following:

```
Floppy Disks Required = (Disk Space in Use) / (Floppy Disk Size)
                      = 11,419,648 / 1,213,952
                      = 9.41
                      = 10 1.2M floppy disks
```

This value is the number of floppy disks required to back up the entire disk. As discussed, your goal is to back up only those files changed since the previous backup.

Using the FORMAT command

```
C> FORMAT A:
```

format the number of diskettes you need to back up your system. When formatting floppy disks for backup operations, do not use the /S switch in the FORMAT command line. The /S switch directs FORMAT to create a bootable system disk, transferring the necessary system files to the disk. Placing the system files on backup disks wastes disk space.

If you have time, consider formatting additional floppy disks for backup use later. Next, determine a safe storage location where you can place the backup floppy disks after the backup operation is complete.

Backing Up an Entire Disk Using BACKUP

Everything has a price. Before you can perform fast backup operations that only back up those files that have been created or changed since the last backup operation, you need to back up the entire hard disk. The amount of time the complete system backup requires depends on the number of files the disk contains. Don't use the complete disk backup operation as a time indicator for future backup operations. The backup operations you will perform regularly should require only one or two disks and only a few minutes of your time.

To back up your entire hard disk to drive A, place a formatted floppy disk in drive A and issue the following command:

```
C> BACKUP C:\*.* A: /S
```

The /S switch directs BACKUP to back up all files in subdirectories that reside below the subdirectory specified. In this case, DOS begins at the root directory and backs up all files in the root directory and below, which is the entire disk.

When the BACKUP command begins, it will display the following message:

```
Warning! Files in the target drive
A:\root directory will be erased
Strike any key when ready
```

213

If you have not placed a formatted floppy disk in drive A, do so now.

The warning message tells you that BACKUP erases all files in the floppy disk's root directory. Since you are using newly formatted diskettes, the error message is purely informational. Press Enter to begin the backup operation.

When the first floppy disk fills, BACKUP will pause, displaying the following message:

```
Insert backup diskette 02 in drive A:

Warning! Files in the target drive
A:\root directory will be erased
Strike any key when ready
```

Remove the floppy disk from drive A and insert another newly formatted floppy disk, pressing Enter to continue the backup operation. Prepare a label that contains the drive letter, backup date, and disk number for the floppy disk you just removed.

Repeat this process each time BACKUP fills a floppy disk until the entire disk backup operation is complete.

Performing Incremental Backup Operations

A complete disk backup operation backs up every file on a disk and can be quite time consuming. An incremental backup operation, on the other hand, backs up only those files that have been created or changed since the last backup operation. Recall that every file on your disk has a 32-byte directory entry. Every directory entry contains a name, extension, the size in bytes, a date and time stamp, an attribute byte, and a starting cluster number. One of the fields in the directory entry contains the file's attribute, as shown in the following figure.

ONE.DAT	Filename.ext
66	Size in bytes
12-31-89	} Date and time stamp
12:00	
ARCHIVE	File attribute
14	Starting disk location
TWO.DAT	
44	
11-31-89	
14:00	
READ-ONLY	
56	
THREE.DAT	
61	
1-14-90	
15:30	
NORMAL	
38	
FOUR.DAT	
140	
3-17-90	
11:55	
READ-ONLY ARCHIVE	
106	
FIVE.DAT	
330	
4-1-90	
15:30	
NORMAL	
38	

In Chapter 5 you learned that DOS uses the file attribute to create hidden, system, and read-only files requiring backup. The DOS ATTRIB command displays a file's read-only and archive required status.

Each time you create or change a file, DOS sets the file's archive attribute to backup required. When you perform incremental backups, DOS examines each file's attribute value and backs up only those files marked *archive required*. When BACKUP successfully backs up a file to disk, BACKUP removes the file's archive required attribute. By using the file attribute, BACKUP can determine which files have been created since the last backup operation and selectively back up only those files.

Assume that the files in a directory contain the attributes shown in the previous figure. If you perform an incremental backup, BACKUP will copy only those files whose archive attribute is set. Once BACKUP successfully copies the file, BACKUP will clear the file's archive attribute, as shown in the next figure. Notice how the archive attribute bytes of ONE.DAT and FOUR.DAT are changed once the backup operation is completed.

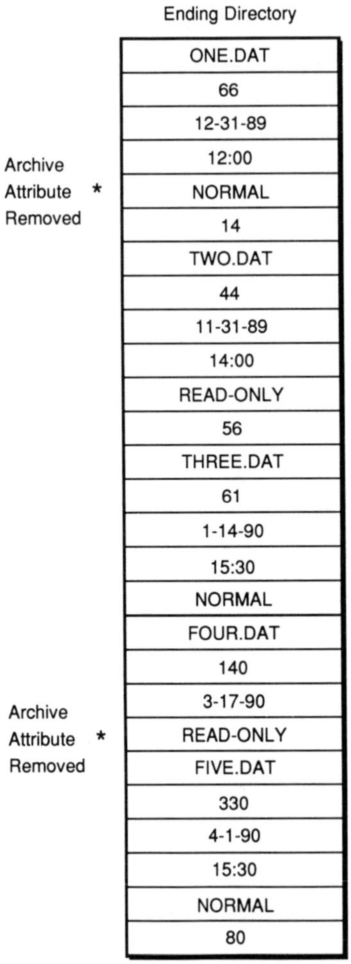

Ending Directory

ONE.DAT
66
12-31-89
12:00
NORMAL
14
TWO.DAT
44
11-31-89
14:00
READ-ONLY
56
THREE.DAT
61
1-14-90
15:30
NORMAL
FOUR.DAT
140
3-17-90
READ-ONLY
FIVE.DAT
330
4-1-90
15:30
NORMAL
80

Archive Attribute * Removed

Archive Attribute * Removed

Other Methods of Changing Attribute Bytes

Since a file's directory entry attribute byte controls whether a file is backed up, you may find it helpful to change manually the archive attribute on some files before doing a backup. You can use the ATTRIB command to do this or the FILEATTR utility provided with the Jamsa Disk Utilities. For more information on FILEATTR, see Chapter 12.

Because an incremental backup is selective, it completes much faster than a disk backup, usually in a few minutes, provided you perform incremental backups regularly.

To perform incremental backups, label a newly formatted floppy disk with the drive letter, backup date, and disk number. You should also note that it is an incremental backup.

Next, issue the following BACKUP command:

```
C:\> BACKUP C:\*.* A: /S /A /M
```

As before, the /S switch directs BACKUP to back up files that reside in subdirectories below the directory specified. The /A switch lets you add files to an incremental backup disk from one day to the next until the disk fills. The /M switch directs BACKUP to perform an incremental backup, selecting only those files whose archive required attribute is set.

In this case, BACKUP will prompt you to insert the last floppy disk used for an incremental backup as shown here.

```
Insert last backup diskette in drive A:
Strike any key when ready
```

To maintain current backup files, you need to issue this incremental backup command on a regular (ideally daily) basis.

If the incremental backup requires more than one floppy disk, BACKUP will prompt you to enter a new disk. Label the disk as previously shown and continue. The next time you perform backup operations, begin with the last disk used. By using the /A switch, you can add files to disk until it fills. Depending upon the number of files you change or create, you may use the same floppy disk for several incremental backups.

Your backup procedures must follow a pattern. Every month you should perform a complete backup of your disk. After the backup operation completes, you can format and reuse the diskettes from your previous incremental backups. Performing your backup operations in this way reduces the amount of time backups require, the number of floppy disks you must track, and the possibility of data loss.

Understanding BACKUP's Command Line Switches

The BACKUP command supports several command line switches.

/S	Directs BACKUP to back up files in subdirectories.
/A	Directs BACKUP to add files to a floppy disk used previously for backup operations.
/M	Directs BACKUP to perform an incremental backup selecting only those files with the archive required attribute.
/F	Directs BACKUP to format each floppy disk before storing files on it. Requires DOS 3.3.
/D:mm:dd:yy	Directs BACKUP to only select files created or changed after the date specified.
/T:hh:mm:ss	Directs BACKUP to select only files created or changed after the time specified.
/L:logfile	Directs BACKUP to record the name of each file it backs up and the disk number to the file specified. Requires DOS 3.3.

If you are using a version of DOS greater than 3.3, the /F switch lets you perform a backup operation using unformatted floppy disks. However, as already discussed, formatting floppy disks during backups greatly slows down the process.

The /D and /T switches let you selectively back up files using the file's date and time stamps. The following command, for example, directs BACKUP to select those files created or changed since noon on Christmas 1989.

```
C:\> BACKUP C:\*.* A: /S /D:12:25:89 /T:12:00
```

If you are using a version of DOS greater than 3.3, the /L switch directs BACKUP to create a log file containing each file it backs up along with the number of the disk containing the file. If you later need to restore a specific file, the backup log tells you which disk the file resides on. A sample log file might contain the following information:

```
1-26-1990  8:50:40
001   \AUTOEXEC.BAT
001   \CONFIG.SYS
001   \DOS\COMMAND.COM
001   \DOS\COUNTRY.SYS
001   \DOS\DISKCOPY.COM
  :         :
002   \DOS\DISPLAY.SYS
002   \DOS\FDISK.COM
002   \DOS\FORMAT.COM
```

The log file is very useful. In this case, the value 001 in the log tells you that the file resides on disk 1. Likewise, 002 tells you a file resides on disk 2 and so on. Although the overhead required to create the log file increases your backup time slightly, the ability to identify quickly the backup disk containing a specific file is very convenient if you ever need to restore one or more files.

Create a directory called BACKUP to store the backup log file.

```
C:\> MKDIR \BACKUP
```

For the name of the log file, you may find it convenient to use the name of current month with the extension LOG. The following command performs a complete disk backup recording file names to the log file MARCH.LOG.

```
C:\> BACKUP C:\*.* A: /S /L:C:\BACKUP\MARCH.LOG
```

If you are not using DOS 3.3, you can create your own log file by redirecting BACKUP's output from the screen to a log file as shown here.

```
C:\> BACKUP C:\*.* A: /S > C:\BACKUP\MARCH.LOG
```

Likewise, change the incremental backup commands. For DOS 3.3, use the following:

```
C:\> BACKUP C:\*.* A: /S /A /M /L:C:\BACKUP\MONTH.LOG
```

For DOS versions prior to 3.3, use the following:

```
C:\> BACKUP C:\*.* A: /S /A /M >> C:\BACKUP\MONTH.LOG
```

Restoring Files from Backup Disks

Hopefully, you will never need to use your backup files. However, if you inadvertently delete files you can't undelete, or your disk becomes damaged requiring a low-level format, the DOS RESTORE command lets you copy files from your backup disk back to your hard disk. Even if you have formatted your hard disk, RESTORE creates your original directory structure placing the correct files into each directory.

If you need to restore files from a backup disk, you will restore either one or more files or the entire disk. For simplicity, lets look at each case individually.

Restoring One or More Files

If you delete one or more files from a certain directory, begin your file restoration by printing a copy of your backup log. Starting at the bottom of the log, search for the disk containing the latest backup of the file. Next, issue the RESTORE command using a complete path name to the file.

For example, the following command restores the file FORMAT.COM to the DOS subdirectory.

```
C:\> RESTORE A: C:\DOS\FORMAT.COM
```

Likewise, the following command restores all files in the DOS subdiretory.

```
C> RESTORE A: C:\DOS\*.*
```

If you don't have a backup log, you can still perform the file restoration: however, it will take a little longer since you must search backup disks until you find the disk containing the desired file. Assume, for example, that you need to restore the file DATABASE.DAT that resided in the subdirectory DBASE. Insert the last incremental backup disk and issue the following command:

```
C:> RESTORE A: C:\DBASE\DATABASE.DAT
```

Because you are starting with the last disk in the backup sequence, RESTORE will display the following warning message:

```
Warning! Diskette is out of sequence
Replace diskette or continue if okay
```

In this case, press Enter to continue the restoration. If RESTORE finds the file, it will restore it to your hard disk. If RESTORE does not find the file, RESTORE will display the following error message:

```
WARNING! No files were found to restore.
```

If this error message occurs, repeat the RESTORE command with the next disk in the backup sequence. By starting with the newest disk and working backward, you ensure that RESTORE places the most recent backup of the file on your hard disk. As you can see, a backup log file is very convenient.

Restoring Your Disk

If you need to restore your entire disk, you'll need to begin with the disks containing your complete system backup. Place a disk in drive A, which contains the RESTORE command, and issue the following command:

```
A:\> RESTORE A: C:\*.* /S
```

In this case, drive A is the drive containing the backup files. The /S switch directs RESTORE to copy all files to the correct directories, creating the directories as necessary. When you press Enter to execute the command, RESTORE will display the following prompt, directing you to place the first backup disk into drive A.

```
Insert backup diskette 001 in drive A:
Strike any key when ready
```

When you press Enter to continue, RESTORE will begin placing files on the hard disk, displaying the name of each file on your screen as the file is restored. When RESTORE is done with the first disk, it prompts you to insert the next disk in drive A, repeating this process until it has restored each of the disks from the complete disk backup.

Next, using the disk from the incremental backups, repeat the RESTORE command.

```
A:\> RESTORE A: C:\*.* /S
```

RESTORE will place each file on the incremental backup disks onto your hard disk, making your hard disk as current as your last incremental backup.

Understanding RESTORE's Command Line Switches

Like BACKUP, the DOS RESTORE command supports several command line switches discussed here.

/S	Directs RESTORE to restore files in subdirectories below the directory specified.
/P	Directs RESTORE to prompt the user before overwriting files marked as read-only on the hard disk.
/M	Directs RESTORE to restore only those files modified since the last backup operation.
/N	Directs RESTORE to restore only those files that no longer exist on the hard disk.
/A:mm-dd-yy	Directs RESTORE to restore only those files changed after the date specified.
/B:mm-dd-yy	Directs RESTORE to restore only those files changed before the date specified.
/E:hh-mm-ss	Directs RESTORE to restore only those files changed before the time specified.
/L:hh:mm:ss	Directs RESTORE to restore only those files changed after the time specified.

The RESTORE date and time switches look at the date and time stamp for files on your hard disk. For example, the following command directs RESTORE to restore all files with the extension DAT that have been changed after Christmas 1989.

```
C:\> RESTORE A: C:\*.DAT /S /A:12-25-89
```

> **WARNING!** RESTORE overwrites files existing on your hard disk with matching files on the backup disk. By default, RESTORE even overwrites files marked as read-only.

The /P switch directs RESTORE to prompt the user before overwriting files marked read-only. The following command directs RESTORE to restore all files on a hard disk, prompting the user before overwriting an existing hard disk file marked read-only.

```
C:\> RESTORE A: C:\*.* /P /S
```

If RESTORE encounters an existing read-only file, RESTORE displays the following prompt:

```
WARNING! File FILENAME.EXT
is a read-only file
Replace the file (Y/N)?
```

If you type **Y**, RESTORE will overwrite the existing read-only file. If you type **N**, the file is left unchanged.

Backing Up Only Specific Files

Depending upon your applications, you may need to copy specific files for another user from time to time. If the number of files you need to copy exceeds one floppy disk, or a single file is larger than one floppy disk, BACKUP may prove quite convenient. If a file is larger than a floppy disk, COPY or XCOPY cannot copy the file to a floppy disk. BACKUP, however, can break the file into multiple pieces across two or more floppy disks. RESTORE later puts the file back together.

To back up a single file, simply specify the file's path name as shown here.

```
C:\> BACKUP C:\PATHNAME\BIGFILE.DAT A:
```

Likewise, to back up the files in a specific subdirectory, specify the subdirectory path and DOS wild cards as shown here.

```
C:\> BACKUP C:\DOS\*.*  A:
```

If the subdirectory contains additional directories, you can use /S to direct BACKUP to back up those files also.

Summary

Hard disks store files and programs. As you store information on your hard disk, you periodically need to make copies of your files to reduce the possibility of data loss in the event of an errant DOS command or, worse yet, a hard disk failure.

The DOS BACKUP command lets you back up your entire disk, or specific files, to floppy disk. Users should back up their hard disk and critical files on a regular basis. Ideally, backups should be made each day. However, most users make backups weekly. Depending on the importance of your data, you may want to back up your files more often. By making incremental backups, you can back up only those files created or modified that day in only a few minutes.

9

Detecting and Correcting File Fragmentation

- ▶ Understanding File Fragmentation
- ▶ Recognizing the Symptoms of File Fragmentation
- ▶ Using CHKDSK to Test Fragmentation
- ▶ Correcting Fragmented Files
- ▶ Eliminating Disk Fragmentation with BACKUP, FORMAT, and RESTORE
- ▶ Undeleting Fragmented Files
- ▶ Reducing Fragmentation with DOS Clusters
- ▶ Summary

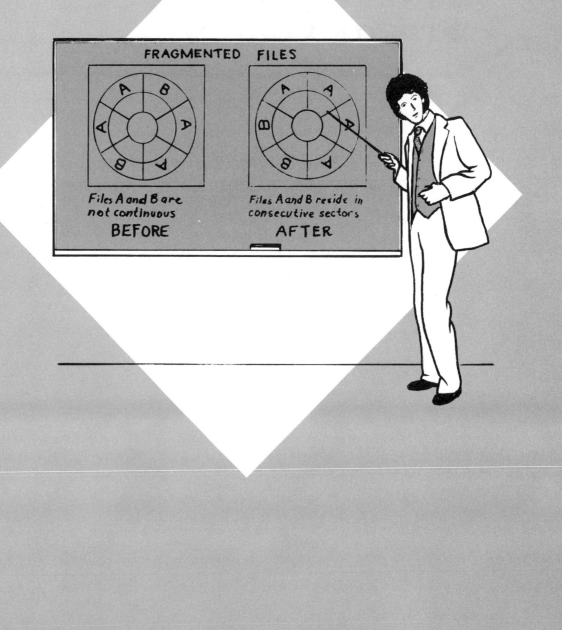

Detecting and Correcting File Fragmentation

This book's general theme is that disks, whether hard or floppy, are slow; any steps you can take to minimize disk use will improve your overall system performance. Chapter 1 discussed several hardware considerations such as faster controllers and RLL (Run Length Limited) encoding, which decrease disk access time. Other chapters have discussed DOS techniques that reduce the number of disk operations DOS must perform such as disk buffers, FASTOPEN tables, and subdirectory optimization.

Unfortunately, even the fastest disk and the most optimized system will eventually experience *file fragmentation*, the single most destructive force against disk performance. File fragmentation occurs when one or more files are stored on disk in sectors physically separated from one another.

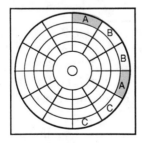
File A is fragmented

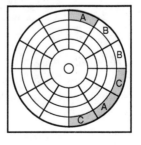
Files A and C are fragmented

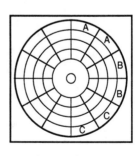
No fragmented files

To read a fragmented file, the disk controller may have to move the disk heads in and out to find the tracks containing the file sectors. The head's slow mechanical movement not only decreases your system performance, but it also adds unnecessary wear to your disk drive.

File fragmentation is a natural occurrence as users create, erase, and expand files on disk. If you are concerned about performance, you need to detect and correct fragmented files. If system performance is not a concern, fragmented files may prevent a third-party UNDELETE utility from successfully recovering inadvertently deleted files.

Understanding File Fragmentation

When your disk is new, DOS is able to store files in consecutive clusters on disk. For example, consider a disk with files ONE, TWO, and THREE as shown in the following figure. We will refer to this figure throughout this chapter.

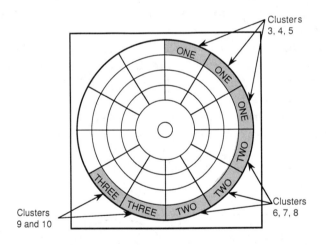

All three files reside in consecutive clusters. If DOS reads file TWO, for example, DOS reads cluster 6, followed by cluster 7, and then cluster 8. Because the file's contents reside on disk in consecutive clusters, the disk controller does not have to move the disk head to read the file.

Contrast the previous (unfragmented) disk with the following disk on which file TWO has become fragmented.

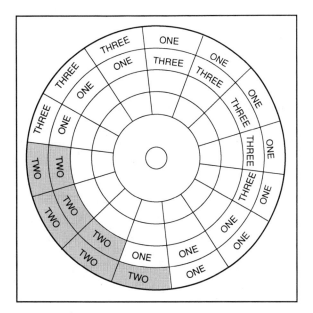

In this case, each file not only has nonconsecutive clusters, but some of the clusters even reside on a different cylinders. When clusters are on different cylinders, the controller must move the disk read and write head back and forth from one cylinder to the next. The additional head movement and disk rotation delay is the *overhead* produced by file fragmentation. The more fragmented files on your disk, the greater the overhead and wear on your disk.

Fragmented Files Reduce Your System Performance

A fragmented file is a file whose sectors are not stored in consecutive clusters. Visualize a fragmented file as a book whose pages are numbered but are not in order. By examining the book's page numbers, you could eventually locate the next page so you could continue reading. However, flipping through the pages takes you much longer than reading the pages that follow one after another. When a file becomes fragmented, DOS can indeed read the file, but doing so takes much longer.

File Fragmentation Is a Natural Occurrence

Although file fragmentation produces tremendous system overhead, which decreases your system performance, you can't prevent it. Fragmentation occurs when existing files grow. Assume, for example, that you place the files ONE, TWO, and THREE on a new disk. As DOS creates the files, DOS is able to store the files in consecutive clusters. The condition of these three files is restored to its previous condition, as shown in the following figure.

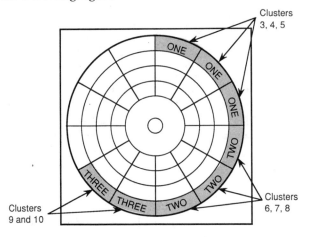

Next, assume that file TWO is a report to which you add several pages. For the file to grow, DOS must allocate additional clusters. In this case, the first available cluster is 11. Assuming you increase the size of the file by two clusters, the new disk layout changes as shown here.

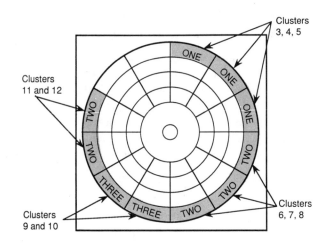

Next, assume the size of file ONE increases, resulting in a disk layout as shown in the next figure.

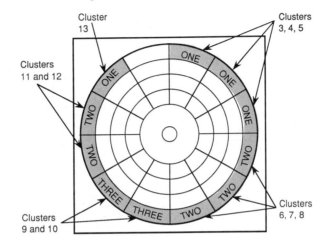

Here a disk with only three files became fragmented when we increased the size of two files. In comparison, consider that a hard disk can contain thousands of files, many of which grow on a regular basis. In most cases, files on your system will become fragmented each day.

File Deletion Can Cause Fragmentation

When a file grows, DOS searches the file allocation table for available clusters. When DOS locates an available cluster, DOS allocates the cluster for the file. Assume that your disk contains the files ONE, TWO, and THREE as shown in the following example.

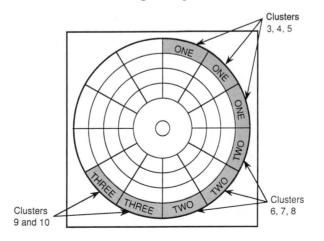

Next, assume the user deletes file THREE freeing up clusters 9 and 10 as shown in the following figure.

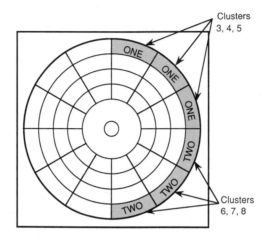

If file ONE grows, DOS will search the FAT for available clusters, allocating the clusters previously used by file THREE. As a result, file ONE becomes fragmented.

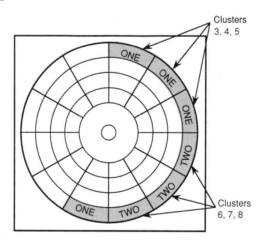

Recognizing the Symptoms of File Fragmentation

If you have worked with DOS for any period of time, you know that deleting and changing files is a common everyday event. Most of us don't stop to think about how file operations affect disk storage; afterall, DOS takes care of all that for us.

Eventually, however, the everyday creation and deletion of files will lead to disk fragmentation. Although fragmentation doesn't prevent DOS from storing files, it will slow disk operations. There are early signs that your disk is becoming fragmented. First, applications that used to start instantly seem to take longer to load. Programs that read or write information to disk will become almost sluggish with poor response times. In many cases, your disk may even become noisy as the controller moves the read and write head from one cylinder to another.

Users who are unfamiliar with disk fragmentation often blame poor system response on the hardware or a new program. By first identifying fragmentation as a cause of the problems, you can eliminate the fragmentation, restoring system performance to its peak level. The CHKDSK command is your first tool for testing file fragmentation.

Using CHKDSK to Test Fragmentation

Chapter 7 examined the CHKDSK command in detail. In addition to checking a disk's FAT and directory entries for consistency, CHKDSK optionally provides disk fragmentation information for a specific subdirectory. For example, the following CHKDSK command displays its default output and lists any files in the DOS subdirectory that are fragmented.

```
C:\> CHKDSK C:\DOS\*.*
```

If CHKDSK finds a fragmented file, CHKDSK displays a message telling you the name of the file that contains the fragmentation and the number of noncontiguous clusters as shown here.

```
C:\PATH\FILENAME.EXT
contains n non-contiguous blocks
```

Clusters are *contiguous* if they reside in consecutive locations. In a fragmented file, therefore, two or more clusters are noncontiguous.

Most directories containing only EXE or COM files will not have fragmented files. Because these files never change, DOS does not have to allocate new clusters for them. The subdirectories containing data files, such as word-processed reports, spreadsheets, or database files are high risks for fragmentation. If fragmentation exists, correct it using the techniques discussed in the next section.

If you suspect a specific file of being fragmented, place the file name in the CHKDSK command line as shown here.

```
C:\>CHKDSK \PATH\FILENAME.EXE
```

In this case, CHKDSK will examine only one file, instead of the entire directory, therefore reducing its processing time.

One drawback to CHKDSK is that it lets you examine only one subdirectory at a time for file fragmentation. The Jamsa Disk Utilities, which accompany this book, contain TESTFRAG, a utility that tests every directory on your disk for fragmented files. For more information on TESTFRAG, see Chapter 21.

Correcting Fragmented Files

If CHKDSK reports that a file is fragmented, your next step is to correct the fragmentation. In some cases, you can simply copy the file to a different disk or directory, delete the fragmented copy, and copy the file back to the directory. For example, assume that you suspect that the file DATABASE.DAT is fragmented. Using CHKDSK you can validate your suspicion as follows:

```
C:\DATA> CHKDSK DATABASE.DAT
```

If CHKDSK reports that the file contains noncontiguous clusters, first copy the file to a different disk.

```
C:\DATA> COPY DATABASE.DAT A:
    1 File(s) copied
```

Next, delete the current fragmented file.

```
C:\DATA> DEL DATABASE.DAT
```

Now restore the file from the disk in drive A.

```
C:\DATA> COPY A:DATABASE.DAT
```

When DOS creates a file, DOS makes its best effort to allocate contiguous clusters for the file. If your disk has sufficient available contiguous clusters, DOS will allocate them, making the restored copy of the file unfragmented. However, if DOS does not have enough contiguous sectors available, DOS must use what it has, and the restored file will still be fragmented, possibly more so than before. When the COPY operation is complete, invoke CHKDSK again to test if fragmentation is improved. If the file is still fragmented, you may want to perform a BACKUP, FORMAT, and RESTORE operation as discussed next.

Third-Party Defragmenters

Many third-party defragmenters are available. The programs improve disk performance by rearranging the layout of files on your disk so that as few files as possible are fragmented. The quality, speed, and value of these programs varies greatly; you are best-off if you test them to make sure they will do the job you expect of them.

When using third-party defragmenters, you must take special care if you also use FASTOPEN. If you install FASTOPEN to track files on your hard disk and later run a third-party disk defragmenter, you must reboot DOS immediately after the defragmenter completes its work. The defragmenter works by moving files around on your disk. The new file locations may not correspond to the values FASTOPEN has recorded. If DOS uses FASTOPEN's values, you may damage your files.

Eliminating Disk Fragmentation with BACKUP, FORMAT, and RESTORE

If you cannot correct fragmentation using the COPY command, your next step is to back up your files, reformat the disk, and then restore the files. When the RESTORE command places the files onto the newly formatted disk, DOS ensures that the files are contiguous. You can use either a third-party software program or the DOS BACKUP command to save your files. If you use BACKUP, format the correct number of floppy disks as discussed in Chapter 8 and issue the following command:

```
C:\> BACKUP C:\*.* A: /S
```

If the BACKUP command is successful, you can continue with the FORMAT operation. If BACKUP did not complete, repeat the backup operation until it is successful. Before you continue, make sure you have a floppy disk containing the file RESTORE.COM or your third-party software so you can perform the file restoration when FORMAT completes.

Next, issue the following FORMAT command:

```
C:\> FORMAT C: /S
```

Recall from Chapter 2 that the /S switch directs FORMAT to create a bootable disk. When the FORMAT command completes, place a DOS disk containing RESTORE.COM in drive A and issue the following command to place your files back onto your disk.

```
A> RESTORE A: C:\*.* /S
```

When the RESTORE operation completes, use the TESTFRAG utility provided on the companion disk to verify that the operation has successfully eliminated disk fragmentation.

Undeleting Fragmented Files

If your files are fragmented, you may not be able to undelete them using a third-party software package. Undelete programs work by rebuilding a file's cluster chain. Assume, for example, that your disk contains files ONE, TWO, and THREE as shown here.

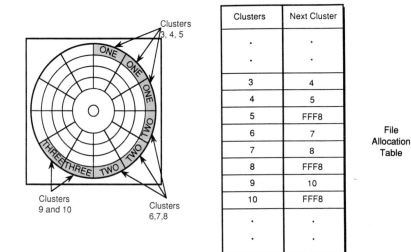

Clusters	Next Cluster
.	.
.	.
3	4
4	5
5	FFF8
6	7
7	8
8	FFF8
9	10
10	FFF8
.	.
.	.

File Allocation Table

Clusters 3, 4, 5

Clusters 9 and 10

Clusters 6,7,8

If you delete file TWO, as shown in the next figure, DOS marks clusters 5, 6, and 7 as available.

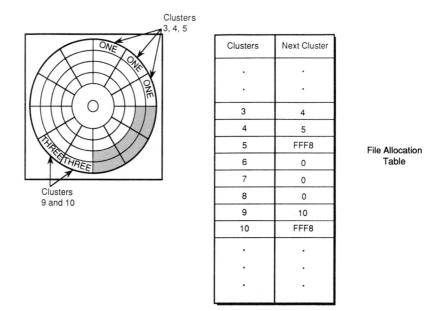

Clusters	Next Cluster
.	.
.	.
3	4
4	5
5	FFF8
6	0
7	0
8	0
9	10
10	FFF8
.	.
.	.
.	.

File Allocation Table

DOS commands ignore deleted files in a directory. When you delete a file, the file's directory entry remains, but DOS marks the entry as unused so the entry does not appear in the directory listing. DOS marks a file as deleted by replacing the first letter of the file's name with another character. When DOS performs a directory listing, DOS does not display the files marked as unused.

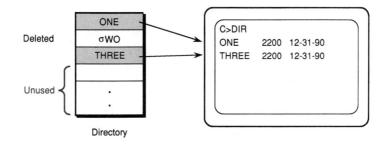

When you invoke the UNDELETE utility provided with the Jamsa Disk Utilities, which accompany this book, UNDELETE displays the deleted files in the directory as shown here.

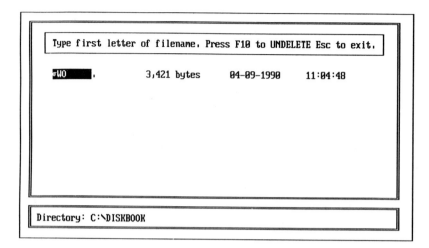

As you can see, each file name begins with a lowercase Greek sigma [σ]. To undelete the file, you must tell UNDELETE the file name's original first letter.

As you create new files, DOS uses the entries marked unused. As a result, if you delete one file and create another, DOS may use the first file's directory entry or overwrite the first file's contents on disk. In either case, a third-party undelete program cannot recover the deleted file. As such, if you inadvertently delete a file, do not create any files on the disk until you have successfully undeleted the lost file.

If you undelete a file using a third-party software utility, the utility first searches the directory for the file's directory entry.

Using the directory entry, the undelete utility can determine the file's starting cluster and size. If the file is contiguous, the utility starts with the FAT entry for the starting cluster and reclaims the number of clusters required to match the file's size.

Assume you have the files ONE, TWO, and THREE on a disk, as shown here.

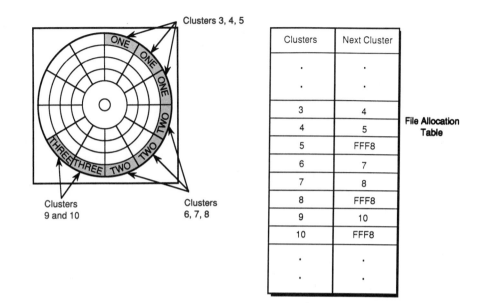

Clusters	Next Cluster
.	.
.	.
3	4
4	5
5	FFF8
6	7
7	8
8	FFF8
9	10
10	FFF8
.	.
.	.

File Allocation Table

Next, assume that you accidentally deleted files TWO and THREE. The disk layout and FAT would appear as shown here.

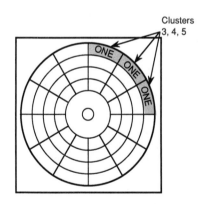

Clusters	Next Cluster
.	.
.	.
3	4
4	5
5	FFF8
6	0
7	0
8	0
9	0
10	0
.	.
.	.
.	.

File Allocation Table

The directory entry for file TWO indicates that it started at cluster 6, and the file size indicates that it required three clusters. Likewise, file THREE started at cluster 9 and required two clusters. When UNDELETE does its work, the disk layout and FAT appear as shown in the following figure.

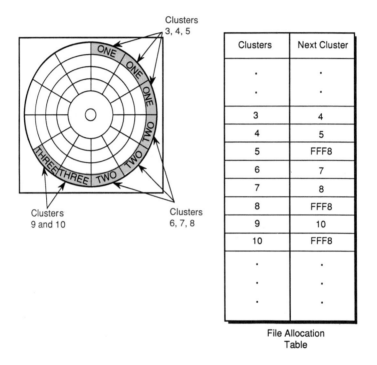

Clusters	Next Cluster
.	.
.	.
3	4
4	5
5	FFF8
6	7
7	8
8	FFF8
9	10
10	FFF8
.	.
.	.
.	.

File Allocation
Table

Now, assume that you had the same three files on disk but that file TWO is fragmented as shown in the next figure.

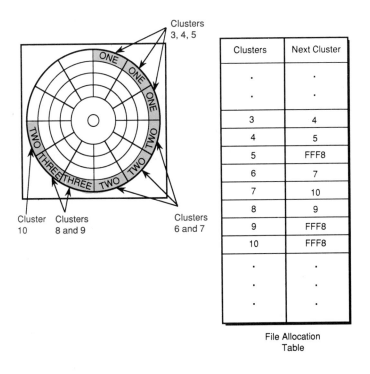

Clusters	Next Cluster
·	·
·	·
3	4
4	5
5	FFF8
6	7
7	10
8	9
9	FFF8
10	FFF8
·	·
·	·
·	·

File Allocation
Table

Delete files TWO and THREE. When you subsequently use the UNDELETE program, remember that the only thing it has to work from is the starting cluster number and the file size. It can only assume that the clusters for the file are contiguous. If you use UNDELETE to recover file TWO, UNDELETE allocates clusters 6, 7, and 8 as shown in the following figure.

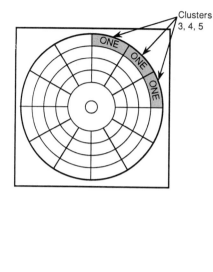

Clusters	Next Cluster
.	.
.	.
3	4
4	5
5	FFF8
6	0
7	0
8	0
9	0
10	0
.	.
.	.
.	.

**File Allocation
Table**

Unfortunately, due to fragmentation, UNDELETE combines part of file TWO's clusters with clusters from file THREE. If a file is fragmented, possible data loss can occur no matter which undelete utility you select. If you are counting on UNDELETE, you'd better make sure your files are contiguous.

Reducing Fragmentation with DOS Clusters

Each time DOS allocates disk space for a file, DOS uses a cluster. For many hard disks, clusters hold four sectors of data. DOS always allocates a cluster for a file, even if it contains only one character.

DOS uses clusters for two reasons. First, by tracking clusters as opposed to sectors, DOS decreases the size of the FAT. Second, clusters reduce disk fragmentation. For example, assume that you create files ONE and TWO and that each file contains 512 bytes. If your hard disk allocates four sectors per cluster, your disk usage resembles that shown in the following figure.

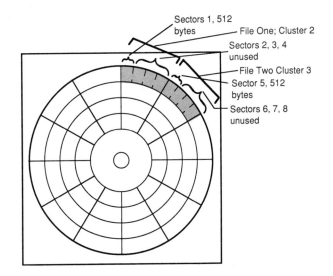

Sectors 1, 512 bytes

File One; Cluster 2

Sectors 2, 3, 4 unused

File Two Cluster 3

Sector 5, 512 bytes

Sectors 6, 7, 8 unused

DOS clusters let files grow by small amounts without disk fragmentation. If the files never grow, the unused clusters are wasted. If, however, you double the size of file ONE to 1,024 bytes, then your layout appears as in the next figure.

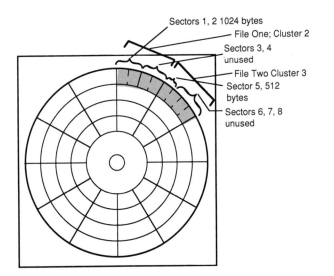

Sectors 1, 2 1024 bytes

File One; Cluster 2

Sectors 3, 4 unused

File Two Cluster 3

Sector 5, 512 bytes

Sectors 6, 7, 8 unused

Because DOS initially assigns a cluster to each file, the files have room to grow. In this case, file ONE can grow an additional 1,024 bytes before it becomes fragmented. As a result, clusters may waste disk space when you create many small files, but they improve your disk utilization for files that grow.

Summary

Disk fragmentation occurs when files are on disk in nonconsecutive sectors. Disk fragmentation decreases your system performance by increasing the number of slow disk head movements the disk drive must perform to read the information stored in a fragmented file, In addition to decreasing your system performance, fragmented files may prevent you from successfully undeleting a file you have accidentally deleted.

The DOS CHKDSK command lets you examine the files in a specific directory for fragmentation. The TESTFRAG Jamsa Disk Utility tests all of the files on your disk for fragmentation. If either CHKDSK or TESTFRAG identifies fragmented files, you may be able to correct the fragmentation by copying the file to another disk, deleting the file, and then copying the file back to your disk. If the file remains fragmented, you can eliminate all of the fragmentation by performing a BACKUP, FORMAT, and RESTORE operation.

If you are concerned about disk performance, test for and eliminate disk fragmentation on a regular basis.

10

Maximizing Your Disk Performance

► DOS Hard Disk Performance Improvement Techniques

► Hardware Performance Considerations

► A Disk Cache

► Summary

Maximizing Your Disk Performance

Users are concerned with hard disk management for three reasons. First, users want to organize their disk to simplify file search operations. Second, hard disk management improves file security by reducing the possibility of an errant DOS command deleting or overwriting your files. Finally, hard disk management improves disk performance, which makes programs execute faster and users more productive. This chapter looks at the steps you can follow to improve your disk performance.

The chapter begins by discussing several DOS commands and concepts relating directly to disk performance. You can easily implement each concept and should do it, if you want the best system performance. The chapter then discusses several hardware considerations that deal primarily with your disk and controller. In some cases, you can implement the recommendations with minimal cost and effort. You may also find that your disk is already optimized. In addition, this section details the performance factors you should consider when purchasing disks.

The chapter ends by discussing several performance enhancements available through third-party software packages.

DOS Hard Disk Performance Improvement Techniques

You should consider several DOS commands and options to improve your performance. The advantage of using DOS to improve disk performance instead of hardware upgrades or third-party software packages is cost and effort. If you are already using a version of DOS greater than 3.3, most of the techniques won't cost you anything. If you are not, you should consider the upgrade. Depending on the current state of your disk's directory structure, several of the techniques require no changes to your disk while others may require some directory restructuring. In many cases the directory manipulation utilities provided in the Jamsa Disk Utilities will save you considerable time and effort as you increase your disk's performance.

Reducing the Number of Directory Entries

As discussed, each time DOS searches a subdirectory for a file, it must sequentially read each directory entry until it locates the file or the end of the directory. The more files in the subdirectory, the longer the search requires. If possible, restrict the number of files in a subdirectory to no more than 64.

As discussed in Chapter 4, DOS treats subdirectories as files containing 32-byte directory entries. Each time DOS allocates disk space for a file, DOS uses a cluster. For most hard disks, DOS uses a cluster size of four sectors, or 2,048 bytes. If a subdirectory uses only a single cluster, it can hold up to 64 entries as shown here.

```
Number of Entries = (Cluster Size) / (Entry Size)
                  = 2,048 / 32
                  = 64
```

Most subdirectories grow over a period of time. Should the subdirectory grow past 64 entries, DOS allocates a second cluster for the subdirectory. In most cases, the second cluster is not adjacent to the first cluster, and the subdirectory becomes fragmented as discussed in Chapter 9. Once a directory becomes fragmented, the performance for every file operation that occurs in the directory decreases.

If your disk already contains directories with more than 64 entries, the directories may already be fragmented. A good first step is to execute the directory compact utility provided with the Jamsa Disk Utilities and as discussed in Chapter 15. Next, create and use subdirectories to logically organize the files, reducing the number of files in the current directory. Once you have copied the files to their new locations and deleted the files from the current directory, execute the directory compress utility for the current directory a second time.

Get into the habit of running the subdirectory compress utility regularly. Doing so will improve the performance of directory search operations.

Optimizing the Command Path

As discussed, the PATH command simplifies your execution of commands and programs by letting you define a list of subdirectories where DOS searches for EXE, COM, and BAT files when it fails to locate the command in the current or specified directory. The following PATH command, for example, directs DOS to search the subdirectories DOS, BATCH, and UTIL (on drive C) in that order.

```
C:\> PATH C:\DOS;C:\BATCH;C:\UTIL
```

Each time you execute a command at the DOS prompt, DOS follows the same steps. First, DOS checks to see if the command is an internal command that resides in memory. These are commands such as CLS, DIR, or DEL. If it is an internal command, DOS executes the command. If it is not, DOS searches the current or specified directory for a file with the extension COM, EXE, or BAT that matches the command name. If DOS locates a matching file, DOS executes it; otherwise, DOS checks for the existence of a command path. If you have reduced the number of files in each directory as just discussed, DOS can quickly determine whether the file is present.

Using the previously defined command path, DOS begins its search in the DOS subdirectory. If DOS locates a matching file, DOS executes the command; otherwise, DOS will continue its search in the next directory in the command path, which in this case is `C:\BATCH`. DOS repeats the process of searching command subdirectories until the file is found or the command path is exhausted.

Obviously, the fewer files DOS has to examine, the faster it can search the command path. As such, don't place subdirectories that aren't likely to contain commonly used commands in the command path. Also decrease the amount of time DOS spends searching directory entries by placing the subdirectories most likely to contain commonly used commands first in the command path.

Finally, if your command path contains more than three or four entries, make sure each directory specified actually contains commonly used commands. In most cases, an excessive number of subdirectories in the command path often corresponds to substantial overhead in command search operations.

Decreasing Disk Input and Output Operations with BUFFERS =

The importance of using a sufficient number of disk buffers cannot be over-stressed. As discussed in Chapter 6, DOS uses disk buffers as an intermediate data stop between an application and the disk. Each time DOS must read a disk sector, DOS first checks to see if the sector already resides in a buffer. If DOS finds the sector in memory, DOS doesn't have to perform a slow disk read operation.

Chapter 6 discussed disk buffers in terms of input or read operations. DOS also uses disk buffers during disk output or write operations. Recall that a sector is the smallest unit of information DOS can transfer to or from disk. Using the birthday database example from Chapter 6, each record in the database contains 64 bytes as shown in the following figure.

Name	Birthday
Kevin	October 18
Stephanie	February 23
Kellie	January 29
Aunt Sandie	April 2
Grandma	December 7
Debbie	December 8

44 bytes   20 bytes

64 bytes

When the database program writes the first record to disk, DOS actually places the data in a disk buffer. As shown in the next figure, it stores information in the DOS buffer until the buffer is full or the file is closed.

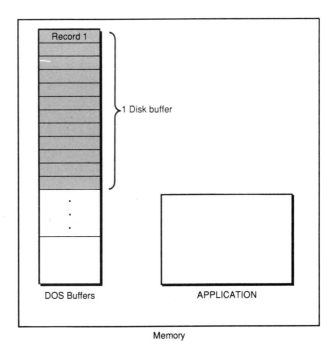

Memory

DOS performs this same operation for records 2 through 7. When the program writes the eight records to disk, the disk buffer becomes full, and DOS transfers the sector from the disk buffer to the disk. As a result, DOS reduces eight disk output operations to one slow disk write. Had the buffer never filled, DOS would have written the buffer to the disk when either the program closed the file containing the database or the program successfully ended.

You must understand the ramifications of DOS using disk buffers for output operations. First, DOS decreases the number of disk write operations, which improves performance. However, because DOS does not actually write data to disk until the buffer is full or the file is closed, a period of time exists where data you assumed was correctly recorded to disk can actually be lost. Assume, for example, the database program has written the first five records to disk. Rather than actually recording the records on disk, DOS stores the records in a disk buffer.

Next, rather than letting the program run to completion, you turn the computer off. As soon as the power is off, the contents of RAM, including the disk buffers, are lost. You leave the computer thinking the records were recorded to disk. In actuality, the records are lost. Because

DOS always uses disk buffers, it is important that you don't turn off your computer unless you are at the DOS prompt.

The number of available disk buffers isn't as critical for output operations as it is for input. As discussed in Chapter 6, you should experiment with the CONFIG.SYS BUFFERS= entry, beginning with a setting of at least 25.

```
BUFFERS=25
```

By changing the value of the CONFIG.SYS BUFFERS= entry, you can determine the setting that provides the best performance without having to make any other changes to your system.

Reducing Directory Search Operations with FASTOPEN

Every time DOS performs a file manipulation operation, DOS must search the current or specified directory for the file's directory entry. By reducing the number of files in the directory, you also decrease the search time. By using the directory compress utility discussed in Chapter 15, you will reduce directory search operations to an even greater extent.

If you are using a version of DOS greater than 3.3, you should place a FASTOPEN command in your AUTOEXEC.BAT file. FASTOPEN installs memory-resident software that directs DOS to save the starting locations of files in a memory table as you access the file from disk. Should DOS later need to access a file for a second file manipulation operation, DOS can quickly locate the file's starting cluster address using the FASTOPEN table instead of having to read the directory from disk and search for the file, which is much more time consuming.

FASTOPEN will not reduce the access time for each file on disk. Instead, FASTOPEN decreases the access time for files that DOS has recently opened. If DOS has not yet opened the file, it won't have a corresponding entry in the FASTOPEN table entry. As such, DOS must read and search the directory. Once DOS locates the file, it places an entry for the file in the FASTOPEN table.

For most users, a FASTOPEN table capable of storing 50 to 75 entries should be sufficient. The following DOS command directs DOS to create a FASTOPEN table of 50 entries.

```
C:\> FASTOPEN C:=50
```

Like all performance-tuning techniques, you will need to experiment with FASTOPEN to determine the optimal performance setting. Once you determine the setting that provides the best performance, place the corresponding entry in AUTOEXEC.BAT.

Like the CONFIG.SYS BUFFERS= entry, the FASTOPEN command lets you improve your system performance without changing your system configuration.

Eliminating Disk Fragmentation

As discussed in Chapter 9, disk fragmentation occurs when one or more files spread out across your disk. Disk fragmentation occurs naturally as files grow over a period of time. Fragmentation decreases your system performance by increasing the amount of disk rotational delay and the number of disk head movements your disk must perform to read or write a file. In the worst case, the clusters that make up a file reside on different cylinders, and the disk head must move in or out, possibly several times depending on the size of the file. Excessive disk head movement results in decreased system performance.

By reducing disk fragmentation following the steps outlined in Chapter 8, you minimize the number of mechanical movements your disk must perform to read a file. Disk fragmentation is one of the largest single causes of slow file access. You may want to review Chapter 9 for use of the CHKDSK command and the TESTFRAG utility to help in determining the degree of file fragmentation on your disk and for methods to correct fragmentation.

Increasing Performance with RAM Drives

Chapter 6 discussed the RAMDRIVE.SYS (VDISK.SYS under PC DOS) device driver and its use in creating RAM drives. RAM drives provide an extremely fast, temporary file storage. Because RAM drives reside in the computer's electronic random-access memory, they don't use any slow mechanical moving parts. RAM drives, therefore, are the fastest file storage alternative. Unfortunately, RAM drives lose their contents when you turn your computer off or reboot. Because of this, you should use

RAM drives only to store temporary files or commonly used programs that you can copy from another disk to the RAM drive.

Get in the habit of using RAM drives as often as possible to create temporary files. Not only will the programs creating the files execute faster, but you will also reduce additional wear and tear on your disk. If you are programming, most compilers create one or more temporary files. By using a RAM drive for the temporary files, you can decrease your compile time significantly.

In Chapter 6, you learned that the COMSPEC environment entry tells DOS where to locate the file COMMAND.COM. In most cases, COMSPEC will either point to the root directory or the subdirectory DOS. Each time your computer starts, DOS loads a copy of COMMAND.COM into memory. In some cases, the programs you execute are so large, DOS allows them to overwrite a portion of COMMAND.COM in memory. When this happens, DOS must reload it from disk when the program is finished as shown in this figure.

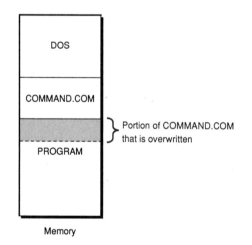

Memory

When the program completes, DOS must reload COMMAND.COM from disk into memory. DOS uses the COMSPEC environment entry to locate COMMAND.COM. If you execute a number of large programs and have extended memory available on your system, you can slightly improve system performance by creating a RAM drive large enough to hold COMMAND.COM and then assigning COMSPEC to point to the RAM drive. In this way, when DOS needs to reload COMMAND.COM, DOS can read the file from your fast RAM drive instead of your hard disk.

To use a RAM drive to hold COMMAND.COM, use the CONFIG.SYS `DEVICE=` entry to install the RAM drive and then place the following commands in your AUTOEXEC.BAT:

```
COPY \DOS\COMMAND.COM D:
SET COMSPEC=D:\COMMAND.COM
```

The previous commands assume that your RAM drive is drive D. If not, use the correct drive letter.

Because of their tremendous speed advantages and the fact that they decrease hard disk wear, more and more users are exploiting RAM drives. To address the data loss possibilities on RAM drives, several hardware manufactures are developing RAM drives with a battery backup that protects the RAM drive's contents when the computer's power is turned off. Although these boards are still fairly expensive, the future should bring reduced prices and general use of battery backup RAM drives.

Suppressing Ctrl+Break Checking

As discussed in Chapter 6, the BREAK command lets you enable and disable extended Ctrl+Break checking. By default, DOS checks for a user-entered Ctrl+Break or Ctrl+C each time it performs input or output to your keyboard, screen, or printer. If DOS encounters either keyboard combination, DOS ends the current program. Many applications programs perform considerable processing without ever writing to the screen or printer or reading from the keyboard. If you use the Ctrl+Break keyboard combination to end such a program, it may take DOS a long time before it realizes you want to end the program. The following BREAK command directs DOS to enable extended Ctrl+Break checking.

```
C:\> BREAK ON
```

When extended Ctrl+Break checking is enabled, DOS checks for a user-entered Ctrl+Break after each DOS system service, including file read and write operations. By testing for Ctrl+Break more often, DOS is more likely to recognize the Ctrl+Break sooner.

Although extended Ctrl+Break checking improves your response time for a DOS acknowledgment of a Ctrl+Break, it results in tremendous system overhead. Basically, each time DOS finishes any operation, DOS must stop the task at hand and check for a user-entered Ctrl+Break. This additional testing consumes much processing time DOS could be using to execute your programs.

If you invoke BREAK without specifying ON or OFF, BREAK will display the current state of extended Ctrl+Break checking as shown here:

```
C:\> BREAK
BREAK is off
```

If extended Ctrl+Break checking is enabled, disable it with the following command:

```
C:\> BREAK OFF
```

Next, examine AUTOEXEC.BAT to ensure that it does not enable extended Ctrl+Break checking. Also, make sure the file CONFIG.SYS does not contain a `BREAK=` entry as discussed in Chapter 6.

Suppressing Disk Verification

Many third-party backup utilities support a verification mode that directs the program to read each sector the utility records on disk to ensure that the information was recorded correctly. Although a verify mode ensures that data is correctly recorded, it nearly doubles the amount of time required to back up a disk. Because disk record errors are rare, most users desire the speed of nonverified backup operations.

DOS provides the VERIFY command that lets you enable and disable disk verification for DOS disk write operations. By default, DOS disables disk verification. When verification is enabled, DOS reads each sector it writes to disk to ensure that the data is recorded correctly. As discussed in Chapter 1, the disk controller calculates a CRC (cyclic redundancy check) value for each sector. The CRC value is determined from the sector's contents. When disk verification is enabled, DOS reads each sector it writes to disk and calculates a CRC value. If the CRC value is equal to the CRC recorded on disk, the sector was recorded correctly. If the CRC differs, DOS can rewrite the sector to disk until it is recorded correctly.

The following command displays the current state of disk verification:

```
C:\> VERIFY
VERIFY is off
```

Because of the system overhead of verifying each sector written to disk, most users leave disk verification disabled. If disk verification is enabled, you can turn it off using the following command:

```
C:\> VERIFY OFF
```

As already stated, disk record errors are rare. If you are performing a critical file copy operation, you might consider enabling disk verification for the file copy operation and later disabling it when the operation completes. The DOS COPY command supports the /V switch, which enables verification for the copy operation. Once the COPY command completes, DOS restores disk verification to its previous state. The following command uses disk verification to copy the file COMMAND.COM from the DOS subdirectory to the floppy disk in drive A:

```
C:\> COPY C:\DOS\COMMAND.COM A: /V
```

Disk verification significantly reduces disk performance. Use it only for critical disk operations.

Hardware Performance Considerations

You can implement many of the DOS disk performance considerations just discussed with little cost or effort. Unfortunately, if you have already purchased your system, changing disk controllers can become quite expensive. If disk performance is critical to your application, a hardware upgrade may be inevitable. In any case, the following discussion will help you better understand the current disk technology and the performance factors you should consider when purchasing your next disk.

As discussed in Chapter 1, the hard disk controller oversees the disk drive operations, moving the disk read and write heads to the correct cylinder and locating the correct sector. The disk controller is involved in virtually every aspect of disk operations. The faster your disk controller works, the better your disk performance is.

To understand the hardware impact upon performance, ask yourself, "What are the time-consuming steps in a disk operation?" First, any step that requires mechanical movement decreases performance. Examples are moving the disk read and write heads to the correct cylinder and waiting for the correct sector to spin past the read and write heads. Once data resides in the controller's memory, the controller can transfer the data to DOS electronically, which is much faster than the mechanical disk access.

Because all hard disks rotate at 3600 RPMs, you can't get faster performance by purchasing a disk that spins more rapidly. Instead, you must determine how to use each disk rotation most effectively. In Chapter 2 you learned that disk interleaving optimizes disk access operations by physically separating consecutively numbered sectors on the disk. Most disk operations require DOS to access several consecutive disk sectors. When the sectors are separate, the controller has time to read a sector and transfer the information to DOS, while preparing to read the next sector. Without interleaving, the controller would most likely miss the next sector and have to wait for the next disk rotation to complete before it could access the missed sector. Continually waiting to access consecutive sectors significantly decreases system performance.

Several third-party software packages exist that determine and then set the correct disk interleave value for your system. Many of these software programs require you to perform a low-level format of your disk. To minimize the impact of incorrect disk sector interleaving, some newer disk controllers buffer each disk sector in the controller's memory as the sector spins past the read and write heads. Assume, for example, that DOS requests sector 5 from the disk. As the disk spins past the read and write heads, the controller reads each sector placing the sector into the controller's memory as shown here.

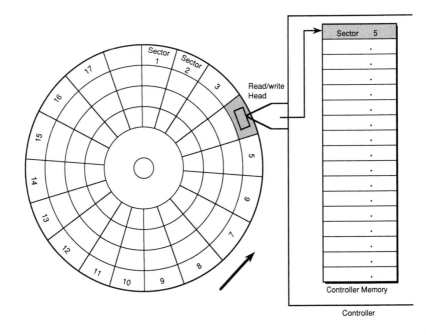

When the controller reads the sector desired, it passes the sector to DOS while continuing to fill its sector buffers from adjacent sectors as shown in the next figure.

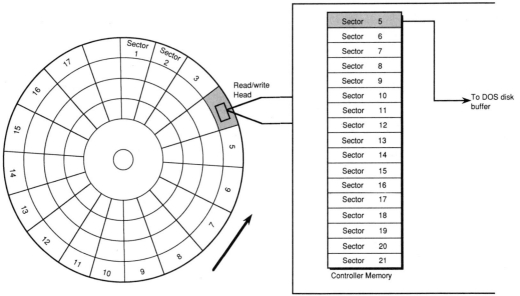

Assuming that DOS later requests sector 6, the controller already has the sector available in its own memory. Because many file operations use successive sectors, buffering the sectors in this manner can be very efficient. Many disk controller manufacturers that do not provide sector-buffering controllers claim that disk performance decreases because the controller must read each sector as it passes by the read and write head. On a single sector comparison, the disk controllers using sector buffering will show slower access times. However, because most file operations use successive sectors, buffering sectors in this way very often leads to better overall system performance.

As hardware capabilities continue to expand, disks can place cylinders closer together, which increases the disk's storage capabilities while decreasing the distance the read and write heads must move to access a different cylinder. Any mechanical movement your disk performs decreases performance. The smaller the movement is, the less the overhead is.

Chapter 1 briefly discussed RLL (Run Length Limited) encoding, which increases disk storage capabilities by decreasing the number of consecutive zeros that can appear on the disk. By storing data more compactly, RLL encoding decreases the number of disk read and write head movements the controller must perform to access specific sectors.

After the data leaves the disk controller and goes to DOS, your system performance depends upon your computer's type and speed, your DOS disk buffers, and the subdirectory structure. The faster your computer is, the faster DOS can transfer data, locate files, and perform other operations. Because it is impossible to continually upgrade your disk and controller, as well as your CPU, your best bet is to concentrate on optimizing the DOS performance considerations. Many users find using third-party disk cache buffers improves their system performance.

A Disk Cache

Chapter 6 discussed the DOS CONFIG.SYS BUFFERS= entry in detail. At that time you learned that disk buffers improve system performance by decreasing the number of slow disk read operations DOS must perform. A *disk cache* is a software program that allocates huge portions of memory to create very large disk buffers. Most cache programs support extended memory, which lets you reserve up to 16M for a cache buffer.

Because cache buffers are so large, a cache might possibly store one or more entire files used in a database application. In Chapter 6, you learned that if you use too many DOS disk buffers, overall system performance could decrease because DOS must spend considerable time searching each buffer. Disk caches, however, store data, using techniques that significantly minimize search time. Using these techniques, even a cache several megabytes in size can determine very quickly if the desired sector is present.

If your system has several megabytes of available memory, a third-party disk cache program may improve your system performance. For systems with 640K of memory, a cache may not provide tremendous performance benefits over DOS disk buffers.

Summary

With computer technology increasing daily, computer users are always searching for ways to improve their system's speed. Unfortunately, it is almost impossible to keep up with new hardware. As such, most users need to maximize the capabilities of their existing hardware. DOS provides several techniques all users can use to improve their system's performance. A major advantage of these techniques is the fact they are free.

A directory is a list of files. Each time you perform a file operation, DOS must search the directory list to locate the file. The longer the list, the more time the directory search takes. By restricting your directories to 64 files or less, you will increase your performance.

The DOS PATH command lets you define the command search directories that DOS searches each time you invoke an external command. If you place directories unlikely to contain commands in the path, DOS will waste considerable time searching them. Likewise, if you place first in the command path the directories most likely to contain commands, you will improve your performance.

Because disks are mechanical, they are much slower than your computer's electronic components. As such, it is desirable to reduce the number of disk operations DOS must perform. The CONFIG.SYS BUFFER= entry reduces disk read and write operations. Likewise, the DOS FASTOPEN command reduces the number of directory search operations DOS must perform. Users who want increased performance should take full advantage of both BUFFERS = and FASTOPEN immediately.

Many third-party software companies sell disk cache software which reduces the number of disk read and write operations by creating large buffers in memory. The disadvantage of disk cache software is that you must purchase additional software.

Two DOS commands don't increase system performance; they decrease it. The DOS VERIFY command directs DOS to perform disk verification operations after each disk write operation. The DOS BREAK command increases the number of times DOS checks for a user-entered Ctrl + Break. Because disk verification errors are very rare, most users improve their performance by leaving verification off. Likewise, if you leave extended Ctrl + Break checking turned off, DOS spends less time checking for a user-entered Ctrl + Break and more time performing other more useful operations.

INSTALLING AND USING THE JAMSA DISK UTILITIES

Chapters 1 through 10 examined hard disk management in detail. You learned how to organize your files using subdirectories, how to configure your system for best performance, and the critical file manipulation commands you'll need on a daily basis. If you haven't read Chapters 1 through 10, make sure you do. The performance tips these chapters provide will save you considerable time and effort each day, making your computer sessions much more productive.

With the importance of Chapters 1 through 10 in mind, I expect most of you to jump right to this section of the book. After all, the capabilities provided by the Jamsa Disk Utilities that accompany this book match or exceed those previously available only through expensive third-party software packages. As such, perform the following steps detailed on the next few pages to install the utilities on your hard disk.

Create the Directory DISKUTIL

Using the MKDIR command, create the subdirectory DISKUTIL on your hard disk as shown here.

```
C:\> MKDIR \DISKUTIL
```

Subdirectories should have meaningful names. In this case, DISKUTIL stands for *disk utilities*. As discussed in Chapter 4, the backslash (\ ) before the directory name is essential.

Copy the Companion Disk Files to Your Hard Disk

The Jamsa Disk Utilities have been compressed so they will fit on two disks. Before you can use the utility programs, you must copy the files stored on the companion disks to your hard disk, and then decompress the files as discussed here.

Place the Jamsa Disk Utilities, disk 1, in drive A and issue the following COPY command:

```
C:\> COPY A:*.* \DISKUTIL
```

When the command completes, insert disk 2 in drive A and repeat the COPY command.

Next, select the DISKUTIL subdirectory as the current directory:

```
C:\> CD \DISKUTIL
```

Before you decompress the files, you will need approximately 1.5 Mbytes of available space on your hard disk. To decompress the files, invoke the batch UNPACK.BAT

```
C:\DISKUTIL> UNPACK
```

The UNPACK batch file displays the name of each file it decompresses. When the batch file completes, the subdirectory DISKUTIL will contain the following files:

```
C:\DISKUTIL> DIR

   Volume in drive C is DOS
   Directory of  C:\DISKUTIL

   .            <DIR>     4-11-90    9:44a
   ..           <DIR>     4-11-90    9:44a
   DATETIME EXE   77032   3-29-90    2:52p
   DISKINFO EXE   59110   3-29-90    2:52p
   DISKSAVE EXE   58014   3-29-90    2:52p
   FILEATTR EXE   72184   3-29-90    2:52p
   FINDFILE EXE   56784   3-29-90    2:52p
```

```
KILLFILE EXE      72694    3-29-90    2:53p
POWER    EXE      66064    3-29-90    2:53p
RENDIR   EXE      64148    3-29-90    2:53p
SELCOPY  EXE      75328    3-29-90    2:53p
SELDEL   EXE      70220    3-29-90    2:53p
SORTDIR  EXE      70860    3-29-90    2:54p
SQUEEZE  EXE      64014    3-29-90    2:54p
TESTFRAG EXE      56470    3-29-90    2:54p
UNDELETE EXE      74424    3-29-90    2:54p
UNFORMAT EXE      60586    3-29-90    2:54p
        17 File(s)   19611648 bytes free
```

Using the DOS PRINT command, print a copy of the file README.DOC which contains additional information on the disk utilities.

```
C:\DISKUTIL> PRINT README.DOC
```

When the file successfully prints, delete it using the DOS DEL command.

Modify Your Search Path

Placing the DISKUTIL subdirectory in your search path (using the PATH command) lets you easily execute the Jamsa Disk Utilities from any disk or subdirectory.

Edit your AUTOEXEC.BAT file and add the DISKUTIL subdirectory to the DOS PATH entry. If you have not yet created AUTOEXEC.BAT, or if you aren't familiar with the DOS PATH command, refer to Chapter 6. The following example adds DISKUTIL to a PATH entry containing only the DOS subdirectory.

```
PATH C:\DOS;C:\DISKUTIL
```

The actual PATH command in your AUTOEXEC.BAT file may differ. In any case, make sure you include the drive letter and backslash (C:\DISKUTIL).

Restart Your System

After you successfully copy the companion disk files to the DISKUTIL subdirectory and add DISKUTIL to the PATH entry in AUTOEXEC.BAT, restart your system using Ctrl + Alt + Del. When the system successfully restarts, invoke the POWER utility as shown here.

```
C:\> POWER
```

If you have successfully installed the utilities, POWER will display the companion disk shell discussed in detail in Chapter 23. If DOS displays the message

```
Bad command or file name
```

you may not have successfully copied all companion disk files to your hard disk, or you may need to provide a correct PATH entry in AUTOEXEC.BAT. In either case, simply repeat the steps discussed in this section.

Using the DISKINFO Utility

- ► Elements of DISKINFO
- ► Understanding DISKINFO Error Messages
- ► How DISKINFO Works

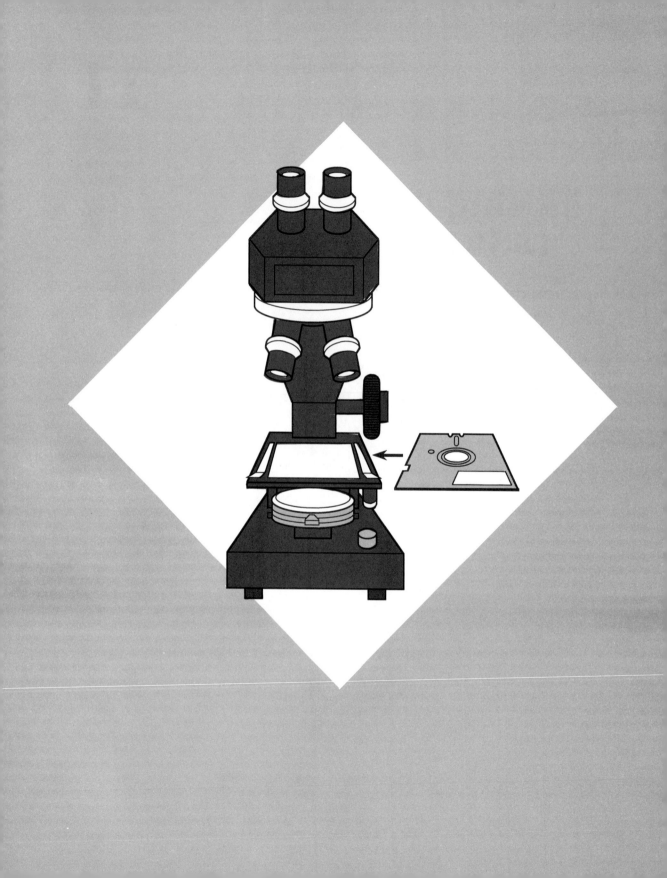

11

Using the
DISKINFO Utility

Chapters 1 through 10 discussed many different disk characteristics such as the number of tracks per disk side, the number of sectors per track, the number of disk clusters, and the maximum number of root directory entries. Using the DISKINFO utility provided on the companion disk, you can display these values for your own disk. Using DISKINFO helps you understand the physical layout of your disk as well as its current usage. You can use DISKINFO to examine hard or floppy disks.

If you have installed the Jamsa Disk Utilities properly, select DISKUTIL as the current directory.

```
C:\> CHDIR \DISKUTIL
```

If you have not installed the utility programs, do so now. (See the introduction to Part 2.)

From the DOS prompt, invoke the `DISKINFO` utility by typing **DISKINFO** and pressing Enter or, if you are using the utilities from the POWER shell, by pressing F9 to select the disk information function.

DISKINFO will clear your screen, displaying the disk specifics for your hard disk as shown in the following figure.

```
┌──────────────────────────────────────────────────────────────┐
│  ┌────────────────────────────────────────────────────────┐   │
│  │   Disk Information, Jamsa Utilities Version 1.0 (C) 1989-90 Kris Jamsa  │  │
│  └────────────────────────────────────────────────────────┘   │
│                                                                │
│   Disk drive letter: C    Boot record system identifier: MSDOS3.3  │
│                                                                │
│   Physical drive number: 2    Bytes/Sector: 512    Sectors/Track: 26  │
│                                                                │
│   Disk type from media descriptor value: F8 - Hard disk        │
│                                                                │
│   Disk sides: 6    Sectors/Cluster: 4    Total sectors: 65,494 │
│                                                                │
│   Number of FATs: 2    Sectors/FAT: 64    FAT entry type: 16 bit  │
│                                                                │
│   Maximum root directory entries: 512    Sectors reserved for root: 32  │
│                                                                │
│   Sectors reserved for boot record, FATs, and root: 161        │
│                                                                │
│   Total clusters: 16,333    Free: 10,025    In use: 6,308      │
│                                                                │
│   Disk Space Total: 33,449,984    Free: 20,531,200    In Use: 12,918,784  │
└──────────────────────────────────────────────────────────────┘
```

`C:\DISKUTIL>`

In this case, DISKINFO displayed the specifics for the current disk. To display disk information for another disk, include a disk drive specifier in the DISKINFO command line as shown here:

`C:\DISKUTIL> DISKINFO A:`

Elements of DISKINFO

The following discussion examines each item DISKINFO displays in detail.

Disk Drive Letter

The disk drive letter field tells you which disk drive DISKINFO is displaying disk specifics for. If you invoke DISKINFO with a drive letter in the command line, DISKINFO displays the corresponding drive letter. If you do not include a drive letter in the command line, DISKINFO displays the default drive.

Boot Record System Identifier

Every DOS disk has a boot record in the first disk sector. In addition to starting the boot process, the boot record contains considerable disk information. The DISKINFO Boot Record System Identifier field contains the operating system that formatted the disk. In this case, the operating system was MS DOS version 3.3.

Physical Drive Number

Every disk drive in your computer has a unique value that DOS uses to access the disk. This value is called the *physical drive number*. Drive A is assigned the physical drive number 0; drive B, the physical drive 1; and drive C, 2 and so on. In this case, the physical drive number 2 corresponds to drive C. If you invoke DISKINFO using drive A, the physical drive number displayed is drive 0.

Bytes/Sector

The DISKINFO Bytes/Sector field tells you the number of bytes per sector for this disk. Although DOS supports sector sizes of 128, 256, 512, and 1,024 bytes, the value is almost always 512.

Sectors/Track

DOS divides every track on your disk into a fixed number of sectors. As just discussed, sectors normally store 512 bytes of data. The DISKINFO Sectors/Track field tells you the number of sectors per track for your disk. Table 11.1 contains common values for different disk types.

In this case, DISKINFO displays the value 26. The hard disk is a 32M disk. Remember that if you use DOS version 4.0, it supports partitions greater than 32M.

Table 11.1. *Common sectors per track settings.*

Disk Type	Sectors Per Track
160K 5¼ floppy disk	8
180K 5¼ floppy disk	9
320K 5¼ floppy disk	8
360K 5¼ floppy disk	9
720K 3½ microfloppy disk	9
1.2M 5¼ floppy disk	15
1.44M 3½ microfloppy disk	18
Hard disk	17

Disk Type from Media Descriptor Value

DOS assigns to the boot record of every disk a two-byte value that defines the disk type. DOS calls this value a *media descriptor* because the value describes the disk media storage type. Table 11.2 defines the DOS media descriptor types.

Table 11.2. *DOS media descriptor values.*

Media Descriptor	Disk Type
F0	1.44M 3½-inch microfloppy disk
F8	Hard disk
F9	1.2M 5¼-inch floppy or 720K 3½-inch microfloppy disk
FC	180K 5¼-inch floppy disk
FD	360K 5¼-inch floppy disk
FE	160K 5¼-inch floppy disk
FF	320K 5¼-inch floppy disk

If CHKDSK reports that a disk is a probable non-DOS disk, use DISKINFO to display the disk's media descriptor value.

Disk Sides

Hard disks have several disk platters for storing information. Depending upon the disk type, the number of platter sides the drive can record on will differ. The DISKINFO Disk Sides field tells you the number of platter sides available on your disk for recording. Using the number of sides, tracks per side, sectors per track, and the sector size, you can determine a disk's total storage capabilities as follows:

```
Storage = (Sides) * (Tracks/Side) * (Sectors/Track) *
          (Sector Size)
```

As discussed in Chapter 1, many disks that use voice coil actuators to move the disk heads from one track to another require positioning data on the disk. In some cases, the controller may record the positioning data between disk tracks. Other controllers use one side of a disk platter to store this information. As such, your disk may not always have an even number of sides for data storage.

Sectors/Cluster

To reduce the size of the FAT and to reduce disk fragmentation, DOS allocates file space using a group of sectors called a cluster. Depending upon the disk type and partition size, the number of sectors in each cluster will differ. Most hard disks use four sectors per cluster.

Each time DOS creates a file, DOS allocates a cluster of disk space for the file. Assuming the cluster size is four sectors, the initial disk space allocated for the file is 2,048 bytes. Even if the file contains only one character (or byte) of information, DOS reserves a cluster of disk space for the file. If the file is larger than a cluster, DOS allocates the number of clusters specified. In Chapter 9 you learned how allocating disk space a cluster at a time reduces disk fragmentation as files grow. However, if you create small files that never grow, the unused sectors in the cluster are wasted. The wasted disk space for small files is a fact of life that you can't change.

The DISKINFO Sectors/Cluster field tells you the number of sectors DOS allocates for each cluster of disk space. You can use this value to better understand file storage. Assume, for example, that your hard disk has only 2,048 free bytes of disk remaining. Next, assume that you want to copy ten files from drive A and that each file is five bytes in size. At first glance, DOS can easily copy the files leaving 1,998 bytes of disk space available.

```
  2,048  bytes available
-    50  bytes (10 files of five bytes each)
  1,998  bytes remaining
```

If you perform the file copy, the operation will fail after the first file is copied, and DOS will display the following error message:

```
Insufficient disk space
```

When DOS copies the first file, DOS allocates a cluster of disk space for the file. Assuming the cluster size is four sectors, DOS allocates the entire 2,048 bytes of available disk space. To copy all 10 five-byte files, the disk would need 20,480 bytes of free disk space.

```
    10  files
×  2,048  bytes (cluster size)
  20,480  bytes
```

Each time the DIR command executes, it displays the amount of free disk space.

```
nn File(s) nnnn bytes free
```

The amount of free disk space DIR displays is always a multiple of the cluster size. DIR does not add file sizes to determine the amount of disk space. Instead, it scans the FAT for available clusters. It then determines the number of bytes free by multiplying the number of available clusters times the cluster size and sector size.

```
Bytes Free = (Available Clusters) * (Sectors/Cluster) *
             (Sector Size)
```

Using the previous DISKINFO output, you can determine the free disk space as follows:

```
Bytes Free = 10,025 * 4 * 512
           = 20,531,200 bytes
```

Total Sectors

The DISKINFO Total Sectors field tells you the number of total sectors on disk. Depending on your disk type, the total sectors is greater than or equal to the following:

```
Total Sectors >= (Total Clusters) * (Sectors/Cluster) +
                  (Reserved Sectors)
```

Depending upon the number of sectors the disk consumes for the partition's master boot record, the total sectors may differ slightly from the result of the previous equation.

Number of FATs

The file allocation table is the disk road map DOS follows to locate files. The FAT tracks the used, unused, and damaged clusters on your disk. The FAT resides on disk immediately following the boot record. To keep a single disk error in any one of the FAT sectors from preventing DOS from accessing the files on disk, DOS places two copies of the FAT on your hard disk. If the first FAT becomes damaged, DOS uses the second.

Sectors/FAT

To store the file allocation table on disk, DOS reserves a specific number of sectors that immediately follow the boot record. The DISKINFO Sectors/FAT field displays the number of sectors DOS allocates for each FAT. Using the previous DISKINFO output, DOS allocates 64 sectors for two FATs (128 sectors total).

FAT Entry Type

For simplicity, each of the examples in this book has assumed that each value in the FAT mapped directly to a cluster. The first five FAT entries, therefore, would point to the first five clusters. For disks 20M or larger, this assumption is valid. Each FAT entry is 16 bits (2 bytes) long and maps to a cluster value.

To reduce the FAT size for smaller disks, however, DOS reduces the FAT entry size to 12 bits. As a result, DOS reduces the FAT size by 25%.

To end users, the FAT entry type is of little importance. For programmers writing disk utility programs, knowledge of the FAT type is essential. In general, DOS uses a 12-bit FAT entry for disks with less than 4,085 clusters and a 16-bit FAT entry for all other disks.

Maximum Root Directory Entries

DOS sets aside a fixed number of sectors to store files in a disk's root directory. Because the size of the root directory is fixed, the root directory can store only a specific number of files or subdirectory entries. The DISKINFO Maximum Root Directory Entries field tells you the number of entries the root directory of your disk can hold. Table 11.3 lists several common root directory entry restrictions.

Table 11.3.   *Maximum root entries per disk type.*

Disk Type	Maximum Root Entries
160K disk	64
360K disk	112
720K disk	112
1.2M disk	224
1.44M disk	224
Hard disk	512

Sectors Reserved for Root

As just discussed, DOS reserves a specific number of sectors on each disk to store the root directory entries. The DISKINFO Sectors Reserved for Root field displays the number of sectors DOS reserves for root entries. Table 11.4 contains the number of sectors DOS reserves for common disk types.

Table 11.4.   *Sectors reserved for root entries by disk type.*

Disk Type	Root Sectors
160K	4
360K	7
720K	7
1.2M	14
1.44M	14
Hard disk	32

Total Clusters

Since DOS allocates file space using groups of sectors called clusters, most hard disks use a cluster size of four sectors. The DISKINFO Total Clusters field contains the number of clusters on your disk. Each cluster has a corresponding file allocation table entry. If you multiply the total number of clusters times the cluster size and sector size, you can determine the disk storage as shown here:

```
Disk Storage = (Total Clusters) * (Sectors/Cluster) *
               (Sector Size)
```

Using the previous DISKINFO output, the total disk space is determined as follows:

```
Disk Storage = 16,333 * 4 * 512
             = 33,449,984 bytes
```

Free Clusters

The DISKINFO Free Clusters field tells you the number of available clusters on your disk. DOS keeps track of available clusters by placing the value 0 in the FAT entry for available clusters. If you multiply the number of free clusters times the number of sectors per cluster and sector size, you can determine the amount of available disk space as follows:

```
Available Disk Space = (Free Clusters) * (Sectors/Cluster) *
                       (Sector Size)
```

Using the previous DISKINFO output, the available disk space is determined as follows:

```
Available Disk Space = 10,025 * 4 * 512
                     = 20,531,200
```

Clusters in Use

The DISKINFO Clusters in Use field tells you the number of clusters either in use for storage or unavailable due to a damaged sector identified by FORMAT. If you need to know the amount of damaged disk space, invoke the CHKDSK command. If you multiply the number of used clusters times the number of sectors per cluster and sector size, you can determine the amount of used or damaged disk space as follows.

```
Used Disk Space = (Used Clusters) * (Sectors/Cluster) *
                  (Sector Size)
```

Using the previous DISKINFO output, the amount of used disk space is determined as follows:

```
Used Disk Space = 6,308 * 4 * 512
                = 12,918,784 bytes
```

Sectors Reserved for Boot Record, FATs, and Root

Every DOS disk begins with a boot record, one or more file allocation tables, and a root directory. Depending on the size of your disk, the amount of disk space DOS allocates for these entries varies. The number of DISKINFO sectors reserved for boot record, FATs, and root field tells you the number of sectors DOS reserves on your disk. The remaining disk sectors are classified as file or data space as shown in the following figure.

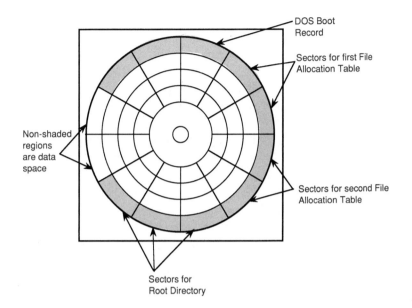

Using the previous DISKINFO output, you can determine the number of reserved sectors as follows:

```
Reserved Sectors = Boot Sector + (Number of FATs *
                   Sectors Per FAT) + Root Sectors

Reserved Sectors = 1 + (2 * 64) + 32
                 = 161 sectors
```

Disk Space Total

The DISKINFO Disk Space Total field tells you the number of bytes your disk can store excluding the sectors reserved by DOS. In other words, this value tells you the number of bytes of file space. DOS does not include the boot, FAT, and root directory sectors in this value.

Free Disk Space

The DISKINFO Free Disk Space field tells you the amount of disk space DOS can still allocate for files. DOS determines this value by searching the file allocation table for available clusters.

Disk Space in Use

The DISKINFO Disk Space in Use field tells you the number of bytes currently used for file storage or unavailable due to damaged sectors. If you divide this value by the total disk space, you can determine the percentage of your disk currently in use.

```
Percent of Disk Space Used = (Space in Use / Total Disk
                              Space) * 100
```

Using the previous DISKINFO output, the percentage of disk space in use becomes the following:

```
Percent of Disk Space Used = (12,918,784 / 33,449,984) * 100
                           = .386 * 100
                           = 38.6%
```

Understanding DISKINFO Error Messages

If DISKINFO cannot access your disk, DISKINFO will display an error message and return control to DOS. The following section discusses DISKINFO error messages and their probable causes.

```
DISKINFO: Requires DOS 2.0 or higher
```

Prior to DOS version 2.0, DOS did not support hard disks. DISKINFO requires DOS version 2.0 or greater to execute.

```
DISKINFO: Invalid disk drive specification
```

This error message tells you that your DISKINFO command line contains an invalid disk drive letter or that the drive letter is not followed by a colon. Reissue the command with a complete drive letter
```
C:\DISKUTIL> DISKINFO A:.
```

```
DISKINFO: Error reading disk storage information
```

DISKINFO displays this error message when either the disk specified in the DISKINFO command line is invalid, or DOS cannot access the drive due to a disk error. For example, if you invoke DISKINFO with an invalid drive, DISKINFO displays the error message shown here:

```
C:\DISKUTIL> DISKINFO E:
DISKINFO: Error reading disk storage information
```

Likewise, if you invoke DISKCOPY to examine an unformatted disk, DISKINFO displays the error. If DISKINFO cannot access your disk and the DOS DIR command also fails, your disk has a serious error. You may need to format your disk and restore your backups.

```
DISKINFO: Error reading boot record
```

If DISKINFO displays this message, DOS is able to access your disk's file allocation table but not the boot record. Reboot your computer and repeat the command. If DOS cannot boot from your hard disk, boot your computer from drive A using the same version of DOS and then issue the following SYS command to rebuild the boot record:

```
A> SYS C:
```

If SYS is not successful, but you can still access the files on your fixed disk, perform a disk backup operation as discussed in Chapter 8. If the backup operation is successful, format your hard disk as shown.

```
A> FORMAT C: /S
```

When FORMAT completes, restore the backup files to your hard disk.

```
DISKINFO: SUBST and ASSIGN not supported
```

As discussed in Chapter 5, DOS lets you create logical disk drives using the SUBST command. Logical drives let users abbreviate long directory names with a single drive letter as shown here.

```
C:\DISKUTIL> SUBST E: C:\DATABASE\JANUARY
```

In this case, DOS will abbreviate the directory name C:\DATABASE\JANUARY with the drive letter E. Most of the utilities in the companion disk do not support logical disk drives. If you invoke DISKINFO with a logical disk drive, DISKINFO will display the following error message:

```
C:\DISKUTIL> DISKINFO E:
DISKINFO: SUBST and ASSIGN not supported
```

How DISKINFO Works

Because every disk is different, DOS and DISKINFO must have a means of finding out the disk's specifics. For example, if you have a 1.2M disk drive, the drive can read both 1.2M and 360K disks. Each time you refer to the drive, DOS must determine the number of sectors, tracks, and sides the current disk contains.

Every DOS disk contains a boot record in the first sector. As discussed, the boot record lets DOS boot from the disk or displays the message:

```
Non-system disk or disk error
Replace and strike any key when ready
```

In addition, the boot record contains specifics about the disk. For example, the boot record for a DOS 3.3 disk contains the fields shown in the following figure.

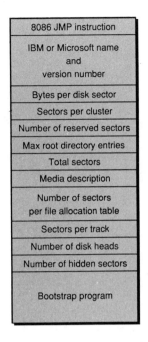

By reading and examining the boot record, DOS is able to determine specifics about your disk. The DISKINFO utility obtains its information in this same way.

12

Working with File Attributes

Working with File Attributes

In Chapter 5 you learned that DOS assigns attribute values to every file on your disk. At that time, you learned that the ATTRIB command lets you set or display a file's archive and read-only attribute settings. As it turns out, DOS actually defines other file attribute values. The FILEATTR utility provided with the Jamsa Disk Utilities lets you easily and quickly set and display a file's archive, read-only, hidden, and system attributes using a menu interface. As you will see, the FILEATTR command is much easier to use and offers more functionality than the ATTRIB command.

Every file on your disk has a date and time stamp that DOS uses to track the date and time you created or last changed a file. The DIR command displays each file's date and time stamp as shown in the following figure.

FORMAT.   COM   22923   06-17-88   12:00p

Date and time
stamp

Remember, DOS only changes a file's date and time stamp when you change the file's contents. Simply reading or displaying the file does not affect the file's contents and, therefore, does not change the date and time stamp.

Assume, for example, that the battery-powered clock that stores your computer's date and time wears out and you inadvertently create files with an incorrect date (many systems will use 01/01/1980). The DATETIME utility provided on the companion disk lets you quickly and easily change a file's date and time stamp using a menu interface. Likewise, many professional software developers assign the same date to all files they distribute to end users. The DATETIME utility makes such operations easy.

Understanding File Attributes

The FILEATTR utility lets you set and display a file's archive, read-only, hidden, and system attributes. The next few sections examine each of these attributes in detail.

The Archive Attribute

The DOS BACKUP command as well as other third-party backup utilities use the archive attribute to perform incremental backup operations. Recall from Chapter 8 that an incremental backup copies only those files that have been created or changed since the last backup operation. For users that perform backups regularly, incremental backups require only a few minutes each day.

To understand how incremental backups work, you must understand how DOS uses the archive attribute. Every time you create or change a file on your disk, DOS sets the file's archive attribute. If you display the attributes for the file in the DISKUTIL directory, for example, the ATTRIB command will display the following.

```
C:\> ATTRIB \DISKUTIL\*.*
    A        C:\DISKUTIL\DATETIME.EXE
    A        C:\DISKUTIL\DISKINFO.EXE
    A        C:\DISKUTIL\DISKSAVE.EXE
    A        C:\DISKUTIL\FILEATTR.EXE
    A        C:\DISKUTIL\FINDFILE.EXE
    A        C:\DISKUTIL\KILLFILE.EXE
    A        C:\DISKUTIL\POWER.EXE
    A        C:\DISKUTIL\RENDIR.EXE
    A        C:\DISKUTIL\SELCOPY.EXE
    A        C:\DISKUTIL\SELDEL.EXE
    A        C:\DISKUTIL\SORTDIR.EXE
    A        C:\DISKUTIL\SQUEEZE.EXE
```

```
A            C:\DISKUTIL\TESTFRAG.EXE
A            C:\DISKUTIL\UNDELETE.EXE
A            C:\DISKUTIL\UNFORMAT.EXE
```

The uppercase A that precedes each file name indicates that the file needs to be archived or backed up. In other words, these files have been added to your disk since the last backup operation.

Assuming that you later back up your disk, DOS will remove the archive attribute for each of these files as it successfully backs them up. If you invoke the ATTRIB command for the same files following a backup operation, the uppercase letter A is no longer displayed.

```
C:\> ATTRIB \DISKUTIL\*.*
            C:\DISKUTIL\DATETIME.EXE
            C:\DISKUTIL\DISKINFO.EXE
            C:\DISKUTIL\DISKSAVE.EXE
            C:\DISKUTIL\FILEATTR.EXE
            C:\DISKUTIL\FINDFILE.EXE
            C:\DISKUTIL\KILLFILE.EXE
            C:\DISKUTIL\POWER.EXE
            C:\DISKUTIL\RENDIR.EXE
            C:\DISKUTIL\SELCOPY.EXE
            C:\DISKUTIL\SELDEL.EXE
            C:\DISKUTIL\SORTDIR.EXE
            C:\DISKUTIL\SQUEEZE.EXE
            C:\DISKUTIL\TESTFRAG.EXE
            C:\DISKUTIL\UNDELETE.EXE
            C:\DISKUTIL\UNFORMAT.EXE
```

Because DOS has successfully backed up these files, the archive attribute is no longer set.

In the case of the disk utilities that already reside on the floppy disks provided with this book, you may not want your backup operation to make unnecessary duplicates of these files. By removing the archive-required attribute before backing up the files using ATTRIB or FILEATTR, you can speed up your backup operation.

Archive File Attribute

DOS uses the archive file attribute to determine which files you have created or changed since the last system backup. By examining the archive attribute, the DOS BACKUP command or other third-party backup software can quickly determine which files on your disk need to be copied to a floppy disk. By performing these incremental backup operations, you spend much less time backing up your disk and much more productive time with your computer.

The Read-Only Attribute

The read-only file attribute lets you protect a file from being deleted, modified, or inadvertently overwritten. If you have key files on your disk whose contents never change, you should set the file to read-only. The commands in your DOS subdirectory are excellent candidates for read-only files.

To better understand the read-only attribute, create the file READONLY.DAT that contains the following:

```
C:\DISKUTIL> COPY CON READONLY.DAT
Read-only files cannot be deleted.
^Z
     1 File(s) copied
```

Next, using the DOS ATTRIB command, set the file to read-only as shown here.

```
C:\DISKUTIL> ATTRIB +R READONLY.DAT
```

Using the DEL command, try to delete the file.

```
C:\DISKUTIL> DEL READONLY.DAT
Access denied
```

The `Access denied` message tells you that DOS did not have access to delete the file. Because the file is read-only, it cannot be changed or deleted.

Using the ATTRIB command, remove the read-only attribute as shown here.

```
C:\DISKUTIL> ATTRIB -R READONLY.DAT
```

Repeating the DEL command

```
C:\DISKUTIL> DEL READONLY.DAT
```

the file READONLY.DAT is no longer protected and is deleted.

A directory listing reveals that the file no longer resides on your disk.

```
C:\DISKUTIL> DIR READONLY.DAT
File not found
```

Using the FILEATTR utility, you can easily assign the read-only attribute to key files in your directory.

Read-Only File Attribute

DOS uses the read-only file attribute to restrict use of a file to read operations only. For example, a program that reads and displays, or reads and copies, a file's contents can access a read-only file as it requires. A program cannot, however, change the contents of a read-only file. Likewise, DOS cannot delete read-only files. Users protect their key files by setting the file's read-only attribute.

The Hidden Attribute

A *hidden file* is a file that exists on your disk but does not appear in the current directory. MS-DOS, for example, assigns the hidden file attribute to the files MSDOS.SYS and IO.SYS that reside in your root directory. DOS hides these files to prevent you from inadvertently deleting, renaming, or moving them.

If you are using a system shared by other users, there may be times when you want to protect your files without actually removing the files from disk. By setting a file's hidden attribute, your file won't appear in DOS directory listings. As such, other users won't know the file exists on disk. When you later need to access the file, you can unhide it. Using FILEATTR, you can hide and unhide files with two keystrokes.

Hidden File Attribute

Hidden files exist on your disk but do not appear in the DOS directory listing. Every time you format a bootable DOS disk, DOS copies two hidden files onto the disk that DOS uses during its start-up process. DOS hides these two key files to prevent you from inadvertently deleting, renaming, or moving them. Using the FILEATTR utility provided on the companion disk, you can hide your own files to protect them from other users who share the system. Unless another user knows that the file is hidden, that user will not be able to find the hidden file.

The System Attribute

In addition to hidden files, DOS supports system files. Like hidden files, system files do not appear in the DOS directory listing. DOS distinguishes hidden files from system files in that *system files* exist to perform an operating system task. The FILEATTR lets you access the system attribute, but in most cases you will not need to.

System File Attributes

DOS uses the system file attribute to hide a file in a directory as well as to specify that the file is an operating system file. Most users will never need to use the system file attribute. You should reserve its use for DOS.

Using the FILEATTR Utility

Invoke FILEATTR by typing its name at the DOS prompt as shown here.

```
C:\> FILEATTR
```

FILEATTR displays its main menu, prompting you to enter a directory name as shown here. If you simply press Enter at the directory name prompt, FILEATTR will use the current directory.

```
┌────────────────────────────────────────────────────────────────────┐
│  ┌──────────────────────────────────────────────────────────────┐  │
│  │  File Attributes, Jamsa Utilities Version 1.0 (C) 1989-90 Kris Jamsa  │  │
│  └──────────────────────────────────────────────────────────────┘  │
│                                                                      │
│  Directory:                                                          │
│  Status: █Press Enter for current directory or Esc to Exit.█        │
└────────────────────────────────────────────────────────────────────┘
```

In this case, type in the subdirectory name DISKUTIL.

```
┌────────────────────────────────────────────────────────────────────┐
│  ┌──────────────────────────────────────────────────────────────┐  │
│  │  File Attributes, Jamsa Utilities Version 1.0 (C) 1989-90 Kris Jamsa  │  │
│  └──────────────────────────────────────────────────────────────┘  │
│                                                                      │
│  Directory: █\DISKUTIL█                                              │
│  Status: ███████████████████████████████████████                    │
└────────────────────────────────────────────────────────────────────┘
```

FILEATTR will display the message "Working.." as it searches the disk for the directory. If FILEATTR successfully locates the directory, FILEATTR will display the files in the directory along with their archive, read-only, hidden, and system attributes.

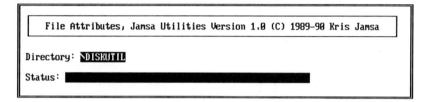

```
┌──────────────────────────────────────────────────────────────────────┐
│  ┌──────────────────────────────────────────────────────────────┐    │
│  │  Use arrow keys to highlight an attribute. Press space bar to select │    │
│  │  or unselect an attribute. Press F10 to update files or Esc to exit. │    │
│  │                                                                │    │
│  │  FILENAME.EXT  Arc R/O Sys Hid      Size      Date     Time    │    │
│  │                                                                │    │
│  │  DATETIME.EXE  █Arc█           77,032 bytes  03-29-90  14:52   │    │
│  │  DISKINFO.EXE  Arc             59,110 bytes  03-29-90  14:52   │    │
│  │  DISKSAVE.EXE  Arc             58,014 bytes  03-29-90  14:52   │    │
│  │  FILEATTR.EXE  Arc             72,184 bytes  03-29-90  14:52   │    │
│  │  FINDFILE.EXE  Arc             56,784 bytes  03-29-90  14:52   │    │
│  │  KILLFILE.EXE  Arc             72,694 bytes  03-29-90  14:53   │    │
│  │  POWER   .EXE  Arc             66,064 bytes  03-29-90  14:53   │    │
│  │  RENDIR  .EXE  Arc             64,148 bytes  03-29-90  14:53   │    │
│  └──────────────────────────────────────────────────────────────┘    │
│  ┌──────────────────────────────────────────────────────────────┐    │
│  │  Directory: C:\DISKUTIL                                        │    │
│  └──────────────────────────────────────────────────────────────┘    │
└──────────────────────────────────────────────────────────────────────┘
```

In this case, the file's archive attributes are set, and FILEATTR in turn displays the letters "Arc" next to the file name. Using the arrow keys, you can examine the attributes for each file in the directory.

To set an attribute, use the right- and left-arrow keys to highlight a specific attribute. Pressing the space bar sets or removes an option. For example, select the file DISKINFO.EXE. Next, highlight the R/O or read-only attribute. When you press the space bar, FILEATTR sets the read-only attribute for DISKINFO.EXE as shown here.

```
┌─────────────────────────────────────────────────────────────────┐
│ ┌─────────────────────────────────────────────────────────────┐ │
│ │ Use arrow keys to highlight an attribute. Press space bar to select │
│ │ or unselect an attribute. Press F10 to update files or Esc to exit. │
│ └─────────────────────────────────────────────────────────────┘ │
│                                                                   │
│   FILENAME.EXT   Arc R/O Sys Hid      Size      Date      Time    │
│                                                                   │
│   DATETIME.EXE   Arc              77,032 bytes  03-29-90   14:52  │
│   DISKINFO.EXE   Arc R/O          59,110 bytes  03-29-90   14:52  │
│   DISKSAVE.EXE   Arc              58,014 bytes  03-29-90   14:52  │
│   FILEATTR.EXE   Arc              72,184 bytes  03-29-90   14:52  │
│   FINDFILE.EXE   Arc              56,784 bytes  03-29-90   14:52  │
│   KILLFILE.EXE   Arc              72,694 bytes  03-29-90   14:53  │
│   POWER   .EXE   Arc              66,064 bytes  03-29-90   14:53  │
│   RENDIR  .EXE   Arc              64,148 bytes  03-29-90   14:53  │
│                                                                   │
│ ┌─────────────────────────────────────────────────────────────┐ │
│ │ Directory: C:\DISKUTIL                                         │ │
│ └─────────────────────────────────────────────────────────────┘ │
└─────────────────────────────────────────────────────────────────┘
```

If you press the space bar a second time, FILEATTR will remove the read-only attribute as shown in the next figure.

```
┌─────────────────────────────────────────────────────────────────┐
│ ┌─────────────────────────────────────────────────────────────┐ │
│ │ Use arrow keys to highlight an attribute. Press space bar to select │
│ │ or unselect an attribute. Press F10 to update files or Esc to exit. │
│ └─────────────────────────────────────────────────────────────┘ │
│                                                                   │
│   FILENAME.EXT   Arc R/O Sys Hid      Size      Date      Time    │
│                                                                   │
│   DATETIME.EXE   Arc              77,032 bytes  03-29-90   14:52  │
│   DISKINFO.EXE   Arc ▮            59,110 bytes  03-29-90   14:52  │
│   DISKSAVE.EXE   Arc              58,014 bytes  03-29-90   14:52  │
│   FILEATTR.EXE   Arc              72,184 bytes  03-29-90   14:52  │
│   FINDFILE.EXE   Arc              56,784 bytes  03-29-90   14:52  │
│   KILLFILE.EXE   Arc              72,694 bytes  03-29-90   14:53  │
│   POWER   .EXE   Arc              66,064 bytes  03-29-90   14:53  │
│   RENDIR  .EXE   Arc              64,148 bytes  03-29-90   14:53  │
│                                                                   │
│ ┌─────────────────────────────────────────────────────────────┐ │
│ │ Directory: C:\DISKUTIL                                         │ │
│ └─────────────────────────────────────────────────────────────┘ │
└─────────────────────────────────────────────────────────────────┘
```

The space bar, therefore, works as a toggle. If an attribute is set, pressing the space bar removes the attribute. If an attribute is not set, pressing the space bar assigns the attributes.

Understanding Hidden Files

A hidden file exists on your disk but does not appear in the directory listing. Invoke FILEATTR and select the file DISKINFO.EXE. Set the file's hidden attribute. Remember, you must press F10 for FILEATTR to record the attribute change on disk. Next, exit FILEATTR and perform a directory listing of DISKUTIL.

```
C:\> DIR \DISKUTIL

   Volume in drive C is DOS
   Directory of  C:\DISKUTIL

DATETIME EXE     77032     3-29-90     2:52p
DISKSAVE EXE     58014     3-29-90     2:52p
FILEATTR EXE     72184     3-29-90     2:52p
FINDFILE EXE     56784     3-29-90     2:52p
KILLFILE EXE     72694     3-29-90     2:53p
POWER    EXE     66064     3-29-90     2:53p
RENDIR   EXE     64148     3-29-90     2:53p
SELCOPY  EXE     75328     3-29-90     2:53p
SELDEL   EXE     70220     3-29-90     2:53p
SORTDIR  EXE     70860     3-29-90     2:54p
SQUEEZE  EXE     64014     3-29-90     2:54p
TESTFRAG EXE     56470     3-29-90     2:54p
UNDELETE EXE     74424     3-29-90     2:54p
UNFORMAT EXE     60586     3-29-90     2:54p
         16 File(s)   19607552 bytes free
```

The file DISKINFO.EXE does not appear in the directory listing. If you invoke DISKINFO, it displays your disk's specifics as discussed in Chapter 11.

If you know a hidden file exists on your disk, you can access the file. If you don't know the file exists, you have no way of discovering it.

Invoke FILEATTR and remove the hidden attribute from DISKINFO.EXE. Hidden attributes may solve some of your problems of preventing other users from accessing your critical files. However, if you forget where you've hidden a file, the only way to locate the file is using FILEATTR. Most users hide files only in very special cases.

FILEATTR lets you first assign all the file attributes you want before it actually updates each file's directory entry on disk. To update the directory entry, press F10. FILEATTR will display its third screen as shown here.

```
┌─────────────────────────────────────────────────────────────────┐
│  ┌─────────────────────────────────────────────────────────────┐ │
│  │ Select Cancel to return to file list.  Select Continue to update files. │ │
│  └─────────────────────────────────────────────────────────────┘ │
│                                                                   │
│  Directory: C:\DISKUTIL                                           │
│                                                                   │
│  Update Operation:    Cancel      Continue                        │
│                                                                   │
│  Status:                                                          │
└─────────────────────────────────────────────────────────────────┘
```

This screen lets FILEATTR ensure that you really want to update the files on disk. If you select the Cancel option, FILEATTR returns to the file screen without updating the files on disk. If you select Continue, FILEATTR records the new file attributes on disk.

In this case, select the Continue option and press Enter, FILEATTR updates the files as shown in the following figure.

```
┌─────────────────────────────────────────────────────────────────┐
│  ┌─────────────────────────────────────────────────────────────┐ │
│  │ Select Cancel to return to file list.  Select Continue to update files. │ │
│  └─────────────────────────────────────────────────────────────┘ │
│                                                                   │
│  Directory: C:\DISKUTIL                                           │
│                                                                   │
│  Update Operation:    Cancel      Continue                        │
│                                                                   │
│  Status:  FILEATTR: Attribute update complete.  Press any key to continue. │
└─────────────────────────────────────────────────────────────────┘
```

When you press Enter, FILEATTR returns to the file menu. You can update additional files repeating this process, or you can press Esc to return to DOS.

Using FILEATTR Fast Keys

By using the arrow key and space bar, you can set the attribute of a specific file. In some cases, you may want to update several files quickly. If you press the F8 function key, FILEATTR toggles the current attribute for the current file and advances the highlight to the next file. By holding the F8 key down, you can quickly toggle the attribute for all files in the directory. The F7 key works in a similar manner, moving the file highlight up toward the first file in the directory list.

Understanding FILEATTR Error Messages

The FILEATTR utility displays several different error messages in its status box. The following section describes the causes and solutions to these error messages.

`FILEATTR: Requires DOS 2.0 or higher`

Prior to version 2, DOS did not provide support for hard disks. The programs on the companion disk, therefore, require DOS 2.0 as a minimum.

`FILEATTR: Only specify .. once in directory name`

The FILEATTR utility supports the use of the parent directory abbreviation (..). For example, assume that you are in a DOS subdirectory. Using the parent directory abbreviation, you can use FILEATTR to access files residing in the parent as shown here.

```
┌──────────────────────────────────────────────────────────────────┐
│ ┌────────────────────────────────────────────────────────────────┐ │
│ │   File Attributes, Jamsa Utilities Version 1.0 (C) 1989-90 Kris Jamsa │ │
│ └────────────────────────────────────────────────────────────────┘ │
│                                                                    │
│ Directory: ██                                                      │
│ Status: ████████████████████████████████████████████              │
└──────────────────────────────────────────────────────────────────┘
```

To avoid confusion when multiple levels of directories are used, FILEATTR lets you specify the parent directory abbreviation only once per directory name. Should this error occur, simply use a complete path name to the directory.

`FILEATTR: The abbreviation .. must appear at start of path name`

As just discussed, FILEATTR fully supports the parent subdirectory abbreviation (..). If you specify this abbreviation, the abbreviation must occur at the beginning of the path name.

`FILEATTR: Invalid file or drive specification`

If the disk drive specified does not exist, FILEATTR displays this error message and returns control to DOS. Should this error occur, make sure you are using a valid disk drive letter. If the disk drive is valid, invoke the DISKINFO utility discussed in Chapter 11 to examine the disk drive.

`FILEATTR: SUBST and ASSIGN not supported`

As discussed in Chapter 5, DOS lets you create logical disk drives using the SUBST command. Logical drives let users abbreviate long directory names with a single drive letter. To prevent confusion from logical drives, FILEATTR simply does not support them.

`FILEATTR: Network drives not supported`

In most cases, running disk management utilities on a disk drive used by a local area network can be quite dangerous. Disk utilities work by accessing individual sectors of a disk. In a network, access to a disk is controlled by network software. To prevent an incompatibility between the network software and the disk utility software from damaging your disk, the low-level utilities on the companion disk do not support network drives.

`FILEATTR: Sector size must be 512 or 1,024 bytes`

Most DOS disks use 512-byte sectors. Several third-party software packages let users format their disks using 1,024-byte sectors. The packages do this to provide support for partitions greater than 32M. The disk utilities provided on the companion disk support these two sector sizes only.

`FILEATTR: Insufficient memory`

To perform its processing, FILEATTR requires memory to hold disk sectors, FAT, and cluster information as well as its own tables. If FILEATTR cannot allocate sufficient memory, it displays an error message and returns control to DOS. Although the memory requirements vary based upon your disk size and the number of files in each directory, most of the companion disk utilities require a maximum of 256K.

`FILEATTR: Error reading file allocation table`

To track files and directories, the disk utilities provided on the companion disk must read cluster information from the FAT. If a utility encounters an error while reading the FAT, the utility displays an error message and exits to DOS.

Should this error occur, test your disk using CHKDSK. File allocation table errors are very serious. Back up your disk immediately. You may need to format your disk and restore backups to correct the error.

`FILEATTR: Directory not found`

If FILEATTR cannot locate the directory containing the desired files, FILEATTR displays an error message and exits to DOS. Should this error message occur, make sure you are using a correct and complete path name to the subdirectory. This error is most often caused by omitting backslashes in the path name.

`FILEATTR: Error reading directory sector`

If this error occurs, FILEATTR encountered an error while attempting to read one of the sectors containing directory information. This error is often a sign of bad times to come. Should this error occur, back up your disk immediately. Next, invoke CHKDSK to examine your disk. You may need to format your disk to remove the damaged sector, restoring your backup files.

`FILEATTR: Error updating FILENAME.EXT. Press any key to continue.`

If FILEATTR is unable to change the attributes of the file specified, FILEATTR displays the error message and continues updating the remainder of the files you selected. FILEATTR should be able to update all files on your disk. Should this error message occur, run CHKDSK to examine your disk. If CHKDSK does not encounter errors, reboot your system and repeat your attempt to modify the file's attributes. If the error persists, try to remove all of the file's attributes.

`FILEATTR: Attribute update complete. Press any key to continue.`

After FILEATTR updates the last file you have selected, FILEATTR will display a completion message and prompt you to press any key to continue. When you press a key, FILEATTR returns to the file menu, allowing you to update additional files or to exit to DOS.

How FILEATTR Works

As shown in the following figure, every directory entry on your disk stores a file attribute byte.

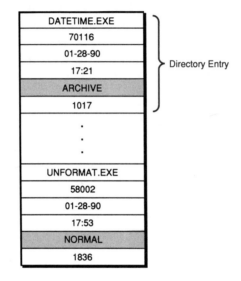

FILEATTR reads each file's attributes displaying them for you on the screen. When you change a file's attribute and press the F10 key to update the disk, FILEATTR records the new attribute on disk as shown in the next figure.

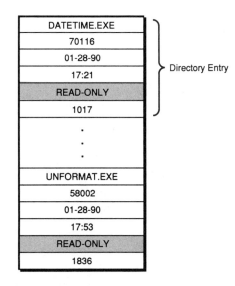

Using the DATETIME Utility

Recall that DOS records the date and time whenever you create or modify a file in the file's directory entry. The DATETIME utility lets you quickly assign a new date and time stamp to one or more files in a directory. Invoke DATETIME from the DOS prompt as follows:

```
C:\> DATETIME
```

DATETIME displays its first screen, prompting you to enter a directory name. Type in the directory name DISKUTIL as shown here.

```
Date and Time Stamps, Jamsa Utilities Version 1.0 (C) 1989-90 Kris Jamsa

Directory: DISKUTIL
Status:
```

DATETIME displays the message "Working.." as it searches your disk for the subdirectory. If DATETIME locates the directory, DATETIME displays its second screen, which prompts you to enter the desired date and time stamp.

```
┌─────────────────────────────────────────────────────────────┐
│ ┌───────────────────────────────────────────────────────────┐ │
│ │  Edit date if necessary. Press Enter to edit time. When date and time │ │
│ │  are correct, press Enter to select files or press Esc to return to DOS. │ │
│ │                                                           │ │
│ │  File Date: ██-09-90                                      │ │
│ │                                                           │ │
│ │  File Time: 12:33                                         │ │
│ └───────────────────────────────────────────────────────────┘ │
└─────────────────────────────────────────────────────────────┘
```

By default, DATETIME displays the current date and time. If you are
satisfied with the date, press Enter; otherwise, type in the date desired.
Next, edit the time as required. When you press Enter, DATETIME
displays the files in the current directory as shown.

```
┌──────────────────────────────────────────────────────────────┐
│ ┌────────────────────────────────────────────────────────────┐ │
│ │ Use arrow keys to highlight. Press Enter to select/unselect files. │ │
│ │ Press F9 to change date. Press F10 to update files or Esc to exit. │ │
│ │                                                            │ │
│ │   DATETIME.EXE    77,032 bytes    03-29-1990    14:52:06   │ │
│ │   DISKINFO.EXE    59,110 bytes    03-29-1990    14:52:14   │ │
│ │   DISKSAVE.EXE    58,014 bytes    03-29-1990    14:52:20   │ │
│ │   FILEATTR.EXE    72,184 bytes    03-29-1990    14:52:28   │ │
│ │   FINDFILE.EXE    56,784 bytes    03-29-1990    14:52:36   │ │
│ │   KILLFILE.EXE    72,694 bytes    03-29-1990    14:53:02   │ │
│ │   POWER   .EXE    66,064 bytes    03-29-1990    14:53:08   │ │
│ │   RENDIR  .EXE    64,148 bytes    03-29-1990    14:53:16   │ │
│ │   SELCOPY .EXE    75,328 bytes    03-29-1990    14:53:26   │ │
│ │   SELDEL  .EXE    70,220 bytes    03-29-1990    14:53:34   │ │
│ └────────────────────────────────────────────────────────────┘ │
│ ┌────────────────────────────────────────────────────────────┐ │
│ │ Directory: C:\DISKUTIL                                     │ │
│ └────────────────────────────────────────────────────────────┘ │
└──────────────────────────────────────────────────────────────┘
```

DATETIME lets you select one or more files for updating. To select a
file, highlight it using the arrow keys and then press either Enter or the
space bar. As shown here, DATETIME places an asterisk next to the file
name letting you know the file is selected.

```
┌─────────────────────────────────────────────────────────────────────┐
│ ┌─────────────────────────────────────────────────────────────────┐ │
│ │ Use arrow keys to highlight. Press Enter to select/unselect files. │ │
│ │ Press F9 to change date. Press F10 to update files or Esc to exit. │ │
│ └─────────────────────────────────────────────────────────────────┘ │
│                                                                       │
│      *DATETIME.EXE      77,032 bytes     03-29-1990     14:52:06       │
│      *DISKINFO.EXE      59,110 bytes     03-29-1990     14:52:14       │
│       DISKSAVE.EXE      58,014 bytes     03-29-1990     14:52:20       │
│       FILEATTR.EXE      72,184 bytes     03-29-1990     14:52:28       │
│      *FINDFILE.EXE      56,784 bytes     03-29-1990     14:52:36       │
│       KILLFILE.EXE      72,694 bytes     03-29-1990     14:53:02       │
│      *POWER   .EXE      66,064 bytes     03-29-1990     14:53:08       │
│       RENDIR  .EXE      64,148 bytes     03-29-1990     14:53:16       │
│       SELCOPY .EXE      75,328 bytes     03-29-1990     14:53:26       │
│       SELDEL  .EXE      70,220 bytes     03-29-1990     14:53:34       │
│                                                                       │
│ ┌─────────────────────────────────────────────────────────────────┐ │
│ │ Directory: C:\DISKUTIL                                            │ │
│ └─────────────────────────────────────────────────────────────────┘ │
└─────────────────────────────────────────────────────────────────────┘
```

The Enter key and space bar work as a toggle. If a file is not currently selected, pressing either Enter or the space bar selects a file. If a file is selected, pressing either of these keys unselects the file and directs DATETIME to remove the asterisk.

Once you select your files, press the F10 key to assign the new date and time stamps. When you do so, DATETIME displays its third screen as shown here.

```
┌─────────────────────────────────────────────────────────────────────┐
│ ┌─────────────────────────────────────────────────────────────────┐ │
│ │ Select Cancel to return to file list.  Select Continue to update files. │ │
│ └─────────────────────────────────────────────────────────────────┘ │
│                                                                       │
│  File Date: 04-09-90  File Time: 12:33                                │
│                                                                       │
│  Directory: C:\DISKUTIL                                               │
│                                                                       │
│  Update Operation:    Cancel     Continue                             │
│                                                                       │
│  Status:                                                              │
└─────────────────────────────────────────────────────────────────────┘
```

This screen lets DATETIME ensure that you really want to update the files. The screen shows your name of the selected directory and the desired date and time stamps. If you select Cancel, DATETIME returns you to the file menu. If you select Continue, DATETIME updates the directory entries on disk and then returns you to the file menu. DATETIME displays the files you previously selected with their new date and time stamps.

Changing the Date and Time Stamp

DATETIME lets you change the desired date and time stamp from the file menu by pressing F9. When you press F9, DATETIME displays the following menu, letting you enter a new date and time.

```
┌──────────────────────────────────────────────────────────────────┐
│ ┌──────────────────────────────────────────────────────────────┐ │
│ │ Edit date if necessary. Press Enter to edit time. When date  │ │
│ │ and time are correct, press Enter to select files or press   │ │
│ │ Esc to return to DOS.                                        │ │
│ └──────────────────────────────────────────────────────────────┘ │
│                                                                  │
│   File Date: ▓4-09-90                                            │
│                                                                  │
│   File Time: 12:33                                               │
│                                                                  │
└──────────────────────────────────────────────────────────────────┘
```

In so doing, DATETIME lets you easily assign several different date and time stamps to several different files in your directory.

Using DATETIME's Fast Keys

By using the space bar, you can quickly select a file for modification by DATETIME. In some cases, you may want to change the date and time for several files in the current directory. The F8 function key toggles the file selection marker and advances the file highlight down to the next file. By holding the F8 key down, you can quickly select all of the files in the current directory. The F7 function key works in a similar manner, advancing the file highlight up toward the beginning of the directory list.

Understanding DATETIME Error Messages

The DATETIME utility displays several possible error messages. The following sections describe in detail the causes and solutions for each error.

`DATETIME: Requires DOS 2.0 or higher`

Prior to version 2, DOS did not provide support for hard disks. The programs on the companion disk, therefore, require DOS 2.0 as a minimum.

```
DATETIME: Only specify .. once in directory name
```

The DATETIME utility supports the use of the parent directory abbreviation (..). For example, assume that you are in a DOS subdirectory. Using the parent directory abbreviation, you can use DATETIME to access files residing in the parent as shown here.

```
┌─────────────────────────────────────────────────────────────────┐
│ ┌─────────────────────────────────────────────────────────────┐ │
│ │ Date and Time Stamps, Jamsa Utilities Version 1.0 (C) 1989-90 Kris Jamsa │ │
│ └─────────────────────────────────────────────────────────────┘ │
│                                                                   │
│ Directory: ▓▓                                                     │
│ Status: ███████████████████████████████████████████████          │
└─────────────────────────────────────────────────────────────────┘
```

To avoid confusion when multiple levels of directories are used, DATETIME lets you specify the parent directory abbreviation only once per directory name. Should this error occur, simply use a complete path name to the directory.

```
DATETIME: The abbreviation .. must appear at start of path
name
```

As just discussed, DATETIME fully supports the parent subdirectory abbreviation (..). If you specify this abbreviation, it must occur at the beginning of the path name.

```
DATETIME: Invalid file or drive specification
```

If the disk drive specified does not exist, DATETIME displays this error message and returns control to DOS. Should this error occur, make sure you are using a valid disk drive letter. If the disk drive is valid, invoke the DISKINFO utility discussed in Chapter 11 to examine the disk drive.

```
DATETIME: SUBST and ASSIGN not supported
```

As discussed in Chapter 5, DOS lets you create logical disk drives using the SUBST command. Logical drives let users abbreviate long directory names with a single drive letter. To prevent confusion from logical drives, DATETIME simply does not support them.

```
DATETIME: Network drives not supported
```

In most cases, running disk management utilities on a disk drive used by a local area network can be quite dangerous. Disk utilities work by accessing individual sectors of a disk. In a network, access to a disk is controlled by network software. To prevent an incompatibility between the network software and the disk utility software from damaging your disk, the low-level utilities on the companion disk do not support network drives.

`DATETIME: Sector size must be 512 or 1,024 bytes`

Most DOS disks use 512-byte sectors. Several third-party software packages let users format their disks using 1024-byte sectors. The packages do this to provide support for partitions greater than 32M. The disk utilities provided on the companion disk support only these two sector sizes.

`DATETIME: Insufficient memory`

To perform its processing, DATETIME requires memory to hold disk sectors, FAT, and cluster information as well as its own tables. If DATETIME cannot allocate sufficient memory, it displays an error message and returns control to DOS. Although the memory requirements vary based upon your disk size and the number of files in each directory, most of the companion disk utilities require a maximum of 256K.

`DATETIME: Error reading file allocation table`

To track files and directories, the disk utilities provided on the companion disk must read cluster information from the FAT. If a utility encounters an error while reading the FAT, the utility displays an error message and exits to DOS.

Should this error occur, test your disk using CHKDSK. File allocation table errors are very serious. Back up your disk immediately. You may need to format your disk and restore backups to correct the error.

`DATETIME: Directory not found`

If DATETIME cannot locate the directory containing the desired files, DATETIME will display an error message and exit to DOS. Should this error message occur, make sure you are using a correct and complete path name to the subdirectory. This error is most often caused by omitting backslashes in the path name.

```
DATETIME: Error reading directory sector
```

If this error occurs, DATETIME encountered an error while attempting to read one of the sectors containing directory information. This error is often a sign of bad times to come. Should this error occur, back up your disk immediately. Next, invoke CHKDSK to examine your disk. You may need to format your disk to remove the damaged sector, restoring your backup files.

```
DATETIME: Error updating FILENAME.EXT. Press any key to
continue.
```

If DATETIME cannot change the date and time stamp of the file specified, DATETIME displays the error message and continues updating the remainder of the files you selected. DATETIME should be able to update all files on your disk. Should this error message occur, run CHKDSK to examine your disk. If CHKDSK does not encounter errors, reboot your system and repeat your attempt to modify the file's date and time stamp.

```
DATETIME: Date and time update complete. Press any key to
continue.
```

After DATETIME updates the last file you have selected, DATETIME displays a completion message and prompts you to press any key to continue. When you press a key, DATETIME returns to the file menu allowing you to update additional files or to exit to DOS.

How DATETIME Works

DOS stores a file's date and time stamp in the file's directory entry. The DATETIME utility reads the specified directory to get each file's date and time.

DATETIME.EXE
70116
01-28-90
17:21
ARCHIVE
1017
.
.
.
UNFORMAT.EXE
58002
01-28-90
17:53
NORMAL
1836

Directory entry

Each time you press F10 to update a file's date and time stamp, DATETIME simply changes the file's directory entry.

DATETIME.EXE
70116
01-28-90
17:21
ARCHIVE
1017
.
.
.
UNFORMAT.EXE
58002
01-28-90
17:53
NORMAL
1836

Directory entry

Renaming
Subdirectories

▶ Renaming a Subdirectory with DOS

▶ Using RENDIR to Rename a Subdirectory

▶ Understanding RENDIR Error Messages

▶ How RENDIR Works

Renaming Subdirectories

In Chapter 4, you learned how to create, select, and remove subdirectories using the MKDIR, CHDIR, and RMDIR commands. As you reorganize your files and directories, it is often desirable to change the name of an existing subdirectory. Unfortunately, although DOS lets you rename files using RENAME, it doesn't provide you with a simple command that renames a subdirectory.

Renaming a Subdirectory with DOS

If you want to rename an existing subdirectory using DOS, you must perform the following steps:

► Create a directory with the desired name.
► Copy all files from the old directory to the new directory.
► Delete the files from the old directory.
► Remove the old directory.

Assume, for example, that you have files residing in the subdirectory DATA. Your goal is to rename the subdirectory to DATA1990. Using the steps just listed, you would rename the directory using the following DOS commands:

```
C:\> MKDIR DATA1990
C:\> COPY DATA\*.* DATA1990
C:\> DEL DATA\*.*
C:\> RMDIR DATA
```

As you can see, you really aren't renaming a directory. In the best case, to rename a DOS subdirectory, you have to perform four commands.

Although it is possible to rename directories this way, you may encounter difficulties that make it much more time consuming. For example, assume that your disk does not contain enough free space to hold the copies of the files during the rename steps. If this occurs, you must first copy the files to floppy disk, delete the existing files, and then copy the files from the floppy disk into the new directory. Depending on the number of files in the directory, you may need to use several floppy disks. Recall that floppy disk operations are much slower than hard disk operations. This fact alone may make the rename process quite time consuming.

Second, if the subdirectory you are renaming contains additional subdirectories, you must create and copy the files in those directories also. For example, assume that the subdirectory DATA contains the subdirectories shown in the following figure:

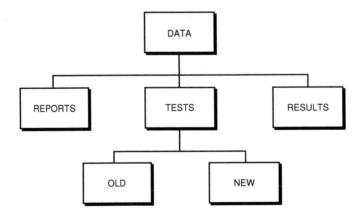

To rename the directory, you must create and copy each subdirectory under the target using the four steps previously mentioned. Thus, the resulting directory structure appears as shown in the next figure:

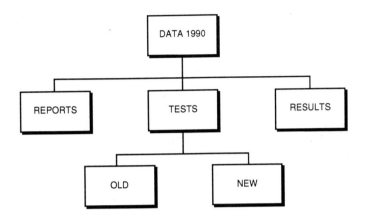

The more subdirectories and files you must copy, the more time consuming and complex the subdirectory rename process becomes.

Using RENDIR to Rename a Subdirectory

The Jamsa Disk Utilities contain a utility called RENDIR. This utility lets you quickly rename a subdirectories in a single step. To begin, create a subdirectory named OLDNAME in the root directory.

```
C:\> MKDIR \OLDNAME
```

Next, at the DOS prompt, invoke RENDIR from the Power Shell or from the DOS prompt, as follows:

```
C:\> RENDIR
```

RENDIR will in turn display the screen shown in the following figure:

```
┌────────────────────────────────────────────────────────────────────┐
│  ┌──────────────────────────────────────────────────────────────┐  │
│  │   Directory Rename, Jamsa Utilities Version 1.0 (C) 1989-90 Kris Jamsa │  │
│  └──────────────────────────────────────────────────────────────┘  │
│                                                                      │
│  Directory:                                                          │
│  New name:                                                           │
│                                                                      │
│  Rename operation: Cancel        Continue                            │
│  Status: Press Esc to Exit.                                          │
│                                                                      │
└────────────────────────────────────────────────────────────────────┘
```

RENDIR prompts you to type in the name of the subdirectory to rename. In this case, type **\OLDNAME**.

Next, RENDIR prompts you to enter the new directory name. Type **NEWNAME** without a leading slash and press Enter.

RENDIR behaves much like the DOS RENAME command in that you cannot specify a drive letter or path name in front of the target name. RENDIR does not move directories; it simply renames them. If you try to enter a backslash or a drive letter followed by a colon in the new name, RENDIR ignores them.

When you press Enter at the end of the new directory name, RENDIR displays the message "Working..". During this time, RENDIR searches your disk to find the original directory, as well as to ensure that the new directory name is not already in use. If all goes well, RENDIR displays a message telling you such and then prompts you to determine whether you want to continue. At this point, your screen should appear similar to that shown here.

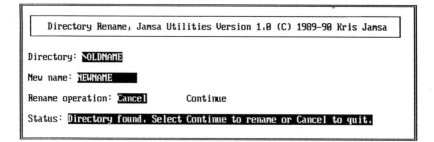

Using either the Tab key or the right- and left-arrow keys, you can highlight the Cancel or Continue option. The Cancel option returns you to the DOS prompt leaving the original directory name unchanged. The Continue option directs RENDIR to rename the directory. In this case, select the Continue option and press Enter. RENDIR will rename the directory notifying you of its success.

A directory listing of the root reveals that the directory has been successfully renamed.

```
C:\> DIR

Volume in drive C is DOS
Directory of  C:\
```

```
AUTOEXEC BAT         128 01-27-90  11:39a
CONFIG   SYS         128 01-23-90   3:39p
DISKBOOK    <DIR>        01-21-90  11:40a
DOS         <DIR>        11-19-89   5:23p
DISKUTIL    <DIR>        01-30-90  10:14a
NEWNAME     <DIR>        01-30-90  11:53a
       6 File(s)    42717184 bytes free
```

Next, create a subdirectory within NEWNAME called LEVEL2 as shown here.

```
C:\> MKDIR \NEWNAME\LEVEL2
```

A directory listing of NEWNAME reveals the following.

```
C:\> DIR \NEWNAME

Volume in drive C is DOS
Directory of  C:\NEWNAME

.           <DIR>        01-30-90  11:53a
..          <DIR>        01-30-90  11:53a
LEVEL2      <DIR>        01-30-90   4:08p
       3 File(s)    42715136 bytes free
```

Using the RENDIR utility, rename the subdirectory LEVEL2 as LEVELTWO as shown in the following figure.

```
┌─────────────────────────────────────────────────────────────────┐
│    ┌───────────────────────────────────────────────────────┐     │
│    │   Directory Rename, Jamsa Utilities Version 1.0 (C) 1989-90 Kris Jamsa │     │
│    └───────────────────────────────────────────────────────┘     │
│                                                                   │
│  Directory: C:\NEWNAME\LEVEL2                                     │
│  New name: LEVELTWO                                               │
│  Rename operation: Cancel      Continue                          │
│  Status: Directory found. Select Continue to rename or Cancel to quit. │
└─────────────────────────────────────────────────────────────────┘
```

As you can see, RENDIR fully supports complete path names (including disk drive letters) in the original directory name. To rename a directory that resides on a disk other than the default drive, simply precede the directory name with the correct drive letter.

Next, select the subdirectory NEWNAME as the current directory.

```
C:\> CHDIR \NEWNAME
```

Next, invoke RENDIR to rename the subdirectory LEVELTWO to SUBDIR as shown here.

```
┌────────────────────────────────────────────────────────────────┐
│ ┌──────────────────────────────────────────────────────────┐   │
│ │ Directory Rename, Jamsa Utilities Version 1.0 (C) 1989-90 Kris Jamsa │ │
│ └──────────────────────────────────────────────────────────┘   │
│                                                                  │
│ Directory: LEVELTWO                                              │
│                                                                  │
│ New name: SUBDIR                                                 │
│                                                                  │
│ Rename operation: Cancel        Continue                         │
│                                                                  │
│ Status: Directory found. Select Continue to rename or Cancel to quit. │
│                                                                  │
└────────────────────────────────────────────────────────────────┘
```

In this case we did not precede the old directory name LEVELTWO with a complete path name. When this occurs, RENDIR searches the current directory for the subdirectory to rename. Because the subdirectory LEVELTWO resided in the current directory, RENDIR successfully locates and renames it.

Understanding RENDIR Error Messages

The RENDIR utility displays several possible error messages in the status box at the bottom of the screen. The following sections explain possible RENDIR error messages in detail.

```
RENDIR: Must specify directory name
```

If you press Enter without typing in the name of the directory to rename, RENDIR will display an error message and prompt you to enter a name. You must specify a source and target directory name.

```
RENDIR: Only specify .. once in directory name
```

The RENDIR utility supports the use of the parent directory abbreviation (..). For example, assume that your directory contains the structure shown in the following figure.

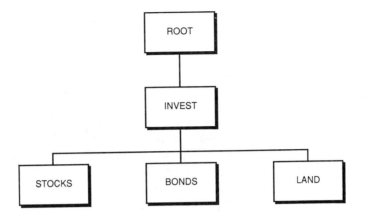

If the current directory is STOCKS, you can use the parent sub-directory abbreviation to rename the subdirectory BONDS, which resides in the parent as shown in the next figure.

```
┌─────────────────────────────────────────────────────────────────┐
│  ┌──────────────────────────────────────────────────────────┐    │
│  │   Directory Rename, Jamsa Utilities Version 1.0 (C) 1989-90 Kris Jamsa │ │
│  └──────────────────────────────────────────────────────────┘    │
│                                                                    │
│   Directory: ..\BONDS                                              │
│   New name: KEYBONDS                                               │
│   Rename operation: Cancel          Continue                       │
│   Status: Directory found. Select Continue to rename or Cancel to quit. │
└─────────────────────────────────────────────────────────────────┘
```

To avoid confusion when you use multiple levels of directories, RENDIR lets you specify only the parent directory abbreviation once per directory name. Should this error occur, simply use a complete path name to the directory.

`RENDIR: The abbreviation .. must appear at start of path name`

As just discussed, RENDIR fully supports the parent subdirectory abbreviation (..). If you specify this abbreviation, it must occur at the beginning of the path name.

`RENDIR: New directory name is invalid`

You must specify a source and target directory name. If you simply press Enter instead of typing a new directory name, RENDIR displays an error message and returns control to DOS.

```
RENDIR:  Invalid file or drive specification
```

If the disk drive specified does not exist, RENDIR displays this error message and returns control to DOS. Should this error occur, make sure you are using a valid disk drive letter. If the disk drive is valid, invoke the DISKINFO utility discussed in Chapter 11 to examine the disk drive.

```
RENDIR:  SUBST and ASSIGN not supported
```

As discussed in Chapter 5, DOS lets you create logical disk drives using the SUBST command. Logical drives let users abbreviate long directory names with a single drive letter. To prevent confusion from logical drives, RENDIR simply does not support them.

```
RENDIR: Network drives not supported
```

In most cases, running disk management utilities on a disk drive used by a local area network can be quite dangerous. Disk utilities work by accessing individual sectors of a disk. In a network, access to a disk is controlled by network software. To prevent an incompatibility between the network software and the disk utility software from damaging your disk, the low-level utilities on the companion disk do not support network drives.

```
RENDIR:  Sector size must be 512 or 1024 bytes
```

Most DOS disks use 512-byte sectors. Several third-party software packages let users format their disks using 1,024-byte sectors. These packages do this to support partitions greater than 32M. The disk utilities provided on the companion disk support only these two sector sizes.

```
RENDIR:  Insufficient memory
```

To perform its processing, RENDIR requires memory to hold disk sectors, FAT, and cluster information as well as its own tables. If RENDIR cannot allocate sufficient memory, it displays an error message and returns control to DOS. Although the memory requirements vary based upon your disk size and the number of files in each directory, most of the companion disk utilities require a maximum of 256K.

`RENDIR:  Error reading file allocation table`

To track files and directories, the disk utilities provided on the companion disk must read cluster information from the FAT. If a utility encounters an error while reading the FAT, the utility displays an error message and exits to DOS.

Should this error occur, test your disk using CHKDSK. File allocation table errors are very serious. Back up your disk immediately. You may need to format your disk and restore backups to correct the error.

`RENDIR:  Directory not found`

If RENDIR cannot locate the directory to rename, RENDIR displays an error message and exits to DOS. Should this error message occur, make sure you are using a correct and complete path name to the subdirectory. This error is most often caused by omitting backslashes in the path name.

`RENDIR:  Cannot rename current directory`

Just as DOS does not let you remove the current directory using RMDIR, the RENDIR utility does not let you rename the current directory. Should this error occur, simply select a different directory as the current directory using CHDIR and then invoke RENDIR once again.

`RENDIR:  Target directory already exists`

If this error message occurs, a subdirectory already exists on disk with the name you entered for the desired directory name. Should this error occur, you must choose a different directory name or remove the existing directory.

`RENDIR:  Target directory name in use for a file`

If this message occurs, a file already exists on disk with the name you entered for the desired directory name. Just as DOS does not let you create a directory with the same name as a file existing on disk, RENDIR does not let you rename a subdirectory to a name in use by a file. Should this error occur, you must select a different name for the subdirectory or rename the existing file.

```
RENDIR: Error reading directory sector
```

If this error occurs, RENDIR encountered an error while attempting to read one of the sectors containing directory information. This error is often a sign of bad times to come. Should this error occur, back up your disk immediately. Next, invoke CHKDSK to examine your disk. You may need to format your disk to remove the damaged sector, restoring your backup files.

```
RENDIR:  Original directory name unchanged
```

RENDIR displays this message when you select the Cancel option to end a rename operation. If any of the error messages previously discussed have occurred, the original directory name remains unchanged.

How RENDIR Works

A directory is a list of file and subdirectory names. When you use RENDIR to rename a subdirectory, RENDIR searches the directory list for the name specified. If RENDIR locates the subdirectory, RENDIR assigns a new name to the directory entry, writing the information back to disk.

To rename the subdirectory OLDNAME to NEWNAME, RENDIR must first find the entry for OLDNAME. If successful, RENDIR can assign the new directory name and record the change on disk, as shown in the second figure.

Assume that your directory contains the entries shown here.

CONFIG.SYS
128
1-23-90
13:39
ARCHIVE
64
AUTOEXEC.BAT
128
1-23-90
11:39
ARCHIVE
81
DOS
0
1-17-90
12:00
138
DIRECTORY
OLDNAME
0
1-30-89
14:59
0
DIRECTORY

Directories have a size of 0

Directories use a directory attribute

CONFIG.SYS
128
1-23-90
13:39
ARCHIVE
64
AUTOEXEC.BAT
128
1-23-90
11:39
ARCHIVE
81
DOS
0
1-17-90
12:00
138
DIRECTORY
NEWNAME
0
1-30-89
14:59
0
DIRECTORY

Root directory contents before

Root directory contents after

14

Selectively Deleting Files

- ▶ Using SELDEL
- ▶ Understanding SELDEL Error Messages
- ▶ How SELDEL Works

Selectively Deleting Files

In Chapter 3, you learned how to delete files using the DEL command. At that time you learned that wildcards let you delete groups of files with similar file names or extensions. Unfortunately, many users inadvertently delete needed files when they issue DEL commands improperly. The SELDEL utility provided as part of the Jamsa Disk Utilities lets you select, from a menu, the files you want to delete. If you use SELDEL, errant DEL commands are a thing of the past.

Using SELDEL

So that you have several files to delete, create the subdirectory DELETE, and copy the files in the directory DISKUTIL to it:

```
C:\> MKDIR \DELETE
C:\> COPY \DISKUTIL\*.* \DELETE
```

To selectively delete files, invoke SELDEL by pressing F4 at the Power Shell or from the DOS command line, as follows:

```
C:\> SELDEL
```

SELDEL displays its first screen, prompting you to enter the directory containing the files to delete. Type DELETE, as shown here.

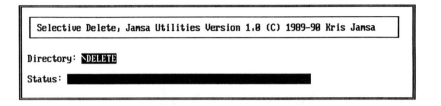

```
┌────────────────────────────────────────────────────────────────────┐
│ ┌──────────────────────────────────────────────────────────────┐   │
│ │ Selective Delete, Jamsa Utilities Version 1.0 (C) 1989-90 Kris Jamsa │ │
│ └──────────────────────────────────────────────────────────────┘   │
│                                                                     │
│ Directory: █DELETE█                                                 │
│                                                                     │
│ Status: █████████████████████████████████████████████              │
│                                                                     │
└────────────────────────────────────────────────────────────────────┘
```

When you press Enter, SELDEL displays the message Working.. as it searches your disk for the directory specified. If SELDEL successfully locates the directory, it displays the files that reside in the directory as shown in the following figure.

```
┌────────────────────────────────────────────────────────────────────┐
│ ┌──────────────────────────────────────────────────────────────┐   │
│ │ Use arrow keys to highlight a file.  Press Enter to select or │   │
│ │ unselect a file.  Press F10 to delete files.  Press Esc to exit. │ │
│ │                                                              │   │
│ │   ▓DATETIME▓.EXE    77,032 bytes    03-29-1990    14:52:06    │   │
│ │    DISKINFO.EXE     59,110 bytes    03-29-1990    14:52:14    │   │
│ │    DISKSAVE.EXE     50,014 bytes    03-29-1990    14:52:20    │   │
│ │    FILEATTR.EXE     72,184 bytes    03-29-1990    14:52:28    │   │
│ │    FINDFILE.EXE     56,784 bytes    03-29-1990    14:52:36    │   │
│ │    KILLFILE.EXE     72,694 bytes    03-29-1990    14:53:02    │   │
│ │    POWER   .EXE     66,064 bytes    03-29-1990    14:53:08    │   │
│ │    RENDIR  .EXE     64,148 bytes    03-29-1990    14:53:16    │   │
│ │    SELCOPY .EXE     75,328 bytes    03-29-1990    14:53:26    │   │
│ │    SELDEL  .EXE     70,220 bytes    03-29-1990    14:53:34    │   │
│ │                                                              │   │
│ └──────────────────────────────────────────────────────────────┘   │
│ ┌──────────────────────────────────────────────────────────────┐   │
│ │ Directory: C:\DELETE                                         │   │
│ └──────────────────────────────────────────────────────────────┘   │
└────────────────────────────────────────────────────────────────────┘
```

Because DOS cannot delete read-only files, SELDEL does not display files whose read-only attribute is set.

To select a file for deletion, use the arrow keys to highlight the file and then press either the space bar or the Enter key. SELDEL displays an asterisk next to the file, indicating that the file has been selected for deletion. The space bar and Enter key work as a toggle. If you press either key for a file selected for deletion, SELDEL removes the asterisk, indicating that the file will not be deleted.

In this case, select the files beginning with the letter D. After doing this, your screen may look similar to that shown in the next figure. Only those files marked with an asterisk will be deleted.

```
┌────────────────────────────────────────────────────────────────────┐
│  ┌──────────────────────────────────────────────────────────────┐   │
│  │ Use arrow keys to highlight a file.  Press Enter to select or │   │
│  │ unselect a file.  Press F10 to delete files.  Press Esc to exit. │ │
│  └──────────────────────────────────────────────────────────────┘   │
│                                                                      │
│      *DATETIME.EXE     77,032 bytes     03-29-1990     14:52:06       │
│      *DISKINFO.EXE     59,110 bytes     03-29-1990     14:52:14       │
│      *DISKSAVE.EXE     58,014 bytes     03-29-1990     14:52:20       │
│       FILEATTR.EXE     72,184 bytes     03-29-1990     14:52:28       │
│       FINDFILE.EXE     56,784 bytes     03-29-1990     14:52:36       │
│       KILLFILE.EXE     72,694 bytes     03-29-1990     14:53:02       │
│       POWER   .EXE     66,064 bytes     03-29-1990     14:53:08       │
│       RENDIR  .EXE     64,148 bytes     03-29-1990     14:53:16       │
│       SELCOPY .EXE     75,328 bytes     03-29-1990     14:53:26       │
│       SELDEL  .EXE     70,220 bytes     03-29-1990     14:53:34       │
│                                                                      │
│  ┌──────────────────────────────────────────────────────────────┐   │
│  │ Directory: C:\DELETE                                          │    │
│  └──────────────────────────────────────────────────────────────┘   │
└────────────────────────────────────────────────────────────────────┘
```

To delete the selected files, press the F10 key. SELDEL displays its third screen as shown here.

```
┌────────────────────────────────────────────────────────────────────┐
│  ┌──────────────────────────────────────────────────────────────┐   │
│  │ Select Cancel to return to file list.  Select Continue to delete files. │ │
│  └──────────────────────────────────────────────────────────────┘   │
│                                                                      │
│   Directory: C:\DELETE                                               │
│                                                                      │
│   Delete Operation:   [Cancel]      Continue                         │
│                                                                      │
│   Status:                                                            │
└────────────────────────────────────────────────────────────────────┘
```

SELDEL prompts you to ensure that you really want to delete the selected files. If you select the Cancel option, SELDEL returns to the menu file, allowing you to view the selected files or to return to DOS. If you select the Continue option, SELDEL begins deleting the selected files. When SELDEL completes, it displays a message informing you that the files have been deleted. Pressing any key returns you to the file menu. From here you can select additional files for deletion or press Esc to exit to DOS.

Using SELDEL's F8 fast key, select the files remaining in the directory and delete them. When the command completes, exit to DOS and remove the directory DELETE with the DOS RMDIR command. The SELDEL command provides more visual control over file deletion than the DOS wildcard characters.

Using Fast Keys with SELDEL

In many cases, you will want to quickly select several files that appear successively in the directory listing. SELDEL uses the F8 function key to toggle a file's current selection status and advance the highlighted file down to the next file in the list. By holding the F8 key down, you can quickly select several files for deletion. The F7 function key works in a similar manner, advancing the file highlight up one file toward the beginning of the list.

Understanding SELDEL Error Messages

The SELDEL utility displays several possible error messages in the status box. The following section describes in detail the causes and solutions for each error.

```
SELDEL: Requires DOS 2.0 or higher
```

Prior to version 2, DOS did not support hard disks. The programs on the companion disk, therefore, require DOS 2.0 as a minimum.

```
SELDEL: Only specify .. once in directory name
```

The SELDEL utility supports the use of the parent directory abbreviation (..). For example, assume that you are in a DOS subdirectory, using the parent directory abbreviation. You can use SELDEL to access files residing in the parent as shown here.

```
Selective Delete, Jamsa Utilities Version 1.0 (C) 1989-90 Kris Jamsa

Directory: ..
Status: 
```

To avoid confusion when you use multiple levels of directories, SELDEL lets you specify only the parent directory abbreviation once per directory name. Should this error occur, simply use a complete path name to the directory.

```
SELDEL: The abbreviation .. must appear at start of path name
```

As just discussed, SELDEL fully supports the parent subdirectory abbreviation (..). If you specify this abbreviation, it must occur at the beginning of the path name.

```
SELDEL: Invalid file or drive specification
```

If the disk drive specified does not exist, SELDEL displays this error message and returns control to DOS. Should this error occur, make sure you are using a valid disk drive letter. If the disk drive is valid, invoke the DISKINFO utility discussed in Chapter 11 to examine the disk drive.

```
SELDEL: SUBST and ASSIGN not supported
```

As discussed in Chapter 5, DOS lets you create logical disk drives using the SUBST command. Logical drives let users abbreviate long directory names with a single drive letter. To prevent confusion from logical drives, SELDEL simply does not support them.

```
SELDEL: Network drives not supported
```

In most cases, running disk management utilities on a disk drive used by a local area network can be quite dangerous. Disk utilities work by accessing individual sectors of a disk. In a network, access to a disk is controlled by network software. To prevent an incompatibility between the network software and the disk utility software from damaging your disk, the low-level utilities on the companion disk do not support network drives.

```
SELDEL: Sector size must be 512 or 1024 bytes
```

Most DOS disks use 512-byte sectors. Several third-party software packages let users format their disks using 1,024-byte sectors. The packages do this to provide support for partitions greater than 32M. The disk utilities provided on the companion disk support only these two sector sizes.

```
SELDEL: Insufficient memory
```

To perform its processing, SELDEL requires memory to hold disk sectors, FAT, and cluster information as well as its own tables. If SELDEL cannot allocate sufficient memory, it displays an error message and returns control to DOS. Although the memory requirements vary based upon your disk size and the number of files in each directory, most of the companion disk utilities require a maximum of 256K.

```
SELDEL: Error reading file allocation table
```

To track files and directories, the disk utilities provided on the companion disk must read cluster information from the FAT. If a utility encounters an error while reading the FAT, the utility displays an error message and exits to DOS.

Should this error occur, test your disk using CHKDSK. File allocation table errors are very serious. Back up your disk immediately. You may need to format your disk and restore backups to correct the error.

```
SELDEL: Directory not found
```

If SELDEL cannot locate the directory containing the desired files, SELDEL displays an error message and exits to DOS. Should this error message occur, make sure you are using a correct and complete path name to the subdirectory. This error is most often caused by omitting backslashes in the path name.

```
SELDEL: Error reading directory sector
```

If this error occurs, SELDEL encountered an error while attempting to read one of the sectors containing directory information. This error is often a sign of bad times to come. Should this error occur, back up your disk immediately. Next, invoke CHKDSK to examine your disk. You may need to format your disk to remove the damaged sector, restoring your backup files.

```
SELDEL: Error deleting FILENAME.EXT. Press any key to
continue.
```

If SELDEL is unable to delete the file specified, SELDEL displays the error message and continues deleting the remainder of the files you selected. SELDEL should be able to delete all files on your disk. Should this error message occur, run CHKDSK to examine your disk. If CHKDSK does not encounter errors, reboot your system and repeat your attempt to delete the file.

```
SELDEL: Selective deletion complete. Press any key to
continue.
```

After SELDEL deletes the last file you have selected, SELDEL displays a completion message and prompts you to press any key to continue. When you press a key, SELDEL returns to the file menu, allowing you to delete additional files or to exit to DOS.

How SELDEL Works

The SELDEL utility locates and reads the directory specified, displaying the files in the directory whose read-only attribute is not set. Once you select files and press F10 , SELDEL deletes the files in the same manner as the DOS DEL command.

Like files deleted by the DEL command, the UNDELETE utility provided on the companion disk can undelete files deleted by SELDEL.

Squeezing Maximum Performance from Your Hard Disk

▶ Using SQUEEZE

▶ Using UNDELETE after SQUEEZE

▶ Understanding SQUEEZE Error Messages

▶ How SQUEEZE Works

15

Squeezing Maximum Performance from Your Hard Disk

A *subdirectory* is a list of file names and specifics about the files on your disk. Each time you create a new file, DOS adds the file name to the list as shown in the following figure.

ONE.DAT
1
1-1-90
11:11
NORMAL
37
TWO.DAT
2
2-2-90
22:22
READ-ONLY
67

Original directory

THREE.DAT

New file

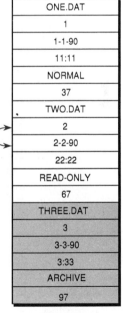

New directory

Every time DOS performs a file operation, DOS must sequentially search the directory specified starting with the first file and working toward the last. The file operation might be a file copy, deletion, or type operation. It also includes creating and opening files with a word processor or other application program. As you might guess, the more files your directory contains, the longer the file search operation takes.

In Chapter 4, you learned how to organize your files and reduce the number of files in a directory by creating additional DOS subdirectories. Chapter 4 also recommended that you restrict the number of files in your directory to 64. Using the DIR command, you can quickly determine the number of files in a directory.

```
C:\> DIR \DISKUTIL

        Volume in drive C is DOS
        Directory of  C:\DISKUTIL

    TESTFRAG EXE      56470    3-29-90    2:54p
    FINDFILE EXE      56784    3-29-90    2:52p
    DISKSAVE EXE      58014    3-29-90    2:52p
    DISKINFO EXE      59110    3-29-90    2:52p
    UNFORMAT EXE      60586    3-29-90    2:54p
    SQUEEZE  EXE      64014    3-29-90    2:54p
    RENDIR   EXE      64148    3-29-90    2:53p
    POWER    EXE      66064    3-29-90    2:53p
    SELDEL   EXE      70220    3-29-90    2:53p
    SORTDIR  EXE      70860    3-29-90    2:54p
    FILEATTR EXE      72184    3-29-90    2:52p
    KILLFILE EXE      72694    3-29-90    2:53p
    UNDELETE EXE      74424    3-29-90    2:54p
    SELCOPY  EXE      75328    3-29-90    2:53p
    DATETIME EXE      77032    3-29-90    2:52p
        17 File(s)   19611648 bytes free
```

The DIR command's last line of output can be misleading. DIR displays only the number of existing files in your directory. As it turns out, each time DOS deletes a file, DOS doesn't remove the file's directory entry. Instead, DOS changes the first letter in the file name to σ, as shown in the next figure.

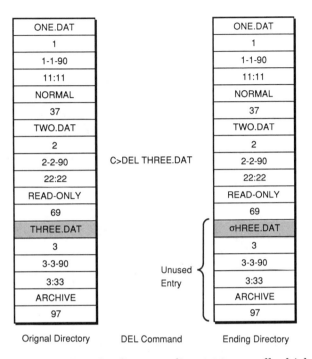

ONE.DAT		ONE.DAT
1		1
1-1-90		1-1-90
11:11		11:11
NORMAL		NORMAL
37		37
TWO.DAT		TWO.DAT
2		2
2-2-90	C>DEL THREE.DAT	2-2-90
22:22		22:22
READ-ONLY		READ-ONLY
69		69
THREE.DAT		σHREE.DAT
3		3
3-3-90	Unused	3-3-90
3:33	Entry	3:33
ARCHIVE		ARCHIVE
97		97

Orignal Directory   DEL Command   Ending Directory

When DOS searches the directory list, DOS can tell which directory entries point to existing files and which are unused, left over from deleted files. If, for example, you delete ten files, DOS leaves ten unused directory entries in the current directory. Every time DOS performs a file operation, DOS must read through these entries. This adds overhead, making every disk operation slower. The more empty entries your directory contains, the more your disk performance suffers.

You may be wondering why DOS leaves the unused entries in the directory if doing so decreases disk performance. First, simply marking a directory entry as unused is much faster than shuffling all the files in the directory up one position to remove the unused entry. As a result, the DEL command is very fast. Second, when you create new files in a directory, DOS reuses old entries. DOS, therefore, assumes that if you delete a file, you'll probably create another, so the directory entry won't be unused long.

Most importantly, because DOS leaves the unused entry in the directory, third-party software packages locate the entry associated with a deleted file and use the entry to undelete the file.

For best disk performance, however, you should remove unused directory entries entirely. The SQUEEZE utility provided with the Jamsa Disk Utilities lets you do just that.

The SQUEEZE utility is so named because it squeezes unused entries out of your directory. Assume, for example, that your directory contains 25 unused entries. DOS has to search through these entries during every file operation. The SQUEEZE utility removes the unused entries, compressing your directory size as shown in the next figure.

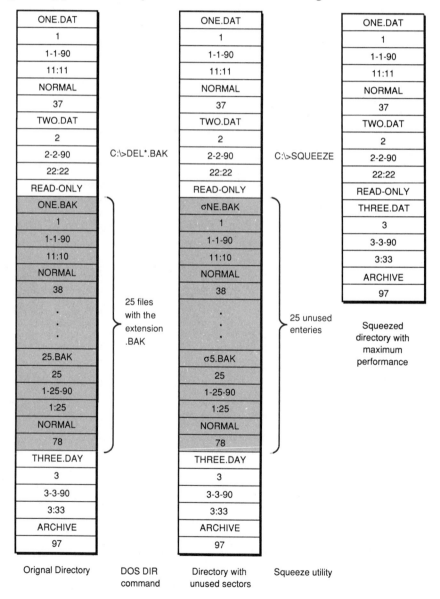

| Orignal Directory | DOS DIR command | Directory with unused sectors | Squeeze utility |

Invoke SQUEEZE by pressing F2 at the Power Shell or from the DOS prompt as follows:

```
C:\> SQUEEZE
```

SQUEEZE displays its only screen, prompting you to enter the name of the directory to squeeze. In this case, use DISKUTIL as shown in the next figure.

```
┌──────────────────────────────────────────────────────────────────┐
│  ┌────────────────────────────────────────────────────────────┐  │
│  │ Directory Squeeze, Jamsa Utilities Version 1.0 (C) 1989-90 Kris Jamsa │
│  └────────────────────────────────────────────────────────────┘  │
│                                                                    │
│  Directory: ▌DISKUTIL                                              │
│                                                                    │
│  Squeeze operation:  Cancel      Continue                          │
│                                                                    │
│  Status: ██████████████████████████████████████████               │
└──────────────────────────────────────────────────────────────────┘
```

If you press Enter at the Directory: prompt, SQUEEZE will use the current directory.

When you press Enter, SQUEEZE displays the message "Working.." as it searching your disk for the directory specified. If SQUEEZE successfully locates the directory, it prompts you to Continue or Cancel the operation. If you select the Cancel operation, SQUEEZE returns you to the DOS prompt leaving the directory unchanged. If you select Continue, SQUEEZE examines the directory, removing unused entries. When SQUEEZE completes its job, it displays a summary of the number of unused entries it removed, as shown in the following figure.

```
┌──────────────────────────────────────────────────────────────────┐
│  ┌────────────────────────────────────────────────────────────┐  │
│  │ Directory Squeeze, Jamsa Utilities Version 1.0 (C) 1989-90 Kris Jamsa │
│  └────────────────────────────────────────────────────────────┘  │
│                                                                    │
│  Directory: ▌DISKUTIL                                             │
│                                                                    │
│  Squeeze operation:  Cancel      Continue                          │
│                                                                    │
│  Status: SQUEEZE: No directory entries removed                     │
└──────────────────────────────────────────────────────────────────┘
```

In this case, the directory did not contain any unused entries.

To better understand how SQUEEZE works, create the files ONE and TWO in the directory DISKUTIL, which contains the following:

```
C:\DISKUTIL> COPY CON ONE
111
^Z
     1 File(s) copied

C:\DISKUTIL> COPY CON TWO
222
^Z
     1 File(s) copied
```

Next, delete the files ONE and TWO using DEL.

```
C:\DISKUTIL> DEL ONE
C:\DISKUTIL> DEL TWO
```

Invoke SQUEEZE and provide DISKUTIL as the directory name. In this case, SQUEEZE removes two unused entries.

If you have directories in which you frequently create and delete files, running SQUEEZE on those directories will improve performance considerably.

Using UNDELETE after SQUEEZE

Third-party undelete utilities work by locating the unused directory entry that corresponds to the file to undelete. Should you squeeze a directory removing the empty directory entries, you will not be able to undelete files from that directory since the unused entries no longer exist.

As such, before you squeeze a directory, make sure it doesn't contain files you need to undelete. The UNDELETE utility discussed in Chapter 18 lets you display the deleted files in a directory.

Understanding SQUEEZE Error Messages

The SQUEEZE command displays several possible error messages in its status box. The following section discusses in detail the cause and solution for each error.

`SQUEEZE: Requires DOS 2.0 or higher`

Prior to version 2, DOS did not support hard disks. The programs on the companion disk, therefore, require DOS 2.0 as a minimum.

`SQUEEZE: Only specify .. once in directory name`

The SQUEEZE utility supports the use of the parent directory abbreviation (..). For example, assume that you are in a DOS subdirectory, using the parent directory abbreviation. You can use DATETIME to access files residing in the parent as shown here.

```
┌──────────────────────────────────────────────────────────────────┐
│ ┌──────────────────────────────────────────────────────────────┐ │
│ │ Directory Squeeze, Jamsa Utilities Version 1.0 (C) 1989-90 Kris Jamsa │ │
│ └──────────────────────────────────────────────────────────────┘ │
│ Directory: ▐▌                                                      │
│ Squeeze operation:  Cancel      Continue                           │
│ Status: ████████████████████████████████████████                  │
└──────────────────────────────────────────────────────────────────┘
```

To avoid confusion when you use multiple levels of directories, SQUEEZE lets you specify only the parent directory abbreviation once per directory name. Should this error occur, simply use a complete path name to the directory.

`SQUEEZE: The abbreviation .. must appear at start of path name`

SQUEEZE fully supports the parent subdirectory abbreviation (..). If you specify this abbreviation, the abbreviation must occur at the beginning of the path name.

`SQUEEZE: Invalid file or drive specification`

If the disk drive specified does not exist, SQUEEZE displays this error message and returns control to DOS. Should this error occur, make sure you are using a valid disk drive letter. If the disk drive is valid, invoke the DISKINFO utility discussed in Chapter 11 to examine the disk drive.

`SQUEEZE:  SUBST and ASSIGN not supported`

As discussed in Chapter 5, DOS lets you create logical disk drives using the SUBST command. Logical drives let users abbreviate long directory names with a single drive letter. To prevent confusion from logical drives, SQUEEZE simply does not support them.

`SQUEEZE: Network drives not supported`

In most cases, running disk management utilities on a disk drive used by a local area network can be quite dangerous. Disk utilities work by accessing individual sectors of a disk. In a network, access to a disk is controlled by network software. To prevent an incompatibility between the network software and the disk utility software from damaging your disk, the low-level utilities on the companion disk do not support network drives.

`SQUEEZE:  Sector size must be 512 or 1024 bytes`

Most DOS disks use 512-byte sectors. Several third-party software packages let users format their disks using 1,024-byte sectors. The packages do this to provide support for partitions greater than 32M. The disk utilities provided on the companion disk support only these two sector sizes.

`SQUEEZE: Insufficient memory`

To perform its processing, SQUEEZE requires memory to hold disk sectors, FAT, and cluster information as well as its own tables. If SQUEEZE cannot allocate sufficient memory, it displays an error message and returns control to DOS. Although the memory requirements vary based upon your disk size and the number of files in each directory, most of the companion disk utilities require a maximum of 256K.

`SQUEEZE:  Error reading file allocation table`

To track files and directories, the disk utilities provided on the companion disk must read cluster information from the FAT. If a utility encounters an error while reading the FAT, the utility displays an error message and exits to DOS.

Should this error occur, test your disk using CHKDSK. File allocation table errors are very serious. Back up your disk immediately. You may need to format your disk and restore backups to correct the error.

```
SQUEEZE:   Directory not found
```

If SQUEEZE cannot locate the directory containing the desired files, SQUEEZE displays an error message and exits to DOS. Should this error message occur, make sure you are using a correct and complete path name to the subdirectory. This error is most often caused by omitting backslashes in the path name.

```
SQUEEZE: Error reading directory sector
```

If this error occurs, SQUEEZE encountered an error while attempting to read one of the sectors containing directory information. This error is often a sign of bad times to come. Should this error occur, back up your disk immediately. Next, invoke CHKDSK to examine your disk. You may need to format your disk to remove the damaged sector, restoring your backup files.

```
SQUEEZE: Error writing directory sector
```

If this error occurs, SQUEEZE encountered an error while attempting to write one of the sectors containing updated directory information. Should this error occur, back up your disk immediately. Next, invoke CHKDSK to examine your disk. You may need to format your disk to remove the damaged sector, restoring your backup files.

How SQUEEZE Works

A DOS directory contains entries for files existing on your disk and may contain unused entries for files that have been deleted from your disk as shown in the following figure.

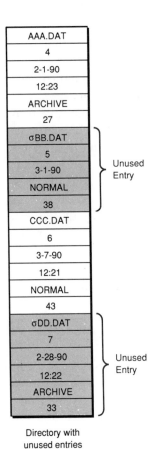

| AAA.DAT |
| 4 |
| 2-1-90 |
| 12:23 |
| ARCHIVE |
| 27 |
| σBB.DAT |
| 5 |
| 3-1-90 |
| NORMAL |
| 38 |
| CCC.DAT |
| 6 |
| 3-7-90 |
| 12:21 |
| NORMAL |
| 43 |
| σDD.DAT |
| 7 |
| 2-28-90 |
| 12:22 |
| ARCHIVE |
| 33 |

Unused Entry

Unused Entry

Directory with
unused entries

SQUEEZE reads your directory and removes each of the unused entries. SQUEEZE then writes the compact directory back out to disk as shown in the next figure.

| AAA.DAT |
| 4 |
| 2-1-90 |
| 12:23 |
| ARCHIVE |
| 27 |
| CCC.DAT |
| 6 |
| 3-7-90 |
| 12:21 |
| NORMAL |
| 43 |

Compressed
directory

16

Locating
Misplaced Files

- ► Using FINDFILE
- ► Understanding FINDFILE Error Messages
- ► How FINDFILE Works

Locating Misplaced Files

Chapter 4 strongly recommended that you create several layers of subdirectories to group your files logically. Using subdirectories improves your system performance by decreasing directory search time. The only possible disadvantage of creating several layers of subdirectories is misplacing a file.

The FINDFILE utility provided on the companion disk lets you quickly search all subdirectories on your disk for one or more files. Using FINDFILE, you can quickly locate misplaced files.

Using FINDFILE

The FINDFILE utility is command line driven. To search for one or more files, you simply place the file name in the command line as shown here.

```
C:\> FINDFILE  FILENAME.EXT
```

FINDFILE searches every directory on your disk for the file specified. Each time FINDFILE locates a matching file, FINDFILE displays the complete path name to the file as follows.

```
Searching for C:FILENAME.EXT
Path: C:\PATHNAME
   FILENAME.EXT    100 bytes  05-15-90  19:30  Attributes: Arc
```

For example, invoke FINDFILE to locate the file DISKINFO.EXE.

```
C:\> FINDFILE DISKINFO.EXE
```

In this case, FINDFILE displays the following output:

```
Searching For: C:DISKINFO.EXE

File Found: C:\DISKUTIL\DISKINFO.EXE
```

If DISKINFO.EXE resides in multiple directories, FINDFILE displays the complete path name to each.

If you invoke FINDFILE without specifying a file name in the command line, FINDFILE displays its command syntax as shown here.

```
C:\> FINDFILE
FINDFILE: usage FINDFILE filename [...]
```

FINDFILE supports DOS wildcards. The following command, for example, displays the path name to every file on your disk with the extension EXE.

```
C:\> FINDFILE *.EXE
```

Likewise, the following command lists every file on your disk.

```
C:\> FINDFILE *.*
```

Using the DOS output redirection operator, you can redirect FIND-FILE's output from the screen to the printer as shown here.

```
C:\> FINDFILE *.* >PRN
```

FINDFILE lets you specify several file names in its command line. The following command, for example, directs FINDFILE to locate SQUEEZE.EXE, AUTOEXEC.BAT, and CONFIG.SYS.

```
C:\> FINDFILE SQUEEZE.EXE AUTOEXEC.BAT CONFIG.SYS
```

Using DOS wildcards, you can list the files with the extension COM and EXE.

```
C:\> FINDFILE *.COM *.EXE
```

Finally, FINDFILE is not restricted to searching only one drive. The following command searches drives C and D for the file BUSINESS.LTR.

```
C:\> FINDFILE BUSINESS.LTR   D:BUSINESS.LTR
```

Temporarily Suspending FINDFILE's Output

Depending upon the number of matching files FINDFILE locates, FIND-FILE's output may quickly scroll past you on the screen. To temporarily stop FINDFILE's output, simply press any key. To resume output again, press any key.

Using FINDFILE, misplaced files won't stay misplaced long.

Understanding FINDFILE Error Messages

The processing that FINDFILE performs is much simpler than the other utility programs in the Jamsa Disk Utilities. As a result, FINDFILE only has one error message.

```
FINDFILE: Invalid specification
```

FINDFILE displays this message when a file name specified in the command line is invalid. The file name may contain an invalid disk drive letter or an invalid DOS path name. Should this error message occur, invoke FINDFILE with a correct name.

To invoke FINDFILE from the Power Shell, press the Alt+F1 keyboard combination. When you do, POWER will prompt you to enter the files for which you want to search. In this case, FINDFILE will search for AUTOEXEC.BAT and CONFIG.SYS.

```
Command Shell, Jamsa Utilities Version 1.0 (C) 1989-90 Kris Jamsa

Parameters: AUTOEXEC.BAT  CONFIG.SYS
```

349

How FINDFILE Works

The FINDFILE utility reads and searches the directories on your disk in the order the directories appear in a directory listing. Assuming that your root directory contains the following.

```
C:\> DIR

 Volume in drive C is DOS
 Directory of  C:\

AUTOEXEC BAT       128 01-27-90  11:39a
CONFIG   SYS       128 01-23-90   3:39p
DISKBOOK     <DIR>     01-21-90  11:40a
DOS          <DIR>     11-19-89   5:23p
DISKUTIL     <DIR>     01-30-90  10:14a
        19 File(s)   41775104 bytes free
```

FINDFILE first searches the root directory, followed by the subdirectories DOS, DISKBOOK, and DISKUTIL in that order. If a directory contains additional subdirectories, FINDFILE examines every file in the directory before processing the subdirectories.

17

Sorting Files in Your Directory

▶ Using SORTDIR

▶ Understanding SORTDIR Error Messages

▶ How SORTDIR Works

17

Sorting Files in Your Directory

A *directory* is a list of file names and characteristics. Each time you create a file on your disk, DOS places an entry for the file in the directory. When DOS adds a file to the directory, DOS uses the fastest technique possible. First, DOS searches your directory for unused entries previously allocated to files you have deleted. If DOS finds an unused entry, DOS uses that entry for the new file.

If the directory does not contain any unused entries, DOS appends an entry to the end of the list. Using this technique, DOS is not concerned with the order in which the files appear on your disk. Instead, DOS is concerned only with speed. If DOS had to place each file into the directory in sorted order, file operations would become very time consuming.

Many users like to examine their directories in sorted order. To do so, they pipe the output of the DIR command into the SORT command as shown here.

```
C:\> DIR ¦ SORT
```

Using the DISKUTIL directory, for example, the sorted output becomes the following.

```
C:\> DIR \DISKUTIL ¦ SORT

        17 File(s)  19601408 bytes free
   Directory of  C:\DISKUTIL
   Volume in drive C is DOS

DATETIME EXE     77032   3-29-90    2:52p
DISKINFO EXE     59110   3-29-90    2:52p
DISKSAVE EXE     58014   3-29-90    2:52p
FILEATTR EXE     72184   3-29-90    2:52p
FINDFILE EXE     56784   3-29-90    2:52p
KILLFILE EXE     72694   3-29-90    2:53p
POWER    EXE     66064   3-29-90    2:53p
RENDIR   EXE     64148   3-29-90    2:53p
SELCOPY  EXE     75328   3-29-90    2:53p
SELDEL   EXE     70220   3-29-90    2:53p
SORTDIR  EXE     70860   3-29-90    2:54p
SQUEEZE  EXE     64014   3-29-90    2:54p
TESTFRAG EXE     56470   3-29-90    2:54p
UNDELETE EXE     74424   3-29-90    2:54p
UNFORMAT EXE     60586   3-29-90    2:54p
```

Notice that while the files appear in sorted order, the first three lines of the sorted output are not in an order consistent with a normal directory listing. The SORT command sorts information starting with the first character of each line. In this case, because the first three lines begin with blanks, SORT displays them first.

Keep in mind that although the SORT command displays the files in sorted order, it does not actually change the order of the files in the directory list. To change the order of the files on disk, you must use the SORTDIR utility provided with the Jamsa Disk Utilities.

Using SORTDIR

The SORTDIR utility lets you sort a directory by name, extension, size, date, or time. Invoke SORTDIR from the Power Shell by pressing F3 or at the DOS prompt as follows.

```
C:\> SORTDIR
```

SORTDIR displays its first screen, prompting you to enter the desired directory name. In this case, type `DISKUTIL` as shown here. If you simply press Enter, SORTDIR uses the current directory.

```
┌─────────────────────────────────────────────────────────────────────┐
│  ┌───────────────────────────────────────────────────────────────┐   │
│  │   Directory Sort, Jamsa Utilities Version 1.0 (C) 1989-90 Kris Jamsa  │
│  └───────────────────────────────────────────────────────────────┘   │
│                                                                       │
│  Directory: ▚DISKUTIL                                                  │
│                                                                       │
│  Sort operation:  Cancel     Name     Extension    Size    Date    Time │
│                                                                       │
│  Status: ██████████████████████████                                   │
└─────────────────────────────────────────────────────────────────────┘
```

When you press Enter, SORTDIR displays the message "Working.." as it searches your disk for the directory. If SORTDIR locates the directory, SORTDIR displays a directory found message and prompts you to select Cancel or the desired sort operation as shown in the next figure.

```
┌─────────────────────────────────────────────────────────────────────┐
│  ┌───────────────────────────────────────────────────────────────┐   │
│  │   Directory Sort, Jamsa Utilities Version 1.0 (C) 1989-90 Kris Jamsa  │
│  └───────────────────────────────────────────────────────────────┘   │
│                                                                       │
│  Directory: ▚DISKUTIL                                                  │
│                                                                       │
│  Sort operation:  Cancel     Name     Extension    Size    Date    Time │
│                                                                       │
│  Status: Directory found. Select Cancel to quit or sort option. │
└─────────────────────────────────────────────────────────────────────┘
```

The Cancel option leaves the specified directory unchanged and returns control to DOS. The Name option sorts files by name. Likewise, the Extension option sorts the files by extension. If two or more files have the same extension, SORTDIR also sorts the files by name. The Size option sorts files by size from smallest to largest. SORTDIR sorts files of the same size by name. The Date and Time options sort files using the date and time stamps. SORTDIR sorts files with identical stamps by name.

In this case, use the arrow keys to highlight the Name option and then press Enter. SORTDIR quickly sorts the directory by name, displaying a message indicating it is completed.

A directory listing reveals the effects of SORTDIR.

```
C:\> DIR \DISKUTIL

   Volume in drive C is DOS
   Directory of  C:\DISKUTIL

DATETIME EXE     77032   3-29-90    2:52p
DISKINFO EXE     59110   3-29-90    2:52p
DISKSAVE EXE     58014   3-29-90    2:52p
FILEATTR EXE     72184   3-29-90    2:52p
FINDFILE EXE     56784   3-29-90    2:52p
KILLFILE EXE     72694   3-29-90    2:53p
POWER    EXE     66064   3-29-90    2:53p
RENDIR   EXE     64148   3-29-90    2:53p
SELCOPY  EXE     75328   3-29-90    2:53p
SELDEL   EXE     70220   3-29-90    2:53p
SORTDIR  EXE     70860   3-29-90    2:54p
SQUEEZE  EXE     64014   3-29-90    2:54p
TESTFRAG EXE     56470   3-29-90    2:54p
UNDELETE EXE     74424   3-29-90    2:54p
UNFORMAT EXE     60586   3-29-90    2:54p
         17 File(s)   19611648 bytes free
```

Invoke SORTDIR again. This time, sort the directory by Size. When SORTDIR completes, a directory listing of DISKUTIL reveals the following:

```
C:\> DIR \DISKUTIL

   Volume in drive C is DOS
   Directory of  C:\DISKUTIL

TESTFRAG EXE     56470   3-29-90    2:54p
FINDFILE EXE     56784   3-29-90    2:52p
DISKSAVE EXE     58014   3-29-90    2:52p
DISKINFO EXE     59110   3-29-90    2:52p
UNFORMAT EXE     60586   3-29-90    2:54p
SQUEEZE  EXE     64014   3-29-90    2:54p
RENDIR   EXE     64148   3-29-90    2:53p
POWER    EXE     66064   3-29-90    2:53p
SELDEL   EXE     70220   3-29-90    2:53p
SORTDIR  EXE     70860   3-29-90    2:54p
```

```
FILEATTR EXE     72184    3-29-90    2:52p
KILLFILE EXE     72694    3-29-90    2:53p
UNDELETE EXE     74424    3-29-90    2:54p
SELCOPY  EXE     75328    3-29-90    2:53p
DATETIME EXE     77032    3-29-90    2:52p
         17 File(s)   19611648 bytes free
```

As you can see, SORTDIR lets you sort a directory quickly and easily.

Understanding SORTDIR Error Messages

The SORTDIR utility displays several possible error messages. The following sections describe in detail the causes and solutions for each error.

```
SORTDIR: Requires DOS 2.0 or higher
```

Prior to version 2, DOS did not support hard disks. The programs on the companion disk, therefore, require DOS 2.0 as a minimum.

```
SORTDIR: Only specify .. once in directory name
```

The SORTDIR utility supports the use of the parent directory abbreviation (..). For example, assume that you are in a DOS subdirectory, using the parent directory abbreviation. You can use SORTDIR to access files residing in the parent as shown here.

```
┌──────────────────────────────────────────────────────────────────┐
│  ┌────────────────────────────────────────────────────────────┐   │
│  │  Directory Sort, Jamsa Utilities Version 1.0 (C) 1989-90 Kris Jamsa │
│  └────────────────────────────────────────────────────────────┘   │
│  Directory: ▮▮                                                     │
│                                                                    │
│  Sort operation:  Cancel     Name     Extension    Size    Date    Time │
│  Status: ███████████████████████████████████                      │
└──────────────────────────────────────────────────────────────────┘
```

To avoid confusion when you use multiple levels of directories, SORTDIR lets you specify only the parent directory abbreviation once per directory name. Should this error occur, simply use a complete path name to the directory.

```
SORTDIR: The abbreviation .. must appear at start of path name
```

SORTDIR fully supports the parent subdirectory abbreviation (..). If you specify this abbreviation, the abbreviation must occur at the beginning of the path name.

`SORTDIR: Invalid file or drive specification`

If the disk drive specified does not exist, SORTDIR displays this error message and returns control to DOS. Should this error occur, make sure you are using a valid disk drive letter. If the disk drive is valid, invoke the DISKINFO utility discussed in Chapter 11 to examine the disk drive.

`SORTDIR: SUBST and ASSIGN not supported`

As discussed in Chapter 5, DOS lets you create logical disk drives using the SUBST command. Logical drives let users abbreviate long directory names with a single drive letter. To prevent confusion from logical drives, SORTDIR simply does not support them.

`SORTDIR: Network drives not supported`

In most cases, running disk management utilities on a disk drive used by a local area network can be quite dangerous. Disk utilities work by accessing individual sectors of a disk. In a network, access to a disk is controlled by network software. To prevent an incompatibility between the network software and the disk utility software from damaging your disk, the low-level utilities on the companion disk do not support network drives.

`SORTDIR: Sector size must be 512 or 1024 bytes`

Most DOS disks use 512-byte sectors. Several third-party software packages let users format their disks using 1,024-byte sectors. The packages do this to provide support for partitions greater than 32M. The disk utilities provided on the companion disk support only these two sector sizes.

`SORTDIR: Insufficient memory`

To perform its processing, SORTDIR requires memory to hold disk sectors, FAT, and cluster information as well as its own tables. If SORTDIR cannot allocate sufficient memory, it displays an error message and returns control to DOS. Although the memory requirements vary based upon your disk size and the number of files in each directory, most of the companion disk utilities require a maximum of 256K.

`SORTDIR: Error reading file allocation table`

To track files and directories, the disk utilities provided on the companion disk must read cluster information from the FAT. If a utility encounters an error while reading the FAT, the utility displays an error message and exits to DOS.

Should this error occur, test your disk using CHKDSK. File allocation table errors are very serious. Back up your disk immediately. You may need to format your disk and restore backups to correct the error.

`SORTDIR: Directory not found`

If SORTDIR cannot locate the directory containing the desired files, SORTDIR displays an error message and exits to DOS. Should this error message occur, make sure you are using a correct and complete path name to the subdirectory. This error is most often caused by omitting backslashes in the path name.

`SORTDIR: Error reading directory sector`

If this error occurs, SORTDIR encountered a disk error while attempting to read one of the sectors containing directory information. This error is often a sign of bad times to come. Should this error occur, back up your disk immediately. Next, invoke CHKDSK to examine your disk. You may need to format your disk to remove the damaged sector, restoring your backup files.

`SORTDIR: Error writing directory sector`

If this error occurs, SORTDIR encountered a disk error while attempting to write one of the sectors containing the sorted directory information. This error is also a sign of bad times to come. Should this error occur, back up your disk immediately. Next, invoke CHKDSK to examine your disk. You may need to format your disk to remove the damaged sector, restoring your backup files.

How SORTDIR Works

The SORTDIR utility begins by reading the directory specified as shown in the following figures.

Unsorted directory
BBB.DAT
32
1-19-90
14:25
ARCHIVE
37
AAA.DAT
67
2-2-90
12:51
READ-ONLY
CCC.DAT
87
3-4-90
15:51
ARCHIVE
118

Sorted directory
AAA.DAT
67
2-2-90
12:51
READ-ONLY
BBB.DAT
32
1-19-90
14:25
ARCHIVE
CCC.DAT
87
3-4-90
15:51
ARCHIVE
118

Once you select a sort option, SORTDIR sorts your directory, shuffling entries as necessary. Once the sort is complete, SORTDIR writes the sorted directory to disk as shown in the second figure.

SORTDIR does not move hidden or system files.

18

Undeleting
Erased Files

- ▶ Using UNDELETE
- ▶ Understanding UNDELETE Error Messages
- ▶ How UNDELETE Works

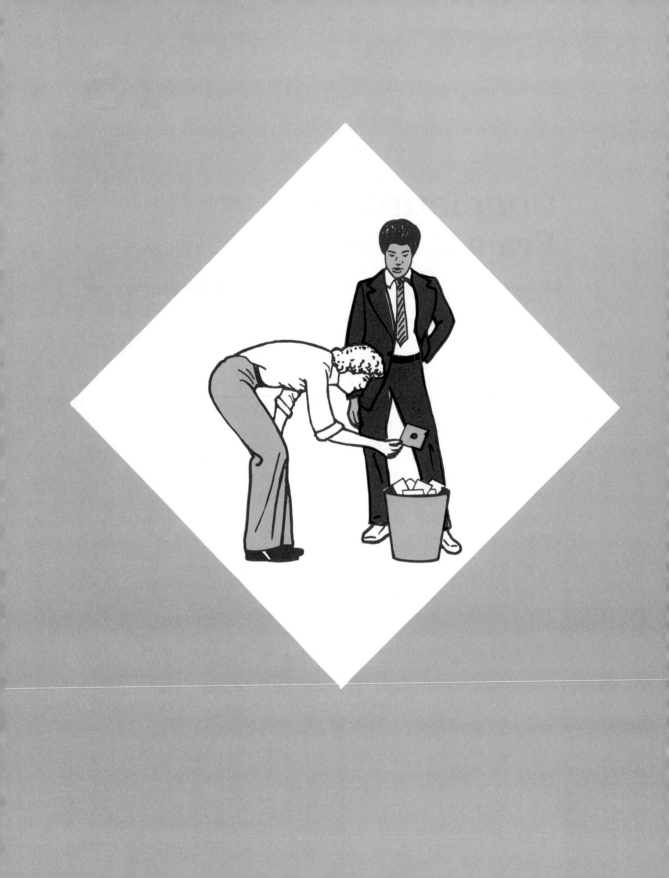

18

Undeleting Erased Files

The more files you create, change, and later delete, the greater your chance of inadvertently deleting a needed file. In Chapter 14, you examined the SELDEL utility which reduces the possibility of erasing needed files by letting you selectively delete files from a menu-driven interface. Even using SELDEL, you may eventually delete one or more files in error. In such cases, the UNDELETE utility provided with the Jamsa Disk Utilities is indispensable. UNDELETE lets you quickly recover one or more deleted files from a menu interface.

Using UNDELETE

When you delete a file using the DEL command, DOS doesn't actually erase the file's contents from your disk. Instead, it marks the file's directory entry and FAT entries as unused. The disk sectors containing the file's data are left unchanged. Because the file's information still actually resides on disk, UNDELETE can rebuild the file.

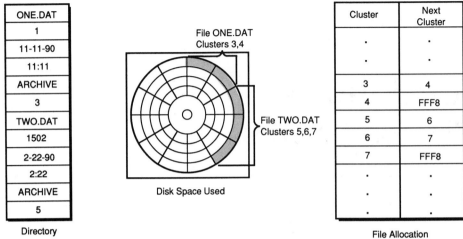

Cluster	Next Cluster
.	.
.	.
3	4
4	FFF8
5	6
6	7
7	FFF8
.	.
.	.
.	.

File Allocation Table

Directory

Disk Space Used

File ONE.DAT Clusters 3,4

File TWO.DAT Clusters 5,6,7

C> DEL TWO.DAT

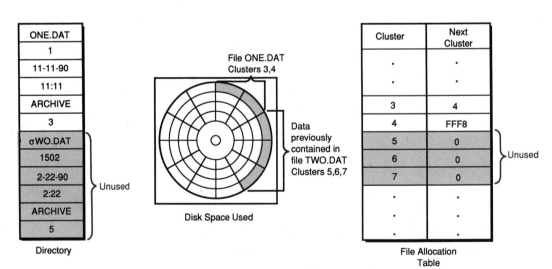

Cluster	Next Cluster
.	.
.	.
3	4
4	FFF8
5	0
6	0
7	0
.	.
.	.
.	.

File Allocation Table

Directory

Disk Space Used

File ONE.DAT Clusters 3,4

Data previously contained in file TWO.DAT Clusters 5,6,7

Unused

When DEL deletes a file, DEL marks the file's directory entry as unused by assigning the σ character to the first letter of the file name DEL. Then DEL sets all of the File Allocation Table clusters associated with the file to 0 indicating they are unused. The rest of the directory entry remains intact. DEL does not erase the file contents on back.

If you inadvertently delete a file, do not create another file on your disk. If you do, DOS may overwrite the deleted file's disk space. Once a file is overwritten, you cannot recover it.

If you inadvertently delete files, immediately invoke UNDELETE from the Power Shell by pressing F1, or from the DOS prompt as follows:

```
C:\> UNDELETE
```

UNDELETE will display its first screen which prompts you to enter the directory containing the files you want to undelete.

```
┌─────────────────────────────────────────────────────────────────────┐
│  ┌─────────────────────────────────────────────────────────────────┐ │
│  │   File Undelete, Jamsa Utilities Version 1.0 (C) 1989-90 Kris Jamsa │ │
│  └─────────────────────────────────────────────────────────────────┘ │
│                                                                       │
│  Directory:                                                           │
│  Status: Press Enter for current directory or Esc to Exit.            │
└─────────────────────────────────────────────────────────────────────┘
```

So that you have two files to undelete, delete the files DISKINFO.EXE and FINDFILE.EXE from the DISKUTIL subdirectory:

```
C:\> DEL \DISKUTIL\DISKINFO.EXE
C:\> DEL \DISKUTIL\FINDFILE.EXE
```

Next, invoke UNDELETE and use the DISKUTIL subdirectory. UNDELETE will display the message `Working..` as it searches your disk for the subdirectory. If it successfully locates the directory, UNDELETE will display the deleted file entries contained in the subdirectory.

```
┌───────────────────────────────────────────────────────────────────────┐
│  ┌─────────────────────────────────────────────────────────────────┐   │
│  │  Type first letter of filename. Press F10 to UNDELETE Esc to exit. │   │
│  └─────────────────────────────────────────────────────────────────┘   │
│                                                                         │
│      ISKINFO.EXE        59,110 bytes      03-29-1990      14:52:14       │
│      INDFILE.EXE        56,784 bytes      03-29-1990      14:52:36       │
│                                                                         │
│                                                                         │
│                                                                         │
│                                                                         │
│                                                                         │
│  ┌─────────────────────────────────────────────────────────────────┐   │
│  │ Directory: C:\DISKUTIL                                            │   │
│  └─────────────────────────────────────────────────────────────────┘   │
└───────────────────────────────────────────────────────────────────────┘
```

When you delete a DOS file, DOS marks the file's directory entry as unused by assigning the character σ to the first letter of the file name. In the preceding figure, DOS has replaced the D of DISKINFO and the F of FINDFILE with σ.

To select a file for undeletion, use the arrow keys to highlight the file and then type the first letter of the original file name. In this case, enter D as the first letter for DISKINFO and F as the first letter of FINDFILE.

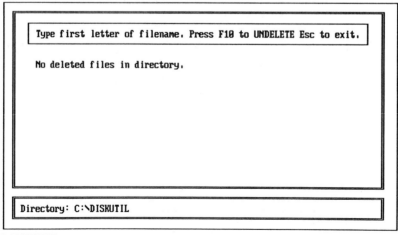

When you enter the first letter for a file, you select that file for undeletion. To actually undelete the files, you must press the F10 function key. In this case when you press F10, UNDELETE will recover both files. Because no other deleted files exist in the directory, UNDELETE displays the following screen.

```
┌──────────────────────────────────────────────────────────────┐
│  ┌──────────────────────────────────────────────────────────┐ │
│  │ Type first letter of filename. Press F10 to UNDELETE Esc to exit. │ │
│  └──────────────────────────────────────────────────────────┘ │
│                                                                │
│     No deleted files in directory.                             │
│                                                                │
│                                                                │
│                                                                │
│                                                                │
│                                                                │
│  ┌──────────────────────────────────────────────────────────┐ │
│  │ Directory: C:\DISKUTIL                                     │ │
│  └──────────────────────────────────────────────────────────┘ │
└──────────────────────────────────────────────────────────────┘
```

C:\DISKUTIL>

A directory listing of DISKUTIL reveals that the files have been successfully restored.

```
C:\> DIR \DISKUTIL

  Volume in drive C is DOS
  Directory of  C:\DISKUTIL

DATETIME EXE      77032    3-29-90    2:52p
DISKINFO EXE      59110    3-29-90    2:52p
DISKSAVE EXE      58014    3-29-90    2:52p
FILEATTR EXE      72184    3-29-90    2:52p
FINDFILE EXE      56784    3-29-90    2:52p
KILLFILE EXE      72694    3-29-90    2:53p
POWER    EXE      66064    3-29-90    2:53p
RENDIR   EXE      64148    3-29-90    2:53p
SELCOPY  EXE      75328    3-29-90    2:53p
SELDEL   EXE      70220    3-29-90    2:53p
SORTDIR  EXE      70860    3-29-90    2:54p
SQUEEZE  EXE      64014    3-29-90    2:54p
TESTFRAG EXE      56470    3-29-90    2:54p
UNDELETE EXE      74424    3-29-90    2:54p
UNFORMAT EXE      60586    3-29-90    2:54p
        17 File(s)   19611648 bytes free
```

So you can experiment with UNDELETE, delete the files DISKINFO.EXE, DISKSAVE.EXE, and DATETIME.EXE from the DISKUTIL subdirectory, as shown here:

```
C:\>DEL \DISKUTIL\D*.EXE
```

Invoke UNDELETE, again using the subdirectory DISKUTIL. In this case, UNDELETE will display the following deleted files.

```
┌─────────────────────────────────────────────────────────────┐
│ ┌───────────────────────────────────────────────────────┐   │
│ │  Type first letter of filename. Press F10 to UNDELETE Esc to exit. │
│ └───────────────────────────────────────────────────────┘   │
│                                                              │
│     █ATETIME.EXE     77,032 bytes     03-29-1990    14:52:06 │
│     σISKINFO.EXE     59,110 bytes     03-29-1990    14:52:14 │
│     σISKSAVE.EXE     58,014 bytes     03-29-1990    14:52:20 │
│                                                              │
│                                                              │
│                                                              │
│ ┌───────────────────────────────────────────────────────┐   │
│ │ Directory: C:\DISKUTIL                                │   │
│ └───────────────────────────────────────────────────────┘   │
└─────────────────────────────────────────────────────────────┘
```

Highlight the entry for DISKINFO.EXE and type D.

```
┌─────────────────────────────────────────────────────────────┐
│ ┌───────────────────────────────────────────────────────┐   │
│ │  Type first letter of filename. Press F10 to UNDELETE Esc to exit. │
│ └───────────────────────────────────────────────────────┘   │
│                                                              │
│     σATETIME.EXE     77,032 bytes     03-29-1990    14:52:06 │
│     D█ISKINFO█.EXE   59,110 bytes     03-29-1990    14:52:14 │
│     σISKSAVE.EXE     58,014 bytes     03-29-1990    14:52:20 │
│                                                              │
│                                                              │
│                                                              │
│ ┌───────────────────────────────────────────────────────┐   │
│ │ Directory: C:\DISKUTIL                                │   │
│ └───────────────────────────────────────────────────────┘   │
└─────────────────────────────────────────────────────────────┘
```

UNDELETE lets you unselect a file using the space bar. If you press the space bar with DISKINFO.EXE highlighted, UNDELETE will restore the σ character indicating that the file is not selected for undeletion. If you select the DISKINFO.EXE file and press the space bar, your screen will again appear. Select the file DISKSAVE.EXE for undeletion and press F10. UNDELETE will undelete that file and remove the file from the list of deleted file names, as shown here.

```
┌──────────────────────────────────────────────────────────────────┐
│ ┌──────────────────────────────────────────────────────────────┐ │
│ │ Type first letter of filename, Press F10 to UNDELETE Esc to exit, │ │
│ └──────────────────────────────────────────────────────────────┘ │
│                                                                    │
│    ▐DATETIME▌.EXE      77,032 bytes      03-29-1990    14:52:06     │
│    σISKINFO.EXE        59,110 bytes      03-29-1990    14:52:14     │
│                                                                    │
│                                                                    │
│                                                                    │
│                                                                    │
│                                                                    │
│                                                                    │
│                                                                    │
│ ┌──────────────────────────────────────────────────────────────┐ │
│ │ Directory: C:\DISKUTIL                                          │ │
│ └──────────────────────────────────────────────────────────────┘ │
└──────────────────────────────────────────────────────────────────┘
```

In this case, select the files DISKINFO.EXE and DATETIME.EXE, and press F10 to undelete the files.

As discussed, UNDELETE cannot undelete a file that has been overwritten. If UNDELETE is unable to undelete a selected file because it was overwritten, UNDELETE will display the following error message.

```
┌──────────────────────────────────────────────────────────────────┐
│ ┌──────────────────────────────────────────────────────────────┐ │
│ │ FILENAME.EXT: sectors have been overwritten, Cannot undelete file, │ │
│ └──────────────────────────────────────────────────────────────┘ │
│                                                                    │
│    ▐FILENAME▌.EXT        13 bytes        04-09-1990    15:26:16     │
│                                                                    │
│                                                                    │
│                                                                    │
│                                                                    │
│                                                                    │
│                                                                    │
│                                                                    │
│ ┌──────────────────────────────────────────────────────────────┐ │
│ │ Directory: C:\DISKUTIL                                          │ │
│ └──────────────────────────────────────────────────────────────┘ │
└──────────────────────────────────────────────────────────────────┘
```

SQUEEZE and UNDELETE

Chapter 15 discussed the use of the SQUEEZE utility, which removes unused (deleted) directory entries for better performance. Because UNDELETE uses the same deleted directory entries to recover a file, you cannot UNDELETE files after SQUEEZE has been used. The directory entries associated with the deleted files no longer exist.

The SQUEEZE utility is fundamental for getting the best performance from your system. Before you invoke SQUEEZE, however, make sure you don't want to undelete any files from the directory. Remember, using UNDELETE, you can display a subdirectory's unused directory entries so you can determine the directory entries SQUEEZE will eliminate.

Understanding UNDELETE Error Messages

The UNDELETE utility displays several possible error messages. The following sections describe the causes and solutions for each error in detail.

```
UNDELETE: Requires DOS 2.0 or higher
```

Prior to version 2, DOS did not provide support for hard disks. The programs on the Jamsa Disk Utilities, therefore, require DOS 2.0 as a minimum.

```
UNDELETE: Only specify .. once in directory name
```

The UNDELETE utility supports the use of the parent directory abbreviation (..). For example, assume that you are in a DOS subdirectory and are using the parent directory abbreviation, you can use UNDELETE to access files residing in the parent, as shown here.

```
    File Undelete, Jamsa Utilities Version 1.0 (C) 1989-90 Kris Jamsa

Directory: ..
Status:
```

To avoid confusion when multiple levels of directories are used, UNDELETE only lets you specify the parent directory abbreviation once per directory name. Should this error occur, simply use a complete path name to the directory.

```
UNDELETE: The abbreviation .. must appear at start of path
name
```

As just discussed, UNDELETE fully supports the parent subdirectory abbreviation (..). If you specify this abbreviation, it must occur at the beginning of the path name.

```
UNDELETE: Invalid file or drive specification
```

If the specified disk drive does not exist, UNDELETE will display this error message and return control to DOS. Should this error occur, make sure you are using a valid disk drive letter. If the disk drive is valid, invoke the DISKINFO utility discussed in Chapter 11 to examine the disk drive.

```
UNDELETE:  SUBST and ASSIGN not supported
```

As discussed in Chapter 5, DOS lets you create logical disk drives using the SUBST command. By using logical drives, users can abbreviate a long directory name with a single drive letter. To prevent confusion from using logical drives, UNDELETE simply does not support them.

```
UNDELETE: Network drives not supported
```

In most cases, running disk management utilities on a disk drive used by a local area network can be quite dangerous. Disk utilities work by accessing individual sectors of a disk. In a network, access to a disk is controlled by network software. To prevent an incompatibility between the network software and the disk utility software from damaging your disk, the low-level utilities on the Jamsa Disk Utilities do not support network drives.

```
UNDELETE:  Sector size must be 512 or 1024 bytes
```

Most DOS disks use 512-byte sectors. To provide support for partitions greater than 32 megabytes, several third-party software packages let users format their disks using 1024-byte sectors. The Jamsa Disk Utilities only support these two sector sizes.

UNDELETE: Insufficient memory

To perform its processing, UNDELETE requires enough memory to hold disk sectors, FAT and cluster information, and its own tables. If UNDELETE cannot allocate sufficient memory, it will display an error message and return control to DOS. Although the memory requirements will vary based upon your disk size and the number of files in each directory, most of the Jamsa Disk Utilities require a maximum of 256K.

UNDELETE: Error reading file allocation table

To track files and directories, the Jamsa Disk Utilities must read cluster information from the FAT. If a utility encounters an error while reading the FAT, it will display an error message and exit to DOS.

Should this error occur, test your disk using CHKDSK. File allocation table errors are very serious. Back up your disk immediately. You may need to format your disk and restore backups to correct the error.

UNDELETE: Directory not found

If UNDELETE cannot locate the directory containing the desired files, UNDELETE will display an error message and exit to DOS. Should this error message occur, make sure you are using a correct and complete path name to the subdirectory. This error is most often caused by omitting back slashes in the path name.

UNDELETE: Error reading directory sector

If this error occurs, UNDELETE encountered a disk error while attempting to read one of the sectors containing directory information. This error is often indicative of serious problems to come. Should this error occur, back up your disk immediately. Then, invoke CHKDSK to examine your disk. You may need to format your disk to remove the damaged sector, and then restore your backup files.

```
UNDELETE: Error writing directory sector
```

If this error occurs, UNDELETE encountered a disk error while attempting to write one of the sectors containing the sorted directory information. This error is also indicative of problems to come. Should this error occur, back up your disk immediately. Then, invoke CHKDSK to examine your disk. You may need to format your disk to remove the damaged sector and then restore your backup files.

```
UNDELETE: No deleted files in directory.
```

The specified directory does not contain any deleted files. Remember, when you delete a file and then create another file in the same directory, DOS uses the first unused directory entry it finds. As a result, you can no longer undelete the overwritten file.

```
FILENAME: sectors have been overwritten. Cannot undelete
file.
```

When you inadvertantly delete one or more files, do not create any other files on your disk. If you create a file, you risk overwriting the information contained in the file you just deleted. When a file is overwritten, UNDELETE cannot recover the information it contained and, as such, displays the previous error message. If this message occurs, you must rely on your latest file backups.

```
FILENAME: partially recovered. Some sectors overwritten.
```

See the previous error message. UNDELETE displays this error message when one or more sectors of the file it was attempting to undelete have been overwritten. When this error occurs, UNDELETE will recover as much of the file as it can. You may have to restore your latest backups to recover the file.

How UNDELETE Works

Each time you create a file on disk, DOS creates a subdirectory entry for the file and tracks the clusters containing the file's data in the file allocation table. Assume that your disk contains the files ONE, TWO, and THREE, as shown here.

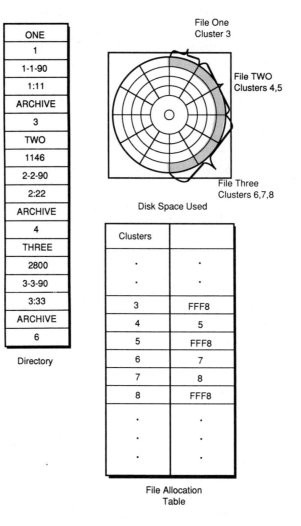

ONE
1
1-1-90
1:11
ARCHIVE
3
TWO
1146
2-2-90
2:22
ARCHIVE
4
THREE
2800
3-3-90
3:33
ARCHIVE
6

Directory

File One
Cluster 3

File TWO
Clusters 4,5

File Three
Clusters 6,7,8

Disk Space Used

Clusters	
.	.
.	.
3	FFF8
4	5
5	FFF8
6	7
7	8
8	FFF8
.	.
.	.
.	.

File Allocation
Table

If you delete file TWO, DOS marks the file's directory entry and file allocation table entries as unused, as shown here.

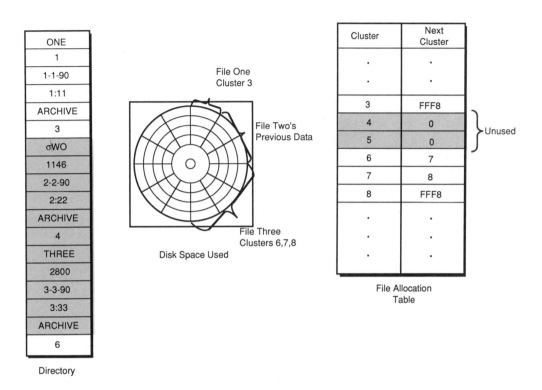

ONE	
1	
1-1-90	
1:11	
ARCHIVE	
3	
σWO	
1146	
2-2-90	
2:22	
ARCHIVE	
4	
THREE	
2800	
3-3-90	
3:33	
ARCHIVE	
6	

Directory

File One
Cluster 3

File Two's
Previous Data

File Three
Clusters 6,7,8

Disk Space Used

Cluster	Next Cluster
.	.
.	.
3	FFF8
4	0
5	0
6	7
7	8
8	FFF8
.	.
.	.
.	.

Unused

File Allocation
Table

If you invoke the UNDELETE utility, it will read the directory displaying the entry for file TWO.

```
┌──────────────────────────────────────────────────────────────┐
│ ┌────────────────────────────────────────────────────────┐   │
│ │ Type first letter of filename, Press F10 to UNDELETE Esc to exit, │
│ └────────────────────────────────────────────────────────┘   │
│                                                                │
│   ▓WO    .        5 bytes      04-09-1990     13:56:42         │
│                                                                │
│                                                                │
│                                                                │
│                                                                │
│ ┌────────────────────────────────────────────────────────┐   │
│ │ Directory: C:\DISKUTIL                                   │   │
│ └────────────────────────────────────────────────────────┘   │
└──────────────────────────────────────────────────────────────┘
```

If you select file TWO for undeletion, UNDELETE uses the deleted file's directory entry to determine file TWO's first cluster and the file's original size.

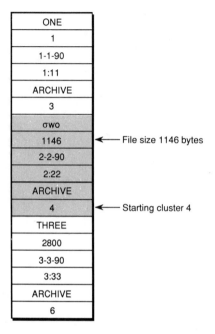

| ONE |
| 1 |
| 1-1-90 |
| 1:11 |
| ARCHIVE |
| 3 |

σWO ← File size 1146 bytes
1146
2-2-90
2:22
ARCHIVE
4 ← Starting cluster 4

| THREE |
| 2800 |
| 3-3-90 |
| 3:33 |
| ARCHIVE |
| 6 |

Using the file size, UNDELETE can determine the number of clusters in the original file. For example, assume that the disk uses two 512-byte sectors per cluster:

```
Number of clusters = File size / (Sectors per Cluster *
                     Sector Size)
                   = 1146 / (2 * 512)
                   = 1146 / 1024
                   = 1.119
                   = 2 clusters
```

Next, UNDELETE assumes that the original file was *contiguous*. Starting at the file's first cluster, UNDELETE assigns the first free clusters to the file.

Cluster	Next Cluster
.	.
.	.
3	FFF8
4	0
5	0
6	7
7	8
8	FFF8
.	.
.	.

Original File
Allocation Table

Cluster	Next Cluster
.	.
.	.
3	FFF8
4	5
5	FFF8
6	7
7	8
8	FFF8
.	.
.	.

File TWO { 4, 5, 6 }

Ending File
Allocation Table

UNDELETE then updates the directory to its previous condition, as shown here.

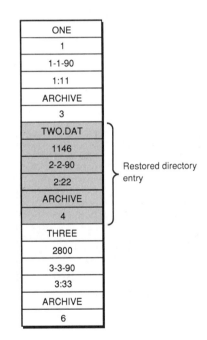

ONE
1
1-1-90
1:11
ARCHIVE
3
TWO.DAT
1146
2-2-90
2:22
ARCHIVE
4
THREE
2800
3-3-90
3:33
ARCHIVE
6

Restored directory entry

Assuming that you had deleted all three files, UNDELETE will determine the number of clusters in each file as follows:

File	Number of Clusters	Starting Cluster
ONE	= 1/1024 = 1	3
TWO	= 1146/1024 = 2	4
THREE	= 2800/1024 = 3	6

UNDELETE Cannot Recover Overwritten Files

As previously stated, if you inadvertently delete one or more files, do not create another file on your disk until you undelete the desired files. If you create new files on your disk, DOS may very likely overwrite the information in a file you want to undelete.

Assume that your disk contains the files ONE, TWO, and THREE, as shown here.

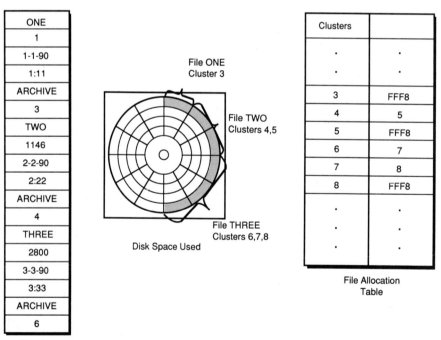

ONE
1
1-1-90
1:11
ARCHIVE
3
TWO
1146
2-2-90
2:22
ARCHIVE
4
THREE
2800
3-3-90
3:33
ARCHIVE
6

Directory

File ONE
Cluster 3

File TWO
Clusters 4,5

File THREE
Clusters 6,7,8

Disk Space Used

Clusters	
.	.
.	.
3	FFF8
4	5
5	FFF8
6	7
7	8
8	FFF8
.	.
.	.
.	.

File Allocation
Table

If you delete file ONE, DOS marks file ONE's directory and FAT entries as unused.

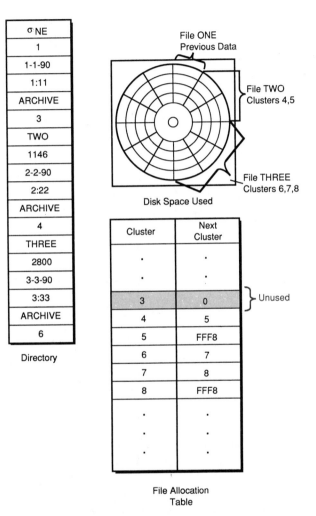

Directory

File ONE
Previous Data

File TWO
Clusters 4,5

File THREE
Clusters 6,7,8

Disk Space Used

Cluster	Next Cluster
.	.
.	.
3	0
4	5
5	FFF8
6	7
7	8
8	FFF8
.	.
.	.
.	.

Unused

File Allocation Table

If you then create file FOUR, DOS will use the first unused directory and FAT entries.

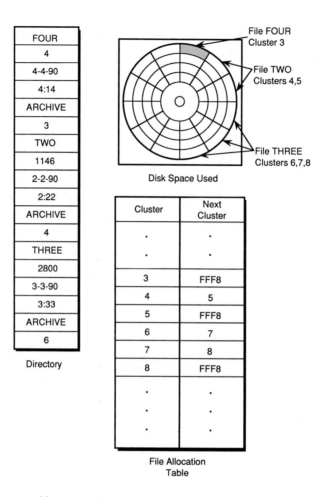

FOUR
4
4-4-90
4:14
ARCHIVE
3
TWO
1146
2-2-90
2:22
ARCHIVE
4
THREE
2800
3-3-90
3:33
ARCHIVE
6

Directory

File FOUR
Cluster 3

File TWO
Clusters 4,5

File THREE
Clusters 6,7,8

Disk Space Used

Cluster	Next Cluster
.	.
.	.
3	FFF8
4	5
5	FFF8
6	7
7	8
8	FFF8
.	.
.	.
.	.

File Allocation
Table

In this case, file FOUR has overwritten the disk locations previously used by file ONE. As a result, you cannot recover file ONE.

Fragmented Files May Prevent Successful Undeletion

Chapter 9 discussed fragmented files in detail. In it, you learned that a fragmented file is a file whose clusters are not consecutive.

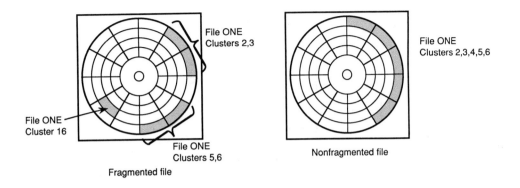

File ONE
Cluster 16

File ONE
Clusters 2,3

File ONE
Clusters 5,6

Fragmented file

File ONE
Clusters 2,3,4,5,6

Nonfragmented file

Assume, for example, that your disk contains fragmented files TWO and THREE, as shown here.

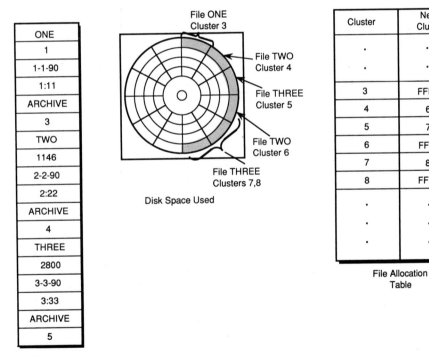

ONE
1
1-1-90
1:11
ARCHIVE
3
TWO
1146
2-2-90
2:22
ARCHIVE
4
THREE
2800
3-3-90
3:33
ARCHIVE
5

Directory

File ONE
Cluster 3

File TWO
Cluster 4

File THREE
Cluster 5

File TWO
Cluster 6

File THREE
Clusters 7,8

Disk Space Used

Cluster	Next Cluster
.	.
.	.
3	FFF8
4	6
5	7
6	FFF8
7	8
8	FFF8
.	.
.	.
.	.

File Allocation
Table

If you inadvertently delete file TWO, UNDELETE can recover the file as shown.

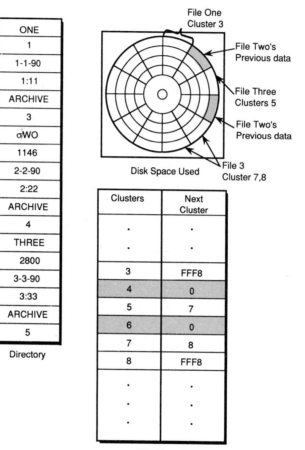

	ONE
	1
	1-1-90
	1:11
	ARCHIVE
	3
	oWO
	1146
	2-2-90
	2:22
	ARCHIVE
	4
	THREE
	2800
	3-3-90
	3:33
	ARCHIVE
	5

Directory

File One
Cluster 3

File Two's
Previous data

File Three
Clusters 5

File Two's
Previous data

Disk Space Used

File 3
Cluster 7,8

Clusters	Next Cluster
.	.
.	.
3	FFF8
4	0
5	7
6	0
7	8
8	FFF8
.	.
.	.
.	.

File Allocation
Table

Deleting file Two marks the files directory
and file allocation table entries unused.

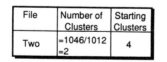

File	Number of Clusters	Starting Clusters
Two	=1046/1012 =2	4

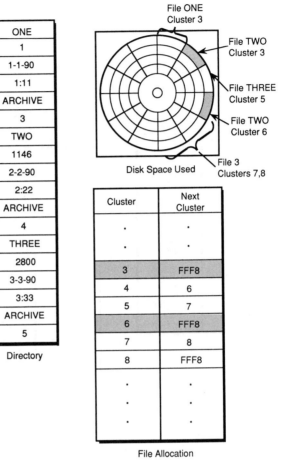

ONE
1
1-1-90
1:11
ARCHIVE
3
TWO
1146
2-2-90
2:22
ARCHIVE
4
THREE
2800
3-3-90
3:33
ARCHIVE
5

Directory

File ONE
Cluster 3

File TWO
Cluster 3

File THREE
Cluster 5

File TWO
Cluster 6

File 3
Clusters 7,8

Disk Space Used

Cluster	Next Cluster
.	.
.	.
3	FFF8
4	6
5	7
6	FFF8
7	8
8	FFF8
.	.
.	.
.	.

File Allocation
Table

To restore file TWO, UNDELETE rebuilds the
File Allocation Table and directory.

However, assume that you delete files TWO and THREE.

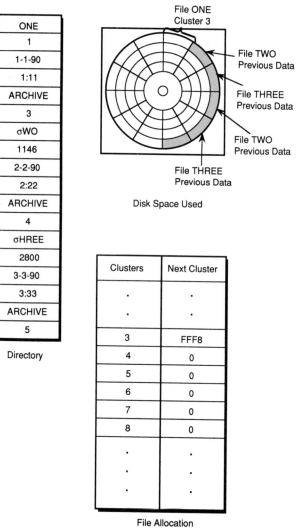

ONE
1
1-1-90
1:11
ARCHIVE
3
σWO
1146
2-2-90
2:22
ARCHIVE
4
σHREE
2800
3-3-90
3:33
ARCHIVE
5

Directory

File ONE
Cluster 3

File TWO
Previous Data

File THREE
Previous Data

File TWO
Previous Data

File THREE
Previous Data

Disk Space Used

Clusters	Next Cluster
.	.
.	.
3	FFF8
4	0
5	0
6	0
7	0
8	0
.	.
.	.
.	.

File Allocation
Table

If you use UNDELETE to recover file TWO, UNDELETE assumes the file is contiguous and restores the following clusters. It has no way of knowing the original file was fragmented.

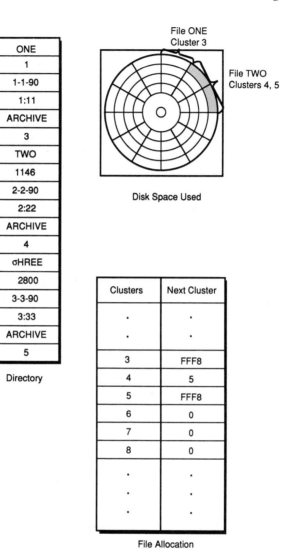

ONE
1
1-1-90
1:11
ARCHIVE
3
TWO
1146
2-2-90
2:22
ARCHIVE
4
σHREE
2800
3-3-90
3:33
ARCHIVE
5

Directory

File ONE
Cluster 3

File TWO
Clusters 4, 5

Disk Space Used

Clusters	Next Cluster
.	.
.	.
3	FFF8
4	5
5	FFF8
6	0
7	0
8	0
.	.
.	.
.	.

File Allocation
Table

Because the files were originally fragmented, UNDELETE has assigned a cluster previously belonging to file THREE to file TWO. Should you undelete file THREE, UNDELETE will assign file THREE a cluster previously belonging to file TWO.

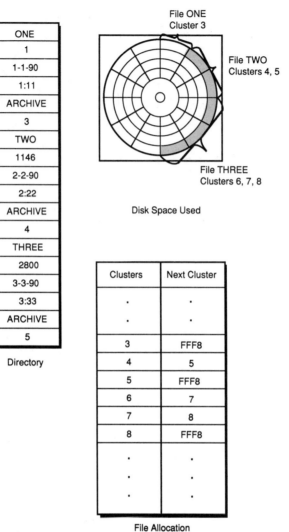

ONE
1
1-1-90
1:11
ARCHIVE
3
TWO
1146
2-2-90
2:22
ARCHIVE
4
THREE
2800
3-3-90
3:33
ARCHIVE
5

Directory

File ONE
Cluster 3

File TWO
Clusters 4, 5

File THREE
Clusters 6, 7, 8

Disk Space Used

Clusters	Next Cluster
.	.
.	.
3	FFF8
4	5
5	FFF8
6	7
7	8
8	FFF8
.	.
.	.
.	.

File Allocation
Table

UNDELETE has no way of knowing the files were originally fragmented. If the files contained text, you can probably correct the mix up using your text editor or a word processor. If the files contained executable programs or other data, you will need to restore the files from your system backups.

As discussed in Chapter 21, you should invoke the TESTFRAG utility on a regular basis to identify fragmented files. Using the techniques discussed in Chapter 9 or a third party defragmentor, you should correct fragmented files. By doing so, you improve your system performance and increase the likelihood of successful file undeletion.

Undeleting An Entire Directory

In some cases, a user may delete all of the files in a directory and then use RMDIR to remove the directory entry only to discover they still need the files. If, for example, you delete the directory DATA that contains 100 data files.

```
C:\> DEL \DATA
All files in directory will be deleted!
Are you sure (Y/N)? Y

C:\> RMDIR \DATA
```

To recover the files, you must first recover the directory. In this case, you would recover DATA from the root directory, as shown here.

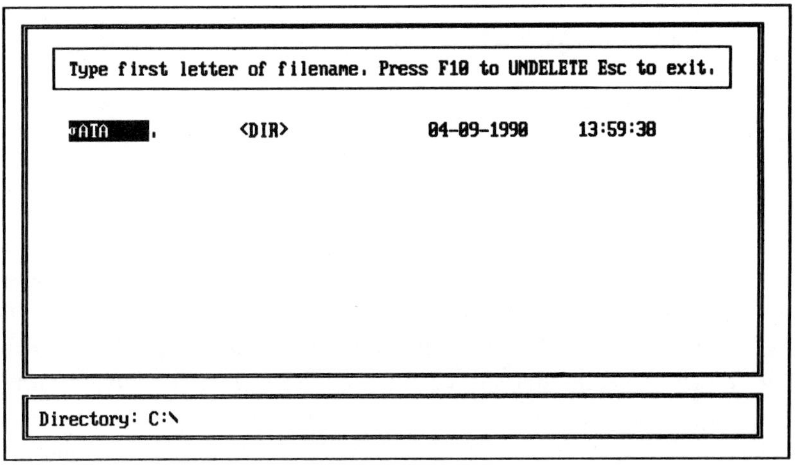

```
Type first letter of filename, Press F10 to UNDELETE Esc to exit,
```

```
?ATA    .    <DIR>        04-09-1990    13:59:30
```

```
Directory: C:\
```

Next, you must invoke UNDELETE with the subdirectory DATA.

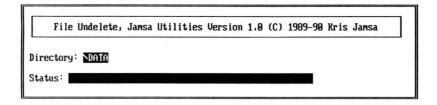

```
┌──────────────────────────────────────────────────────────────┐
│  ┌────────────────────────────────────────────────────────┐  │
│  │   File Undelete, Jamsa Utilities Version 1.0 (C) 1989-90 Kris Jamsa │  │
│  └────────────────────────────────────────────────────────┘  │
│                                                                │
│   Directory: █DATA                                             │
│                                                                │
│   Status: ██████████████████████████████████████              │
│                                                                │
└──────────────────────────────────────────────────────────────┘
```

If UNDELETE is successful, UNDELETE will display the deleted data files.

```
┌──────────────────────────────────────────────────────────────────┐
│  ┌────────────────────────────────────────────────────────────┐  │
│  │  Type first letter of filename. Press F10 to UNDELETE Esc to exit.│  │
│  └────────────────────────────────────────────────────────────┘  │
│                                                                    │
│     ▓0        .        14 bytes    04-09-1990    14:04:00          │
│     ⌐1        .        14 bytes    04-09-1990    14:04:00          │
│     ⌐2        .        14 bytes    04-09-1990    14:04:00          │
│     ⌐3        .        14 bytes    04-09-1990    14:04:00          │
│     ⌐4        .        14 bytes    04-09-1990    14:04:00          │
│     ⌐5        .        14 bytes    04-09-1990    14:04:00          │
│     ⌐6        .        14 bytes    04-09-1990    14:04:00          │
│     ⌐7        .        14 bytes    04-09-1990    14:04:00          │
│     ⌐8        .        14 bytes    04-09-1990    14:04:02          │
│     ⌐9        .        14 bytes    04-09-1990    14:04:02          │
│                                                                    │
│  ┌────────────────────────────────────────────────────────────┐  │
│  │  Directory: C:\DATA                                         │  │
│  └────────────────────────────────────────────────────────────┘  │
└──────────────────────────────────────────────────────────────────┘
```

Recovering a deleted subdirectory is UNDELETE's biggest challenge.

Because most directories grow over a period of time, directories are almost guaranteed to be fragmented. As a result, if UNDELETE does not find the end of the directory marker in the directory's first disk cluster, UNDELETE begins searching the disk's unused clusters for the directory's next cluster.

In most cases, UNDELETE will locate the correct directory cluster. However, if you have recently deleted several directories, UNDELETE may possibly include entries from a different directory in the directory you are attempting to undelete, just as UNDELETE may periodically intermix fragmented files. If this occurs, undelete as many files as possible, and then restore the remaining files from your backups. In this case, UNDELETE has made its best attempt to minimize the damage of a subdirectory deletion.

In most cases, UNDELETE will successfully and quickly recover inadvertently deleted files. As you have seen, there may be obstacles that prevent UNDELETE from successfully recovering all of your files. For those cases, you must rely on your recent backups.

19

Ensuring File Deletions

- ► Using KILLFILE
- ► Understanding KILLFILE Error Messages
- ► How KILLFILE Works

Ensuring File Deletions

In Chapter 14, you learned how to selectively delete files using the SELDEL utility provided with the Jamsa Disk Utilities. For most file delete operations, you will use SELDEL to quickly select and delete files without the risk of an errant DEL command. However, as you will learn in this chapter, deleting "sensitive" files with DEL or SELDEL does not guarantee that the file is gone forever.

In Chapter 18, you learned how to use the UNDELETE utility to recover previously deleted files. Although UNDELETE is probably the most commonly used utility in the Jamsa Disk Utilities, there may be rare instances when you wish it didn't exist. For example, assume that you have written and printed a critical office memo that you don't want your employees to see. If you delete the file using the DEL command, an employee with access to your computer may be able to undelete the file using UNDELETE. As a result, the important memo you thought you had safely erased is back.

As long as third-party undelete programs exist, you need a way to ensure that specific files that you delete cannot be undeleted. The KILLFILE utility on the companion disk does just that.

When DEL deletes a file, it does not actually remove the file's data from disk. Instead, DEL marks the file's directory entry as unused and the file clusters in the FAT as available. Third-party undelete programs reverse this process to recover deleted files.

The KILLFILE utility deletes a file by first overwriting every byte of the file's previous contents on disk with ones. Then, KILLFILE overwrites the file's contents with zeros. KILLFILE repeats this process for three series of zeros and ones in accordance with the Department Of Defense

Security Specification DOD 52220.22M. KILLFILE then overwrites the file with a final series of ones. Each time KILLFILE overwrites the file's contents, KILLFILE reads the file's contents to verify that the overwrite was successful.

Next, KILLFILE changes the file's directory entry and marks the file's clusters as unused. KILLFILE makes file undeletion impossible.

Using KILLFILE

So that you have a file to KILL, issue the following commands:

```
C:\> COPY CON \DISKUTIL\SECURE.LTR
This letter is a secure memo.
It should not be available to
undelete.
^Z
    1 File(s) copied
```

Invoke KILLFILE to KILL the file from the Power Shell by pressing the Alt +F2 keyboard combination, or invoke it from the DOS prompt as follows:

```
C:\> KILLFILE
```

KILLFILE will display its first screen, prompting you to enter the directory containing the files to KILL. Type in DISKUTIL, as shown here.

```
┌──────────────────────────────────────────────────────────────┐
│  ┌──────────────────────────────────────────────────────────┐ │
│  │ File Kill Utility, Jamsa Utilities Version 1.0 (C) 1989-90 Kris Jamsa │ │
│  └──────────────────────────────────────────────────────────┘ │
│                                                                │
│  Directory: \DISKUTIL                                          │
│                                                                │
│  Status: ████████████████████████████████████████████         │
│                                                                │
└──────────────────────────────────────────────────────────────┘
```

When you press Enter, KILLFILE will display the message Working.. as it searches your disk for the directory specified. If KILLFILE successfully locates the directory, it will display the files that reside in the directory.

```
┌──────────────────────────────────────────────────────────────────┐
│ ┌────────────────────────────────────────────────────────────┐   │
│ │  Use arrow keys to highlight a file.  Press Enter to select or │
│ │  unselect a file.  Press F10 to KILL files.  Press Esc to exit. │
│ └────────────────────────────────────────────────────────────┘   │
│                                                                    │
│     DATETIME.EXE     77,032 bytes    03-29-1990    14:52:06        │
│     DISKINFO.EXE     59,110 bytes    03-29-1990    14:52:14        │
│     DISKSAVE.EXE     58,014 bytes    03-29-1990    14:52:20        │
│     FILEATTR.EXE     72,184 bytes    03-29-1990    14:52:28        │
│     FINDFILE.EXE     56,784 bytes    03-29-1990    14:52:36        │
│     KILLFILE.EXE     72,694 bytes    03-29-1990    14:53:02        │
│     POWER   .EXE     66,064 bytes    03-29-1990    14:53:08        │
│     RENDIR  .EXE     64,148 bytes    03-29-1990    14:53:16        │
│     SELCOPY .EXE     75,328 bytes    03-29-1990    14:53:26        │
│     SELDEL  .EXE     70,220 bytes    03-29-1990    14:53:34        │
│                                                                    │
│ ┌────────────────────────────────────────────────────────────┐   │
│ │ Directory: C:\DISKUTIL                                          │
│ └────────────────────────────────────────────────────────────┘   │
└──────────────────────────────────────────────────────────────────┘
```

Because DOS cannot delete read-only files, KILLFILE does not display files whose read-only attributes are set. You can change file attributes (including the read-only attribute) with the FILEATTR utility.

To select a file for deletion, use the arrow keys to highlight the file, and then press either the space bar or the Enter key. KILLFILE will display an asterisk next to the file, indicating the file has been selected for deletion. Both the space bar and the Enter key work as toggles. If you press either key for a file selected for deletion, KILLFILE will remove the asterisk, indicating that the file will not be killed. In this case, select the file SECURE.LTR, ensuring that an asterisk appears only to the left of this filename.

To KILL the selected file, press the F10 key. KILLFILE will display its third screen, as shown here.

```
┌──────────────────────────────────────────────────────────────────┐
│ ┌────────────────────────────────────────────────────────────┐   │
│ │  Select Cancel to return to file list.  Select Continue to KILL files. │
│ └────────────────────────────────────────────────────────────┘   │
│                                                                    │
│  Directory: C:\DISKUTIL                                            │
│                                                                    │
│  Delete Operation:   Cancel      Continue                          │
│                                                                    │
│  Status:                                                           │
└──────────────────────────────────────────────────────────────────┘
```

KILLFILE prompts you to verify that you really want to kill the selected files. If you select the Cancel option, KILLFILE will return to the previous screen, allowing you to view the selected files or return to DOS.

If you select the Continue option, KILLFILE will begin to work on the selected files. When it is completed, KILLFILE displays a message indicating it is complete.

When you press any key at this point, KILLFILE will return to the file menu and let you select additional files or press Esc to exit to DOS. In this case, exit KILLFILE to DOS. Next, invoke UNDELETE to examine the directory DISKUTIL. In this case, UNDELETE will display the following.

```
┌─────────────────────────────────────────────────────────────┐
│ ┌─────────────────────────────────────────────────────────┐ │
│ │ Type first letter of filename. Press F10 to UNDELETE Esc to exit. │ │
│ └─────────────────────────────────────────────────────────┘ │
│                                                              │
│    ?122      .          73 bytes      04-09-1990    14:11:44 │
│                                                              │
│                                                              │
│                                                              │
│                                                              │
│                                                              │
│                                                              │
│ ┌─────────────────────────────────────────────────────────┐ │
│ │ Directory: C:\DISKUTIL                                   │ │
│ └─────────────────────────────────────────────────────────┘ │
└─────────────────────────────────────────────────────────────┘
```

Unlike many third-party kill-file programs, KILLFILE does not remove the file's directory entry. Instead, it renames the entry with a unique name. KILLFILE does this so you can ensure the file's contents were actually overwritten. Recover this file using the name 1122.

From the DOS prompt, display the file's contents using the TYPE command.

```
C:\> TYPE \DISKUTIL\1122
☺☺☺☺☺
```

The ASCII value 1, which was the last value written to the file, creates the smiling face. As you can see, the file was overwritten. To delete this temporary file, use the DEL command, SELDEL, or KILLFILE. To remove the unused directory entry, invoke the SQUEEZE utility, discussed in Chapter 15.

As you can see, when you kill a file using KILLFILE, you can't get it back.

Understanding KILLFILE Error Messages

The KILLFILE utility displays several possible error messages. The following section describes the causes and solutions for each error in detail.

```
KILLFILE: Requires DOS 2.0 or higher
```

Prior to version 2, DOS did not provide support for hard disks. The programs on the Jamsa Disk Utilities, therefore, require DOS 2.0 as a minimum.

```
KILLFILE: Only specify .. once in directory name
```

The KILLFILE utility supports the use of the parent directory abbreviation (..). For example, assuming that you are in a DOS subdirectory, using the parent directory abbreviation, you can use KILLFILE to access files residing in the parent, as shown here.

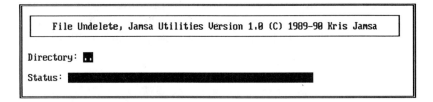

To avoid confusion when multiple levels of directories are used, KILLFILE only lets you specify the parent directory abbreviation once per directory name. Should this error occur, simply use a complete path name to the directory.

```
KILLFILE: The abbreviation .. must appear at start of path
name
```

As just discussed, KILLFILE fully supports the parent subdirectory abbreviation (..). If you specify this abbreviation, it must occur at the beginning of the path name.

```
KILLFILE: Invalid file or drive specification
```

If the disk drive specified does not exist, KILLFILE will display this error message and return control to DOS. Should this error occur, make sure you are using a valid disk drive letter. If the disk drive is valid, invoke the DISKINFO utility discussed in Chapter 11 to examine the disk drive.

```
KILLFILE:  SUBST and ASSIGN not supported
```

As discussed in Chapter 5, DOS lets you create logical disk drives using the SUBST command. By using logical drives, the user can abbreviate a long directory name with a single drive letter. To prevent confusion from logical drives, KILLFILE simply does not support them.

```
KILLFILE: Network drives not supported
```

In most cases, running disk management utilities on a disk drive used by a local area network can be quite dangerous. Disk utilities work by accessing individual sectors of a disk. In a network, access to a disk is controlled by network software. To prevent an incompatibility between the network software and the disk utility software from damaging your disk, the low-level utilities on the Jamsa Disk Utilities do not support network drives.

```
KILLFILE:  Sector size must be 512 or 1024 bytes
```

Most DOS disks use 512-byte sectors. To provide support for partitions greater than 32 megabytes, several third-party software packages let users format their disks using 1024-byte sectors. The Jamsa Disk Utilities only support these two sector sizes.

```
KILLFILE:  Insufficient memory
```

KILLFILE requires enough memory to hold disk sectors, FAT and cluster information, and its own tables. If KILLFILE cannot allocate sufficient memory, it displays an error message and returns control to DOS. Although the memory requirements will vary based upon your disk size and the number of files in each directory, most of the Jamsa Disk Utilities require a maximum of 256K.

```
KILLFILE:  Error reading file allocation table
```

To track files and directories, the Jamsa Disk Utilities must read cluster information from the FAT. If a utility encounters an error while reading the FAT, it will display an error message and exit to DOS.

If you get this error, test your disk using CHKDSK. File allocation table errors are very serious. Back up your disk immediately. You may need to format your disk and restore backups to correct the error.

`KILLFILE:  Directory not found`

If it cannot locate the directory containing the desired files, KILLFILE will display an error message and exit to DOS. Should this error message occur, make sure you are using a correct and complete path name to the subdirectory. This error is most often caused by omitting back slashes in the path name.

`KILLFILE: Error reading directory sector`

If this error occurs, KILLFILE encountered an error while attempting to read one of the sectors containing directory information. This error frequently signals serious problems to come. Should this error occur, back up your disk immediately. Next, invoke CHKDSK to examine your disk. You may need to format your disk to remove the damaged sector and then restore your backup files.

`KILLFILE: Error deleting FILENAME.EXT. Press any key to continue.`

If it is unable to delete the file specified, KILLFILE displays this error message and continues deleting the remainder of the selected files. KILLFILE should be able to delete all of the files on your disk. If this error message occurs, run CHKDSK to examine your disk. If CHKDSK does not encounter errors, reboot your system and repeat your attempt to modify the file's date and time stamp.

`KILLFILE: Selective deletion complete. Press any key to continue.`

After it deletes the last selected file, KILLFILE will display a completion message and prompt you to press any key to continue. When you press a key, KILLFILE will return to the file menu and allow you to delete additional files or to exit to DOS.

How KILLFILE Works

The KILLFILE utility locates and reads the directory specified, displaying the files in the directory whose read-only attribute is not set. Once you select files and press the F10 function key, KILLFILE first overwrites the file's contents with a series of ones. Then, KILLFILE overwrites the file's contents with a series of ones. KILLFILE repeats this process three times.

Finally, KILLFILE overwrites the file with a final set of ones. KILLFILE reads the file's contents to verify that the overwrite was successful.

20

Copying Only Selected Files

- ► Using SELCOPY
- ► Understanding SELCOPY Error Messages
- ► How SELCOPY Works

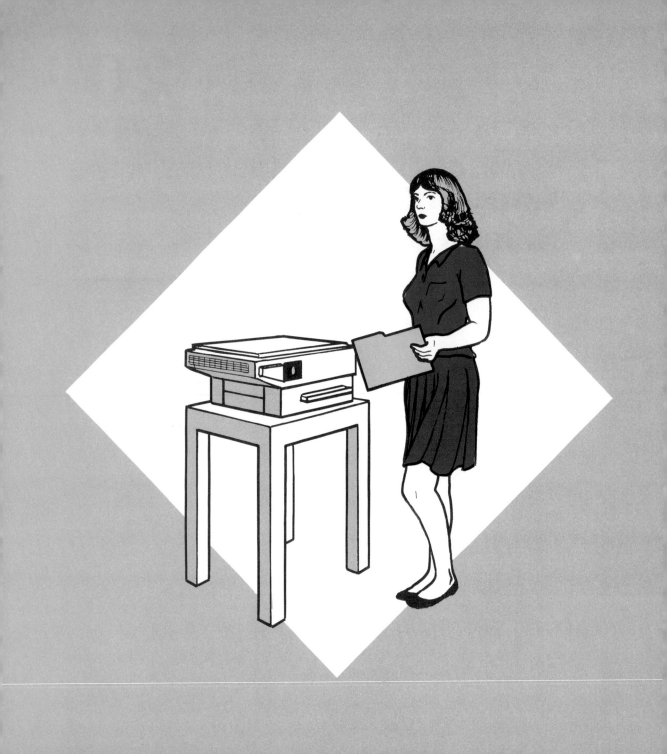

20

Copying Only Selected Files

In Chapter 3, you learned how to use the COPY command and wild-cards to copy groups of files with similar names or extensions. In Chapter 5, you used the XCOPY command to copy only those files whose archive-required attribute was set. In this chapter, you will learn how to use the SELCOPY utility provided on the Jamsa Disk Utilities that accompanies this book. With SELDEL's easy-to-use menu interface, you can quickly select one or more files to copy.

If you are copying files to a floppy disk and completely fill it up, SELCOPY lets you quickly continue a copy operation with the correct file.

Using SELCOPY

Invoke SELCOPY from the Power Shell by pressing F5, or invoke it from the DOS prompt as shown:

```
C:\> SELCOPY
```

The SELCOPY utility displays its first screen and prompts you to enter the name of the subdirectory containing the files to copy. If you simply press Enter, SELCOPY will use the current directory. In this case, type in DISKUTIL, as shown here.

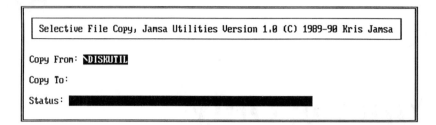

```
┌──────────────────────────────────────────────────────────────────┐
│  ┌──────────────────────────────────────────────────────────────┐ │
│  │ Selective File Copy, Jamsa Utilities Version 1.0 (C) 1989-90 Kris Jamsa │ │
│  └──────────────────────────────────────────────────────────────┘ │
│                                                                    │
│  Copy From: █DISKUTIL                                              │
│  Copy To:                                                          │
│  Status: ████████████████████████████████████████                 │
│                                                                    │
└──────────────────────────────────────────────────────────────────┘
```

SELCOPY will display the message Working.. as it searches your disk for the specified subdirectory. If SELCOPY successfully locates the directory, it will prompt you to enter the target directory. In this case, place a formatted floppy disk in drive A and enter A: as the Copy To drive.

When you press Enter, SELCOPY will again display the message Working.. as it searches your disk for the destination directory. If SELCOPY successfully locates both directories, it will display the files that reside in the source directory, as shown here.

```
┌──────────────────────────────────────────────────────────────────┐
│  ┌──────────────────────────────────────────────────────────────┐ │
│  │ Use arrow keys to highlight a file.  Press Enter to select or  │ │
│  │ unselect a file.  Press F10 to copy files.  Press Esc to exit. │ │
│  └──────────────────────────────────────────────────────────────┘ │
│                                                                    │
│      █DATETIME.EXE      77,032 bytes    03-29-1990    14:52:06     │
│      DISKINFO.EXE       59,110 bytes    03-29-1990    14:52:14     │
│      DISKSAVE.EXE       58,014 bytes    03-29-1990    14:52:20     │
│      FILEATTR.EXE       72,104 bytes    03-29-1990    14:52:28     │
│      FINDFILE.EXE       56,704 bytes    03-29-1990    14:52:36     │
│      KILLFILE.EXE       72,694 bytes    03-29-1990    14:53:02     │
│      POWER   .EXE       66,064 bytes    03-29-1990    14:53:08     │
│      RENDIR  .EXE       64,148 bytes    03-29-1990    14:53:16     │
│      SELCOPY .EXE       75,328 bytes    03-29-1990    14:53:26     │
│      SELDEL  .EXE       70,220 bytes    03-29-1990    14:53:34     │
│                                                                    │
│  ┌──────────────────────────────────────────────────────────────┐ │
│  │ Directory: C:\DISKUTIL                                        │ │
│  └──────────────────────────────────────────────────────────────┘ │
└──────────────────────────────────────────────────────────────────┘
```

To select a file to copy, use the arrow keys to highlight the file and then press either the space bar or Enter. SELCOPY acknowledges a file selection by displaying an asterisk next to the file name. In this case, select the files DISKINFO.EXE and DISKSAVE.EXE, verifying that only these files have asterisks next to their file names.

SELCOPY uses the space bar and the Enter key as a toggle. If a file is currently selected, pressing either key unselects the file. After you select the files you want to copy, press the F10 key and SELCOPY will display its final screen, as shown here.

```
┌─────────────────────────────────────────────────────────────┐
│  ┌────────────────────────────────────────────────────────┐  │
│  │ Select Cancel to return to file list.  Select Continue to copy files. │  │
│  └────────────────────────────────────────────────────────┘  │
│                                                               │
│  Directory: C:\DISKUTIL                                       │
│                                                               │
│  Copy Operation:      █Cancel█      Continue                  │
│                                                               │
│  Status:                                                      │
└─────────────────────────────────────────────────────────────┘
```

SELCOPY prompts you to verify that you really want to perform the file copy operation. If you select the `Cancel` option, SELCOPY will return to the file menu so that you can review, add, or remove files from the copy list. If you select the `Continue` option, SELCOPY will begin the file operation.

If successful, SELCOPY will display a message indicating that the file copying is complete. If SELCOPY is unable to successfully copy a file, it will display a message specifying the file name that could not be copied.

The most common cause for this error is an existing file in the target directory that is marked read-only. As you will recall, DOS is unable to overwrite read-only files. SELCOPY obeys this same rule. If this error occurs, simply press any key to continue the file copy operation with the next file.

If the target disk fills up before SELCOPY is completed, SELCOPY will display the following message.

```
┌─────────────────────────────────────────────────────────────┐
│  ┌────────────────────────────────────────────────────────┐  │
│  │ Select Cancel to return to file list.  Select Continue to copy files. │  │
│  └────────────────────────────────────────────────────────┘  │
│                                                               │
│  Directory: C:\DISKUTIL                                       │
│                                                               │
│  Copy Operation:      Cancel       █Continue█                 │
│                                                               │
│  Status: █SELCOPY: Disk Full-Files marked with * not copied. Press any key.█ │
└─────────────────────────────────────────────────────────────┘
```

When you press a key to continue, SELCOPY returns you to the file menu. If SELCOPY was unable to copy a file due to insufficient disk space, it will leave the asterisk highlight next to the file's name. If you are copying files to floppy disk, simply insert a formatted floppy disk in the drive and press F10 to continue the file copy operation. If the file copy operation requires several floppy disks, simply repeat this process until the operation completes.

> **Warning!** The SELCOPY command is similar to the COPY command. If a file exists in the target directory with the same name as the source file, the existing file is overwritten. The only exception to this rule is a file marked read-only.

As you select files for copying, SELCOPY builds a list containing the name of each file. When you press F10 to copy the files, SELCOPY tries to copy the files in the same order they appear in the source directory. If you are copying files to a disk with limited disk space, SELCOPY may not be able to copy the current file. When this occurs, SELCOPY searches its list until it locates a file that will fit in the remaining disk space. SELCOPY repeats this process until no more files can fit on the target disk.

Using Fast Keys with SELCOPY

In many cases, you will want to quickly select several files that appear successively in your directory listing. The F8 function key toggles a file's current selection state and advances the file highlight down to the next file. If you hold the F8 key down, you can quickly select all of the files in the directory listing. The F7 function key works in a similar manner, advancing the file highlight upward, toward the first file in the list.

Understanding SELCOPY Error Messages

The SELCOPY utility displays several possible error messages. The following sections describe the causes and solutions for each error in detail.

```
SELCOPY: Requires DOS 2.0 or higher
```

Prior to version 2, DOS did not provide support for hard disks. The programs on the companion disk, therefore, require DOS 2.0 as a minimum.

```
SELCOPY: Source and target directories must differ
```

SELCOPY lets you quickly copy files from a directory to a different directory or disk. SELCOPY cannot create identically named copies of the same files in the same directory.

```
SELCOPY: Target directory not found
```

SELCOPY displays this error message when it cannot locate the target directory specified. If this error occurs, make sure you are specifying a correct and complete directory path name.

```
SELCOPY: Only specify .. once in directory name
```

The SELCOPY utility supports the use of the parent directory abbreviation (..). For example, if you are in a subdirectory and are using the parent directory abbreviation, you can use SELCOPY to access files residing in the parent, as shown here.

```
┌──────────────────────────────────────────────────────────────┐
│ ┌──────────────────────────────────────────────────────────┐ │
│ │ Selective File Copy, Jamsa Utilities Version 1.0 (C) 1989-90 Kris Jamsa │ │
│ └──────────────────────────────────────────────────────────┘ │
│ Copy From: ..\SYSTEM                                          │
│                                                              │
│ Copy To:                                                     │
│ Status: ████████████████████████████████████████████        │
│                                                              │
└──────────────────────────────────────────────────────────────┘
```

To avoid confusion when multiple levels of directories are used, SELCOPY only lets you specify the parent directory abbreviation once per directory name. Should this error occur, simply use a complete path name to the directory.

```
SELCOPY: The abbreviation .. must appear at start of path
name
```

As just discussed, SELCOPY fully supports the parent subdirectory abbreviation (..). If you specify this abbreviation, it must occur at the beginning of the path name.

```
SELCOPY: Invalid file or drive specification
```

If the specified disk drive does not exist, SELCOPY will display this error message and return control to DOS. If this error occurs, make sure you are using a valid disk drive letter. If the disk drive is valid, invoke the DISKINFO utility discussed in Chapter 11 to examine the disk drive.

```
SELCOPY:  SUBST and ASSIGN not supported
```

As discussed in Chapter 5, DOS lets you create logical disk drives using the SUBST command. By using logical drives, the user can abbreviate a long directory name with a single drive letter. To prevent confusion from using logical drives, SELCOPY simply does not support them.

```
SELCOPY: Network drives not supported
```

In most cases, running disk management utilities on a disk drive used by a local area network can be quite dangerous. Disk utilities work by accessing individual sectors of a disk. In a network, access to a disk is controlled by network software. To prevent an incompatibility between the network software and the disk utility software from damaging your disk, the low-level utilities on the Jamsa Disk Utilities do not support network drives.

```
SELCOPY:  Sector size must be 512 or 1024 bytes
```

Most disks use 512-byte sectors. To provide support for partitions greater than 32 megabytes, several third-party software packages let users format their disks using 1024-byte sectors. The Jamsa Disk Utilities only support these two sector sizes.

```
SELCOPY:  Insufficient memory
```

To process, SELCOPY requires enough memory to hold disk sectors, FAT and cluster information, and its own tables. If SELCOPY cannot allocate sufficient memory, it will display an error message and return control to DOS. Although the memory requirements will vary based upon your disk size and the number of files in each directory, most of the companion disk utilities require a maximum of 256K.

```
SELCOPY:  Error reading file allocation table
```

To track files and directories, the Jamsa Disk Utilities must read cluster information from the FAT. If a utility encounters an error while reading the FAT, it will display an error message and exit to DOS.

Should this error occur, test your disk using CHKDSK. File allocation table errors are very serious. Back up your disk immediately. You may need to format your disk and restore backups to correct the error.

```
SELCOPY:  Directory not found
```

If SELCOPY cannot locate the directory containing the desired files, it will display an error message and exit to DOS. Should this error message occur, make sure you are using a correct and complete path name to the subdirectory. This error is most often caused by omitting back slashes in the path name.

```
SELCOPY: Error reading directory sector
```

If this error occurs, SELCOPY encountered an error while attempting to read one of the sectors containing directory information. This error is frequently a prelude to more problems to come. Should this error occur, back up your disk immediately. Next, invoke CHKDSK to examine your disk. You may need to format your disk to remove the damaged sector, and then restore your backup files.

```
SELCOPY: Error copying FILENAME.EXT. Press any key to
continue.
```

If SELCOPY is unable to copy the file specified, it displays the error message and continues copying the remainder of the selected files. The most common cause of this error is an existing read-only file in the target directory that SELCOPY cannot overwrite.

```
SELCOPY: Selective file copy complete. Press any key to
continue.
```

After it copies the last selected file, SELCOPY will display a completion message and prompt you to press any key to continue. When you press a key, SELCOPY will return to the file menu, allowing you to copy additional files or to exit to DOS.

How SELCOPY Works

SELCOPY reads the directory specified and displays a list of files you can select for copying. When you press the F10 key to initiate the file copy operation, SELCOPY will begin copying files to the target directory, just as the COPY command would do.

If SELCOPY is successful, it will return to the file menu where you can select additional files to copy or exit to DOS. If the target disk fills,

SELCOPY returns to the file menu with the uncopied files still high-lighted. If you are copying to floppy disk, insert a second disk and continue the file copy operation. If you are not copying to floppy disk, record the names of the uncopied files, so you can copy them later after you have made disk space available on the target disk.

21

Testing Your Disk for Fragmented Files

- ► Using TESTFRAG
- ► Understanding TESTFRAG Error Messages
- ► How TESTFRAG Works

21

Testing Your Disk for Fragmented Files

Chapter 9 discussed fragmented files in detail. In it, you learned that a fragmented file is one that is stored on nonconsecutive disk sectors. Fragmented files slow disk operations by adding mechanical disk head movements or rotational delays. You also learned that fragmented files may be impossible to undelete. Unfortunately, fragmented files are an unavoidable result of creating and deleting files. Testing and correcting fragmented files should be an exercise you perform regularly.

The CHKDSK command lets you examine the files in a specific directory for fragmentation. For example, the following command examines the files in the DISKUTIL subdirectory:

```
C:\> CHKDSK \DISKUTIL\*.*
```

If CHKDSK encounters a fragmented file, the following message is displayed:

```
C:\PATH\FILENAME.EXT
   Contains n non-contiguous blocks.
```

A non-contiguous block is a block of two disk-cluster groups that are not consecutive. The following illustration shows a file with two non-contiguous blocks and a file with three non-contiguous blocks.

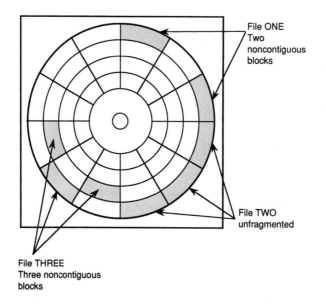

Chapter Twenty-One

File ONE
Two
noncontiguous
blocks

File TWO
unfragmented

File THREE
Three noncontiguous
blocks

If CHKDSK identifies fragmented files, repair the files as discussed in Chapter 8. CHKDSK is limited in that it can only examine one subdirectory at a time. If your disk contains many commonly used directories, testing each directory with CHKDSK can become very time consuming. Fortunately, the TESTFRAG utility provided with the Jamsa Disk Utilities lets you examine your entire disk for fragmented files in one step.

To invoke TESTFRAG from the Power Shell, press the F10 function key. When you do, Power will prompt you to enter the drive letter of the desired drive as follows.

```
Type in the command line for TESTFRAG and press Enter. Press Esc to exit.

Parameters:
```

If you simply press Enter, TESTFRAG will use the current drive.

Temporarily Suspending TESTFRAG's Output

Depending on the number of fragmented files on your disk, TESTFRAG may scroll many files names past you on the screen. To temporarily stop TESTFRAG's output, simply press any key. To resume TESTFRAG's output, again press any key.

Using TESTFRAG

Invoke TESTFRAG at the DOS prompt, as shown:

```
C:\> TESTFRAG
```

TESTFRAG will test every file on your disk for fragmentation. If TESTFRAG encounters a fragmented file, it will display the following:

```
C:\PATH\
   FILENAME.EXT contains n non-contiguous cluster groups
```

Keep in mind, TESTFRAG examines every file on your disk. If TESTFRAG isn't displaying output, it hasn't found any fragmented files (yet). You can verify that TESTFRAG is running simply by watching your disk activation light.

TESTFRAG lets you examine disks other than the current drive by specifying the drive letter in the TESTFRAG command line, as shown here:

```
C:\> TESTFRAG A:
```

You can obtain a printout of the names of their fragmented files by redirecting TESTFRAG's output to the printer, as shown:

```
C:\> TESTFRAG > PRN
```

If your disk contains a large number of fragmented files, you should eliminate fragmentation by performing a backup, format, and restore operation, as discussed in Chapter 9.

Understanding TESTFRAG Error Messages

The TESTFRAG utility displays several possible error messages. The following sections describe the causes and solutions for each error in detail.

```
TESTFRAG: Requires DOS 2.0 or higher
```

Prior to version 2, DOS did not provide support for hard disks. The programs on the Jamsa Disk Utilities, therefore, require DOS 2.0 as a minimum.

`TESTFRAG: Invalid file or drive specification`

If the specified disk drive does not exist, TESTFRAG will display this error message and return control to DOS. Should this error occur, make sure you are using a valid disk drive letter. If the disk drive is valid, invoke the DISKINFO utility discussed in Chapter 11 to examine the disk drive.

`TESTFRAG:  SUBST and ASSIGN not supported`

As discussed in Chapter 5, DOS lets you create logical disk drives using the SUBST command. By using logical drives, users can abbreviate a long directory name with a single drive letter. To prevent confusion from using logical drives, TESTFRAG simply does not support them.

`TESTFRAG: Network drives not supported`

In most cases, running disk management utilities on a disk drive used by a local area network can be quite dangerous. Disk utilities work by accessing individual sectors of a disk. In a network, access to a disk is controlled by network software. To prevent an incompatibility between the network software and the disk utility software from damaging your disk, the low-level utilities on the Jamsa Disk Utilities do not support network drives.

`TESTFRAG:  Sector size must be 512 or 1024 bytes`

Most disks use 512-byte sectors. To provide support for partitions greater than 32 megabytes, several third-party software packages let users format their disks using 1024-byte sectors. The Jamsa Disk Utilities support these two sector sizes.

`TESTFRAG:  Insufficient memory`

To process, TESTFRAG requires enough memory to hold disk sectors, FAT and cluster information, and its own tables. If TESTFRAG cannot allocate sufficient memory, it will display an error message and return control to DOS. Although the memory requirements will vary based upon your disk size and the number of files in each directory, most of the Jamsa Disk Utilities require a maximum of 256K.

TESTFRAG: Error reading file allocation table

To track files and directories, the Jamsa Disk Utilities must read cluster information from the FAT. If a utility encounters an error while reading the FAT, it will display an error message and exit to DOS.

Should this error occur, test your disk using CHKDSK. File allocation table errors are very serious. Back up your disk immediately. You may need to format your disk and restore the backups to correct the error.

TESTFRAG: Error reading directory sector

If this error occurs, TESTFRAG encountered an error while attempting to read one of the sectors containing directory information. This error frequently signifies difficulties to come. Should this error occur, back up your disk immediately. Then, invoke CHKDSK to examine your disk. You may need to format your disk to remove the damaged sector, and then restore your backup files.

How TESTFRAG Works

The TESTFRAG utility reads every directory listing on your disk and traces the file allocation table entries for each. A nonfragmented file will have consecutive cluster entries in the FAT. A fragmented file, however, will have disjointed cluster entries.

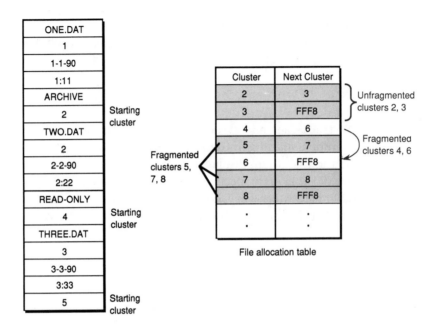

When TESTFRAG encounters a fragmented file, TESTFRAG displays the file's complete path name on the screen.

22

Recovering after a FORMAT Operation

- ▶ Using DISKSAVE
- ▶ Understanding DISKSAVE Error Messages
- ▶ How DISKSAVE Works
- ▶ Using UNFORMAT
- ▶ Understanding UNFORMAT Error Messages
- ▶ How UNFORMAT Works

Recovering after a FORMAT Operation

Throughout this book, you have learned different techniques you can use to protect your files, such as setting files to read-only to prevent inadvertent deletion and restricting the number of files in a subdirectory. As you have learned, most DOS commands only effect files in a single directory. By logically organizing your files into distinct subdirectories, you reduce the number of files that an errant DOS command can effect. Several of the utilities on the companion disk reduce the possibility of deleting or changing files by visually performing directory operations in a menu interface. If you inadvertently delete a file, the Jamsa UNDELETE utility can recover it. Unfortunately, even if you follow these precautions, the information on your disk can be quickly destroyed with just one DOS FORMAT command.

As discussed in Chapter 2, the FORMAT command prepares your disk for use by DOS. Most users rarely need to reformat a hard disk. However, because you will periodically need to format floppy disks, you can't remove the FORMAT command from your DOS vocabulary.

To reduce the risk of overwriting the contents of your hard disk, the FORMAT command displays the following warning message when your hard disk is the target of a format operation:

```
WARNING, ALL DATA ON NON-REMOVABLE DISK
DRIVE C: WILL BE LOST!
Proceed with Format (Y/N)?
```

If you get this message and don't want to format your disk, type **N** to cancel the operation.

As you will recall from Chapter 2, the FORMAT command initializes the FAT and creates the root directory. For floppy disks, FORMAT normally writes the hexadecimal value F6 to every byte of each sector of the disk.

In the past, a user who inadvertently formatted his hard disk needed to have good backups. As you will learn in this chapter, by correctly using the DISKSAVE and UNFORMAT utilities provided on the companion disk, you can recover a large percentage of your files following a hard disk format and, in some cases, 100% of your disk!

The DISKSAVE and UNFORMAT utilities work in conjunction to restore your disk following an inadvertent disk format. You should invoke DISKSAVE each time your system starts. The DISKSAVE utility sets aside information on your disk that UNFORMAT uses to rebuild your directories. If you don't invoke DISKSAVE, UNFORMAT cannot rebuild your disk.

Using DISKSAVE

The DISKSAVE utility stores several critical pieces of information UNFORMAT needs to rebuild your disk. You should place DISKSAVE in your AUTOEXEC.BAT file to ensure that it runs each time your system boots. To do so, simply place the following entry in AUTOEXEC.BAT:

```
DISKSAVE
```

If you don't include a disk drive in the DISKSAVE command line, DISKSAVE uses the default drive. The following command, for example, saves the key information for drive D (on drive D):

```
DISKSAVE D:
```

When you invoke the DISKSAVE utility, DISKSAVE will display copyright information followed by the message Working.. as it records information to the file DISKSAVE.DAT.

If you have created the DISKUTIL directory, DISKSAVE creates the file DISKSAVE.DAT in that directory. If you have not created the directory, DISKSAVE creates the file in the root.

Invoking DISKSAVE is not restricted to system start-up. Any time you complete major file operations, such as installing a new software package, you should invoke DISKSAVE.

Understanding DISKSAVE Error Messages

The DISKSAVE utility displays several possible error messages. The following sections describe the causes and solutions for each error in detail.

```
DISKSAVE: Requires DOS 2.0 or higher
```

Prior to version 2, DOS did not provide support for hard disks. The programs on the companion disk, therefore, require DOS 2.0 as a minimum.

```
DISKSAVE: SUBST and ASSIGN not supported
```

As discussed in Chapter 5, DOS lets you create logical disk drives using the SUBST command. By using logical drives, users can abbreviate a long directory name with a single drive letter. To prevent confusion from using logical drives, DISKSAVE simply does not support them.

```
DISKSAVE: Network drives not supported
```

In most cases, running disk management utilities on a disk drive used by a local area network can be quite dangerous. Disk utilities work by accessing individual sectors of a disk. In a network, access to a disk is controlled by network software. To prevent incompatibility between the network software and the disk utility software from damaging your disk, the low-level utilities on the Jamsa Disk Utilities do not support network drives.

```
DISKSAVE: Sector size must be 512 or 1024 bytes
```

Most DOS disks use 512-byte sectors. Several third-party software packages let users format disks using 1024-byte sectors. The packages do this to provide support for partitions greater than 32 megabytes. The disk utilities provided on the Jamsa Disk Utilities only support these two sector sizes.

```
DISKSAVE: Insufficient memory
```

To perform its processing, DISKSAVE requires enough memory to hold disk sectors, FAT and cluster information, and its own tables. If DISKSAVE cannot allocate sufficient memory, it will display an error

423

message and return control to DOS. Although the memory requirements will vary based upon your disk size and the number of files in each directory, most of the companion disk utilities require a maximum of 256K.

`DISKSAVE:  Error reading file allocation table`

To track files and directories, the Jamsa Disk Utilities must read cluster information from the FAT. If a utility encounters an error while reading the FAT, the utility will display an error message and exit to DOS.

Should this error occur, test your disk using CHKDSK. File allocation table errors are very serious. Back up your disk immediately. You may need to format your disk and restore backups to correct the error.

`DISKSAVE: Error reading disk sector`

If this error occurs, DISKSAVE encountered a disk error while attempting to read one of the sectors containing directory or file allocation table information. This error frequently signals problems to come. If you get this error, back up your disk immediately. Then, invoke CHKDSK to examine your disk. You may need to format your disk to remove the damaged sector, and then restore your backup files.

`DISKSAVE: Error opening the file DISKSAVE.DAT`

DISKSAVE records the file allocation table and root directory information in the file DISKSAVE.DAT. In this case, DISKSAVE tells you that it cannot open the file. If this error occurs, make sure that the number of files in your root directory will not prevent DISKSAVE from creating another file and that your disk contains sufficient disk space for another file.

`DISKSAVE: Error writing to the file DISKSAVE.DAT`

In this case, DISKSAVE was unable to write file allocation table or directory information to the file DISKSAVE.DAT. Should this error occur, make sure that your disk has sufficient disk space available. The size of the file DISKSAVE creates is dependent on your disk partition size.

`DISKSAVE: Disk specified must be a hard disk`

Because FORMAT actually overwrites the contents of a floppy disk during a disk format operation, the UNFORMAT utility can only restore hard disks. As a result, DISKSAVE only lets you save root directory and file allocation table information for a hard disk.

How DISKSAVE Works

For hard disks, the FORMAT command overwrites the FAT and root directory. FORMAT does not overwrite existing information stored on your disk. Unfortunately, with the FAT and root directory destroyed, DOS has no way to locate the data or to determine if the data exists.

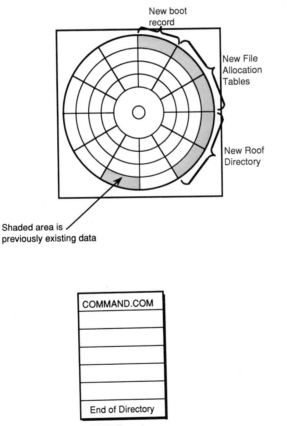

New boot record

New File Allocation Tables

New Roof Directory

Shaded area is previously existing data

Cluster	Next
.	.
.	.
10	0
11	0
12	0
13	0
14	0
15	0
16	0
.	.
.	.
.	.

FORMAT marks each File Allocation Table entry as unused.

```
COMMAND.COM




End of Directory
```

FORMAT creates a new root directory

DISKSAVE lets you recover the files and subdirectories on disk by saving a copy of the root directory and FAT in a file. If your disk is inadvertently formatted, the UNFORMAT utility can rebuild your disk using DISKSAVE's copy of the FAT and root.

Keep in mind that DOS changes the FAT each time you create, delete, or significantly modify the length of a file. The DISKSAVE utility stores the state of the FAT and root at a given time. The more often you invoke DISKSAVE, the fewer files you may lose should you need to unformat your disk.

DISKSAVE and UNFORMAT are disaster-relief utilities. Inadvertently formatting a hard disk is a disaster. The goal of DISKSAVE and UNFORMAT is to minimize the damage. No third-party unformat or backup utility can provide 100% data recovery, 100% of the time. The more frequently you perform preventive steps, such as backups or DISKSAVE, the safer your data will be.

Using UNFORMAT

Hopefully, you will never have to use the UNFORMAT utility. If you do, however, you will probably have to invoke it from floppy disk. Make a copy of UNFORMAT.COM on a floppy disk, and store the floppy in a convenient location. Unformatting a disk is similar to undeleting a file in one aspect. Should you inadvertently delete files, don't create other files on the same disk because you may overwrite the data you want to recover. If you inadvertently format a disk, don't create files on the disk because you will probably overwrite existing files.

The following scenario assumes that you need to unformat drive C. As such, place the floppy disk containing UNFORMAT in drive A and invoke UNFORMAT, as shown:

```
A:\> UNFORMAT C:
```

Note that the UNFORMAT command line contains the disk drive to unformat. UNFORMAT will display the following screen as it begins searching the formatted disk for the information previously saved by DISKSAVE.

```
┌─────────────────────────────────────────────────────────────────┐
│ ┌─────────────────────────────────────────────────────────────┐ │
│ │    Unformat, Jamsa Utilities Version 1.0 (C) 1989-90 Kris Jamsa │ │
│ └─────────────────────────────────────────────────────────────┘ │
│                                                                   │
│ Disk Drive: C                                                     │
│                                                                   │
│ Unformat Operation: Exit      Continue Search     Restore This File │
│                                                                   │
│ Status: Searching sector:  2221                                   │
└─────────────────────────────────────────────────────────────────┘
```

UNFORMAT searches your disk a sector at a time for the file DISKSAVE.DAT. Because FORMAT has overwritten the FAT and the root directory, UNFORMAT has no way of determining where the file DISKSAVE.DAT actually resides on disk. If UNFORMAT does not locate the information after searching the entire disk, it will display a message indicating that the file containing the FAT and root directory was not found.

However, if UNFORMAT locates the file, it will display the following screen:

```
┌─────────────────────────────────────────────────────────────────┐
│ ┌─────────────────────────────────────────────────────────────┐ │
│ │    Unformat, Jamsa Utilities Version 1.0 (C) 1989-90 Kris Jamsa │ │
│ └─────────────────────────────────────────────────────────────┘ │
│                                                                   │
│ Disk Drive: C                                                     │
│                                                                   │
│ Unformat Operation: Exit      Continue Search     Restore This File │
│                                                                   │
│ Status: DISKSAVE file found from: 04-09-90 at 15:46               │
└─────────────────────────────────────────────────────────────────┘
```

The Exit option cancels the unformat operation and returns control to DOS. The Continue Search option lets you continue searching the disk for a different copy of DISKSAVE.DAT. It is possible for your disk to contain more than one copy of DISKSAVE.DAT.

If for example, you invoked DISKSAVE prior to creating the directory DISKUTIL. DISKSAVE will create the file DISKSAVE.DAT in the root directory. If you later create the directory DISKUTIL and invoke DISKSAVE again, DISKSAVE will this time create the file DISKSAVE.DAT in the DISKUTIL directory. To make sure it restores the correct file, UNFORMAT displays the date and time the version of the file DISKSAVE.DAT it has found was created. If the date and time correspond with the last time your invoked DISKSAVE, restore the current file. If the date and time do not agree with the last time you invoked DISKSAVE or if you aren't sure, select the `Continue Search` option.

If you select Continue Search and UNFORMAT does not locate another copy of DISKSAVE.DAT, UNFORMAT will display a message indicating that the file containing the FAT and root directory was not found.

If you select the `Restore This File` option, UNFORMAT will display the message `Working..` as it restores the disk's root directory and FAT. When the unformat operation is complete, UNFORMAT will display a message to that effect. At this point, UNFORMAT has recovered as much of your disk as it can.

Accessing the Damage

As stated, UNFORMAT is a disaster recovery procedure. UNFORMAT does not provide 100% protection of your data. Instead, UNFORMAT reduces the damage to your files.

When UNFORMAT completes, your disk and directory structure may appear intact. To determine which files may be damaged, invoke the CHKDSK command:

```
C:\> CHKDSK
```

If CHKDSK locates damaged files, CHKDSK will display the following message:

```
C:\PATHNAME\FILENAME.EXT
   First allocation unit is invalid, entry truncated
```

The file names displayed will correspond to the files that you have created or changed since your last DISKSAVE operation. If CHKDSK does not encounter errors, your disk may be completely recovered. To print the names of the damaged files, redirect CHKDSK's output to your printer, as shown here:

```
C:\> CHKDSK > PRN
```

Understanding Truncated Files

When you create or change files, DOS keeps track of the file's location on the disk. In addition, DOS stores the file's size in the directory entry. Each time you perform file operations, DOS uses the directory and FAT to locate your files. The DISKSAVE utility stores the current state of the file allocation table.

Assume that you use DISKSAVE to save the contents of your disk when the system starts. The file DISKSAVE.DAT will contain the starting state for the FAT. Assume that you later increase the size of files A and B and create file C, and they all reside in the subdirectory DISKUTIL.

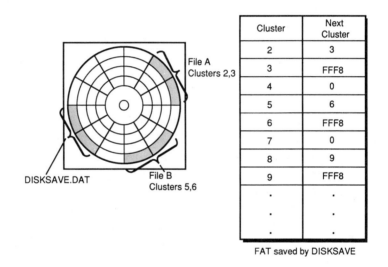

Cluster	Next Cluster
2	3
3	FFF8
4	0
5	6
6	FFF8
7	0
8	9
9	FFF8
.	.
.	.
.	.

FAT saved by DISKSAVE

DISKSAVE saves the original contents of your root directory and file allocation table.

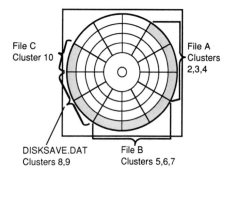

Cluster	Next Cluster
2	3
3	4
4	FFF8
5	6
6	7
7	FFF8
8	9
9	FFF8
10	FFF8
.	.
.	.
.	.

Current FAT after increasing the size of A and B and creating C

Cluster	Next Cluster
2	3
3	FFF8
4	0
5	6
6	FFF8
7	0
8	9
9	FFF8
.	.
.	.
.	.

FAT saved by DISKSAVE

Once you create or change files like this, the current FAT will differ from the one saved by DISKSAVE. If you later unformat the disk due to an inadvertent format, the restored FAT will not show the increased file sizes. In addition, the restored FAT will have no reference to file C which was created after the DISKSAVE invocation.

Unfortunately, the restored directory listing will contain the increased sizes for files A and B, as well as an entry for file C. When CHKDSK compares the directory size to the number of clusters allocated for the file, it will discover the inconsistency and truncate the file size in the directory listing to match the size that corresponds to the number of clusters found. Actually, CHKDSK doesn't truncate the directory entry until you include the /F qualifier.

As you can see, the more frequently you invoke DISKSAVE, the less risk you have of losing files due to truncation.

Possible Data Overwrite Errors

UNFORMAT, like most third-party unformat utilities, is designed to recover from an inadvertent format performed under the same version of DOS that currently resides on your disk. As you will recall from Chapter 2, the FORMAT /S command copies hidden system files to your disk, as well as the file COMMAND.COM.

If you FORMAT your disk with a version of DOS other than the one currently on your disk, the new hidden files and the new COM-MAND.COM may be larger than their counterparts originally stored on your disk. Because they are larger, the new versions may overwrite information previously stored on the disk. Because UNFORMAT only restores the root directory and FATs, it cannot recover the overwritten data. In such cases, you must rely on your backups to recover overwritten data. However, UNFORMAT will recover as much of your disk as possible.

Understanding UNFORMAT Error Messages

The UNFORMAT utility displays several possible error messages. The following sections describe the causes and solutions for each error in detail.

```
UNFORMAT: Requires DOS 2.0 or higher
```

Prior to version 2, DOS did not provide support for hard disks. The programs on the Jamsa Disk Utilities, therefore, require DOS 2.0 as a minimum.

```
UNFORMAT: Invalid file or drive specification
```

If the specified disk drive does not exist, UNFORMAT will display this error message and return control to DOS. Should this error occur, make sure you are using a valid disk drive letter. If the disk drive is valid, invoke the DISKINFO utility discussed in Chapter 11 to examine the disk drive.

```
UNFORMAT:  SUBST and ASSIGN not supported
```

As discussed in Chapter 5, DOS lets you create logical disk drives using the SUBST command. By using logical drives, the user can abbreviate long directory names with a single drive letter. To prevent confusion from logical drives, UNFORMAT simply does not support them.

```
UNFORMAT: Disk specified must be a hard disk
```

Because FORMAT actually overwrites the contents of a floppy disk during a disk format operation, the UNFORMAT utility can only restore hard disks. If you attempt to unformat a disk other than a hard disk, UNFORMAT will display this error message:

```
UNFORMAT: Network drives not supported
```

In most cases, running disk management utilities on a disk drive used by a LAN can be quite dangerous. Disk utilities work by accessing individual sectors of a disk. In a network, access to a disk is controlled by network software. To prevent compatibility problems between the network and the disk utility software from damaging your disk, the low-level utilities within the Jamsa Disk Utilities do not support network drives.

```
UNFORMAT:  Sector size must be 512 or 1024 bytes
```

Most disks use 512-byte sectors. Several third-party software packages let users format their disks using 1024-byte sectors. The packages do this to provide support for partitions greater than 32 megabytes. The Jamsa Disk Utilities only support these two sector sizes.

```
UNFORMAT:  Insufficient memory
```

To perform its processing, UNFORMAT requires enough memory to hold disk sectors, FAT and cluster information, and its own tables. If UNFORMAT cannot allocate sufficient memory, it will display an error message and return control to DOS. Although the memory requirements will vary based upon your disk size and the number of files in each directory, most of the Jamsa Disk Utilities require a maximum of 256K.

```
UNFORMAT: Error reading disk sector
```

If this error occurs, UNFORMAT encountered a disk error while attempting to read one of the sectors containing the information stored in the file DISKSAVE.DAT. Should this error occur, a successful disk recovery is dependent upon the current state of your backup files.

```
UNFORMAT: Error writing disk sector
```

If this error occurs, UNFORMAT encountered a disk error while attempting to write one of the sectors containing the root directory or file allocation table information. If this error occurs, you may be able to restore a portion of your disk that you can back up to floppy disks. A successful disk recovery may require a disk FORMAT and a backup RESTORE operation.

How UNFORMAT Works

When you begin an unformat disk operation, UNFORMAT assumes that your root directory and file allocation table have been overwritten by the DOS FORMAT command. As such, UNFORMAT searches your disk a sector at a time for the file DISKSAVE.DAT.

As discussed, your disk may contain multiple copies of the file. Carefully examine the date and time stamp UNFORMAT displays to ensure you restore the most recent version.

If UNFORMAT successfully locates the correct file and you select the `Restore this file` option, UNFORMAT will copy the previously saved root directory and file allocation tables back to your disk.

Although you may have damaged files, most of the files on your disk should be accessible. As you will recall, UNFORMAT is a disaster recovery utility. Its goal is to minimize file loss.

23

Using the POWER Command Shell

▶ Specifying Command Line Parameters

▶ Understanding POWER Error Messages

▶ How POWER Works

23

Using the POWER
Command Shell

Until now, you have invoked each of the companion disk utility programs using the program's command line interface. For example, to undelete files, you invoked the UNDELETE utility from the DOS prompt, as follows:

```
C:\> UNDELETE
```

To simplify your use of the utilities, the Jamsa Disk Utilities provides a menu-driven shell interface that lets you quickly invoke each utility without needing to remember the utility's correct name or spelling. To invoke the shell, type the following at the DOS prompt:

```
C:\> POWER
```

The POWER utility provides you with an easy to use menu interface. When you invoke POWER, the utility displays the following screen.

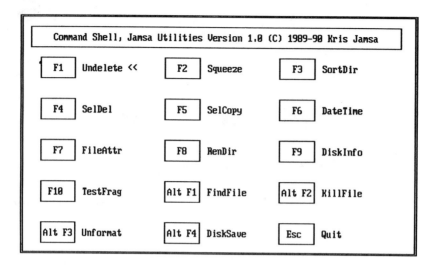

As you can see, all 14 of the companion disk utilities are available from the shell menu. POWER provides two ways to execute a command. First, you can simply press the function key that corresponds to a command name. To invoke UNDELETE, for example, you would press F1. Four of the commands use the Alt key. To invoke these commands, hold down the Alt key and press the function key specified.

The second method of executing a program is to highlight the program using the arrow keys, and then press Enter. POWER highlights a utility by displaying two less than characters (<<) next to the utility name. To simplify selection, POWER supports the Tab, PgUp, PgDn, Home, and End keys.

When you invoke a utility from within the shell, the utility will display its first screen, just as if you had invoked the utility from the command line. Press F3 to invoke the SORTDIR utility and display its first screen, as follows.

```
┌─────────────────────────────────────────────────────────────┐
│  ┌─────────────────────────────────────────────────────────┐ │
│  │  Directory Sort, Jamsa Utilities Version 1.0 (C) 1989-90 Kris Jamsa │ │
│  └─────────────────────────────────────────────────────────┘ │
│ Directory:                                                    │
│ Sort operation:  Cancel    Name    Extension    Size    Date    Time │
│ Status: Press Enter for current directory                     │
└─────────────────────────────────────────────────────────────┘
```

In this case, sort DISKUTIL subdirectory. When the sort operation completes, your screen will contain the following.

```
┌─────────────────────────────────────────────────────────────┐
│  ┌─────────────────────────────────────────────────────────┐ │
│  │  Directory Sort, Jamsa Utilities Version 1.0 (C) 1989-90 Kris Jamsa │ │
│  └─────────────────────────────────────────────────────────┘ │
│  Directory: ▉DISKUTIL                                          │
│                                                                │
│  Sort operation:  Cancel      Name      Extension   Size   Date   Time │
│                                                                │
│  Status: SORTDIR: Directory sort complete                      │
│                                                                │
│                                                                │
│                                                                │
│                                                                │
│                                                                │
│                                                                │
│                                                                │
│  Press any key to continue...                                  │
└────────────────────────────────────────────────────────────────┘
```

The message `Press any key to continue...` that appears at the lower left corner of your screen lets you view SORTDIR's completion message before returning to the shell. When you press a key, execution continues in the shell.

Now that you are back within the command shell, select the SQUEEZE utility. When SQUEEZE prompts you to enter a subdirectory name, press Esc to cancel the command. Your screen will again display the `Press any key to continue...` message in the lower left corner. When you press a key, control returns to the shell. Using POWER, you can quickly and easily invoke each of the Jamsa Utilities.

Specifying Command Line Parameters

Several of the Jamsa Disk Utilities support command line parameters. FINDFILE, for example, requires you to specify the file name it is to search for in the command line, as shown:

```
C:\> FINDFILE FILENAME.EXT
```

If you invoke FINDFILE from within the shell, POWER displays the following prompt.

```
┌─────────────────────────────────────────────────────────────────┐
│ ┌───────────────────────────────────────────────────────────────┐ │
│ │ Type in the command line for FINDFILE and press Enter. Press Esc to exit. │ │
│ └───────────────────────────────────────────────────────────────┘ │
│                                                                   │
│   Parameters:                                                     │
│                                                                   │
└─────────────────────────────────────────────────────────────────┘
```

To search for a file, simply type in the file name. To cancel the command and return to the shell, press Esc. In this case, type POWER.EXE.

When you press Enter to execute the command, your screen will display the following.

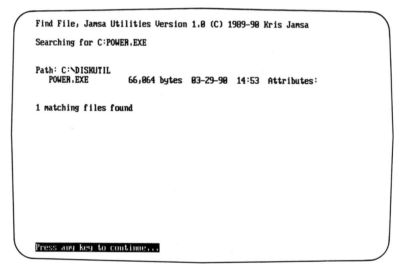

```
Find File, Jamsa Utilities Version 1.0 (C) 1989-90 Kris Jamsa

Searching for C:POWER.EXE


Path: C:\DISKUTIL
    POWER.EXE          66,064 bytes   03-29-90   14:53   Attributes:

1 matching files found




Press any key to continue...
```

Note that if you include the DOS output redirection operator in the command line, POWER will redirect FINDFILE's output as desired.

The DISKINFO, TESTFRAG, UNFORMAT and DISKSAVE utilities use this technique to determine the desired disk drive. If you simply press Enter for these commands at the command line prompt, each will use the default drive.

Understanding POWER Error Messages

POWER displays four primary error messages. The following sections discuss each message, its cause and the steps you should take to solve the error.

```
Bad command or file name
```

POWER displays this message when it is unable to locate the program you have selected. POWER supports the PATH entry. If you correctly include the DISKUTIL subdirectory in the command path, as discussed in the installation procedure, POWER should be able to locate the command specified. If your PATH entry is correct and POWER still displays the error message, make sure the DISKUTIL directory contains all the utility programs.

```
Unable to find COMMAND.COM
```

POWER displays this message when it cannot locate COMMAND.COM using the PATH entry. If POWER displays this message, refer to the discussion on setting the PATH entry in Chapter 5.

```
Insufficient Memory
```

If there is not enough available memory to load and execute the program specified, POWER will display the insufficient memory message. This error occurs when you have installed a very large RAM drive or installed memory resident programs leaving less than 256K of available RAM.

```
Invalid COMMAND.COM
```

POWER displays this message when the version of COMMAND.COM it has located is not consistent with the version of COMMAND.COM that is currently running. It is possible that an older version of COMMAND.COM is still on your disk following an upgrade to a new version of DOS. If this error occurs, use FINDFILE to locate every occurrence of COMMAND.COM on your disk.

```
C:\> FINDFILE COMMAND.COM
```

If FINDFILE locates different versions, delete the older version after copying it to a backup disk.

Chapter Twenty-Three

How POWER Works

The POWER shell lets you invoke each of the Jamsa Disk Utilities quickly and easily from a menu driven interface. Each time you select a command for execution, POWER first searches the current directory for the command. If the command resides within the current directory, POWER executes the command. Otherwise, POWER begins searching the directories specified in your command path. As such, executing a utility from within the shell is identical to invoking the utility from the DOS prompt.

Because POWER searches the directories specified in the command path, it is possible for POWER to invoke another program with the same name as one of the Jamsa Disk Utilities. For example, if you have an existing utility named FINDFILE, and the existing FINDFILE appears in the command path before the directory containing the Jamsa Disk Utilities, POWER will invoke the existing command. Although such naming conflicts are rare, you need to know that such possibilities exist.

With the POWER shell as your interface, the Jamsa Disk Utilities should give you complete control over the files on your disk.

Index

WARNING: Before using any of the disk utility programs, back up your disk or make copies of critical files.

Disclaimer

Kris Jamsa Software, Inc. will not be liable to you for any damages (including any lost profits, lost savings, or other incidental or consequential damages arising out of the use of or inability to use such programs even if Kris Jamsa Software Inc. has been advised of the possibility of such damages) or for any claim by any other party.

The Jamsa Disk Utilities access your disk's file allocation tables and sectors using DOS system services. If the file allocation table is inconsistent, or if your disk contains unmarked damaged sectors, or if you have installed third-party memory-resident software that intercepts DOS system services, the Jamsa Disk Utilities may not be compatible.

The Jamsa Utilities (or any other third-party disk utility) do not eliminate your need to perform regular file backup operations. Unfortunately, hard disks eventually wear out. Likewise, software is never guaranteed as 100 percent error free. It is possible that, without warning, a disk or software error may someday cause you to lose information. Depending on the severity of the error, you may not be able to recover the information. If you do not perform regular backup operations as discussed in this book, you should be prepared to reconstruct lost or damaged files.

CONGRATULATIONS ON YOUR PURCHASE

Please send in this product registration card today. By registering your product with Kris Jamsa Software, Inc. you become first on our list for receiving update notices, and product information as soon as they become available.

Your ability to receive technical support starts the moment we receive your registration card, so it's very important we get your card right away. Please take a few minutes to fill out this card and drop it in the mail.

Please print or type all information

RETURN IMMEDIATELY TO QUALIFY FOR FREE TECHNICAL SUPPORT AND UPGRADE INFORMATION

Name   Last   First   Middle Initial

Company Name (if applicable)   Division

Street Address

City   State   Zip

Daytime Telephone   Date of Purchase   Month   Day   Year

How did you learn about this product?

Place of purchase

Computer Type   DOS Version   Disk Size

To insure our records are always current, please notify
Kris Jamsa Software, Inc. of any address changes.

- -

If your computer uses 3 1/2-inch disks...

While most personal computers use 5 1/4-inch disks to store information, some newer computers are switching to 3 1/2-inch disks for information storage. If your computer uses 3 1/2-inch disks, you can return this form to Sams to obtain a 3 1/2-inch disk to use with this book.

Simply complete the information on this reply card and return to:

Jamsa Disk Exchange
Sams
11711 N. College Ave.
Carmel, IN 46032

Title _____

Name _____

Address _____

City _____

State _____

Zip _____

Phone _____

KRIS JAMSA SOFTWARE, INC.
Product Registration
P.O. Box 26179
Las Vegas, NV 89126